Constitutional Rights
of College Students

A Study in Case Law

by

RICHARD C. RATLIFF

The Scarecrow Press, Inc.

Metuchen, N. J.   1972

Library of Congress Cataloging in Publication Data

Ratliff, Richard C
    Constitutional rights of college students.

    Thesis--University of Oklahoma, 1970.
    Bibliography: p.
    1. Students--Legal status, laws, etc.--United
States. 2. Civil rights--United States. I. Title.
KF4243.R38   344'.73'0793   72-5729
ISBN 0-8108-0532-4

CONTENTS

Page

APR 1 5 1980

ACKNOWLEDGMENTS

A considerable debt is owed by the writer to numerous persons whose inspiration, assistance, suggestions and encouragement contributed substantially to the preparation of this book.

First to Dr. Richard S. Wells and Dr. Joseph C. Pray of the Department of Political Science, University of Oklahoma. For the direction of my efforts and their many helpful suggestions, I am most grateful. Dr. John W. Wood, Chairman of the Department of Political Science, was especially helpful with his criticism of the manuscript. The encouragement which he and Dr. Walter F. Scheffer of the same department were able to offer proved invaluable. The willing encouragement of Dr. C. Joe Holland of the School of Journalism was of great value in achieving fruition. Irving Achtenberg, Kansas City legal counsel for the American Civil Liberties Union, may never realize that his was the germinal influence. To my many students during twenty years of college teaching must go credit for the imperative which preceded the inspiration which made this study necessary. For proofreading the finished manuscript, H. H. Herbert, Emeritus Professor of Journalism, has earned the writer's profound gratitude. Gratitude is due, too, to my wife, Dorothy Claire Ratliff, for her patience as a dissertation widow, my daughter, Valerie, for leaving the door closed, and to Ketha Bollinger for typing and manuscript assistance.

INTRODUCTION

On August 4, 1961, the United States Court of Appeals, Fifth Circuit, delivered a two-to-one opinion in the case of Dixon v. Alabama State Board of Education[1] which declared in essence that "due process requires notice and some opportunity for hearing before students at a tax-supported college are expelled for misconduct." In finding for the expelled appellants, six Negro students, and against the state of Alabama, the court laid the foundation for a new body of case law in the federal courts. For the first time, students in their relationships with tax-supported institutions of higher learning, were held to come under the aegis of the fourteenth amendment's ban on arbitrary state action directed at individuals.

Charles Alan Wright, Professor of Law at the University of Texas, has pointed out that the Dixon decision marked a rare 180-degree turn in the law.[2] This turn was dramatized by the fact that the Fifth Circuit handed down its opinion in Dixon less than two years after the Second Circuit had sustained a decision that federal courts lack jurisdiction in college-discipline cases.[3] The Fifth Circuit not only accepted jurisdiction, but found for the plaintiffs while issuing a general caveat of procedural safeguards due college students in expulsion cases.

Dixon was born of the Negro-rights demonstrations which were flaring up throughout much of the country in 1961. But the classification addressed by the Fifth Circuit's sweeping opinion was not the American Negro. It was the American college student.

The significance of the Fifth Circuit's decision can be viewed from a number of different perspectives. Of undeniable primary importance is the fact that it created a new legal relationship between the American college student and the tax-supported institution--at least insofar as disciplinary action is concerned, replacing the predominant in loco parentis and contractual concepts with a broad concept of constitutional rights for college students.

1

As will be seen in Chapters IV and V, Dixon is most noted for its declarations that (1) students at tax-supported colleges have a property right in their status--a right which they cannot be arbitrarily denied; and (2) included under the penumbra of the fourteenth amendment, students at tax-supported colleges may not be required to surrender constitutional rights at the campus gate. This new rationale terminated the legal legitimacy of the predominant in loco parentis and contract concepts of the status of students at public colleges.

Ten years after the Fifth Circuit handed down its opinion in Dixon, that case remained the controlling precedent for challenge to arbitrary expulsions of college students. Moreover, the constitutional-rights rationale of the student-college relationship had been effectively expanded into the arena of substantive rights for college students, [4] and the Dixon precedent was being used to protect high school students against the arbitrary actions of school administrators. [5] After ten years in the field, Dixon was not only being sustained as the leading precedent, [6] but had been substantially expanded by subsequent decisions which followed its authority. [7]

Dixon and subsequent decisions relying on its precedent have attracted much scholarly attention to the subject of student rights from the ranks of American legal writers. Legal journals probably published as many articles on the subject of student rights in the seven years following Dixon as they had published during the preceding four decades. [8] Of significance, too, is the tone of the literature, sometimes seemingly based on an a priori of a shameless denial of basic fairness in disciplinary proceedings conducted on college campuses and an almost shocked realization that a citadel of freedom in the United States--the college campus--had timidly succumbed in a disquieting number of cases to the pressures of public opinion and administrative expediency in an aura of judicial self-restraint.

If recent developments in procedural rights for college students have constituted something of a revolution, then one might wish to grant the same status to gains scored in the area of substantive rights on the college campus. The simple truth is that college students have won impressive judicial support for their rejection of much of the paternalism that has characterized the administration of tax-supported higher education in the United States. The first amendment means much more to the college student today than it did a decade ago. Nonetheless, paternalism remains on campus. In 1967, six years after Dixon, Phillip Monypenny, Professor of Political Science at the University of Illinois, observed that, "The traditional opinion is that for the student's own protection he needs to be controlled in his choice of residences, including closing hours for women, his use of liquor, possible departures from sexual abstinence, his published expressions, the organizations he forms and joins. . . . "9 If one judges by the number of cases reaching the courts which represent paternalism, one is forced to wonder if the judicial demise federal courts have written for the in loco parentis doctrine was not prematurely noted. For, regardless of how the courts view the college-student relationship, it remains apparent that many college administrators cling to the discredited in loco parentis view of that relationship.

And what does Professor Monypenny consider an appropriate remedy for the situation he has described? "Regulations must start," he says, "with the premise that the student body is a body of relatively mature people with an inherent right to self direction so long as they do not seriously interfere with others."

Can it be assumed that Professor Monypenny yielded to rhetoric and overstated the case? A survey of the literature indicates otherwise. For example, Roy Lucas, Assistant Professor of Law at the University of Alabama, observed in 1968 that, "universities have a vested interest in avoiding the wrath of conservative alumni and, where the institution is public, the legislators."10 Reflecting on the effects of such pressures in his state of Alabama and in the Deep South, Lucas added that "students have too little freedom and are seldom, if ever, encouraged to participate in movements to improve society." He points out that in Alabama, "where the plague of government corruption, poverty, and crude racism reign, these topics are still taboo at institutions which regard themselves as the most progressive in the region."11

Reflecting on the same sort of non-academic campus regulations which attracted Professor Monypenny's attention, William W. Van Alstyne, Professor of Law at Duke University, has decried campus rules, "which do not so much cultivate a high academic life style as they communicate to our students a degree of peevishness, thin-skinned intolerance, and staid prejudice enforced by supererogatory regulations."

Van Alstyne bemoans "the teaching of John Stuart Mill in the classroom, but the preachments of Anthony Comstock in our rules."[12]

The Harvard Law Review has acknowledged a legislative reluctance to meddle with affairs interior to the operation of state colleges and universities "to preserve the freedom of the academic community." "Yet," the author adds, "even though such freedom should be safeguarded primarily as a means for furthering the freedom of individual scholars, including students, institutional autonomy has generally allowed the repression of individuals within the community."[13]

Professor Van Alstyne has published results of a survey he made of seventy-two major universities to determine their procedural practices in disciplinary cases. He concluded that 43 per cent did not provide students with a reasonably clear description of misconduct subject to discipline; 53 per cent did not provide students with written statements of the particular misconduct charged; 16 per cent did not provide hearings when the students disputed charges or contested the penalty; 47 per cent did not exclude students or administrators who appeared as witnesses or brought the charges from the disciplinary hearing board; 26 per cent did not allow accused students to cross-examine witnesses; 85 per cent permitted the hearing board to consider statements by witnesses not available for cross-examination; and 47 per cent permitted the hearing board to consider evidence "improperly" acquired.[14]

Commenting on the facts revealed by his survey, Van Alstyne noted that, "While the situation is brighter in some regards (ninety per cent provide for some type of appeal, typically to the dean of students or to the university president), it is obviously a far cry from what normally obtains in a court of law, and would seem to warrant some explanation."[15]

A number of explanations have been offered to justify the authoritarian role of colleges in relationships with students. Among these are the in loco parentis doctrine, which views the student as a legal infant and college authorities as fulfilling the role of parent. A second justification advanced is that college matriculation is a privilege, not a right,[16] and that the college student usually assumes a contractual relationship which justifies his arbitrary suspension or other arbitrary punishment as college officials deem it necessary.

Van Alstyne points out that "less than ten per cent of the students deny the misconduct with which they are charged, or take exception to the discipline imposed."[17]

A third argument is that providing procedural due process for student offenders would be unduly costly. A fourth most telling argument is that the colleges lack the necessary authority to conduct adversary-type hearings. Cross-examination, for example, is a vacuous right if witnesses cannot be compelled to appear at a hearing, and colleges are without the power to require appearance.

A fifth argument against the applicability of due process considerations to college disciplinary proceedings is the contention that disciplinary sanctions are intended to rehabilitate, rather than to punish. Due process requirements, it is proposed, apply only to punitive action of the state.[18] The United States District Court for the Western District of Missouri, en banc, added some legitimacy to this contention in an extraordinary set of college-controversy guidelines declaring, "The attempted analogy of student discipline to criminal proceedings against adults and juveniles is not sound," and then added that, "federal processes of criminal law, ... are far from perfect, and designed for circumstances and ends unrelated to the academic community."[19]

Yet a sixth argument against judicial intervention in college disciplinary matters is the traditional view that the college should be largely immune to political and judicial pressures. This injunction for judicial self-restraint has been articulated many times, perhaps most recently in the extraordinary guidelines cited above, which state that, "the courts should exercise caution when importuned to intervene in the important processes and functions of education."[20]

Reflecting on Van Alstyne's survey of seventy-two major universities, Robert S. Powell, Princeton student participant in a 1968 conference on student rights, observed, "It is ironic--and for students, enraging--that in America, one of the last of our institutions to reflect our national passion for justice and democratic processes is the university."[21]

It must be remembered that the United States Supreme Court has not ruled on the question of procedural rights for college students. One may make what he wishes of the fact that certiorari was denied in both Dixon and a Second Circuit decision which went roughly opposite to Dixon two years

earlier. It is apparent that <u>Dixon</u> represents an unsettled
legal rationale. However, two important facts would seem
to lend dignity to <u>Dixon's</u> authority: (1) As previously indicated, during its first ten years in the field, its authority
has not been directly denied by either a state or federal
court; and (2) On at least one occasion, it has been cited
favorably by the United States Supreme Court. 22

Regarding the extent of the <u>Dixon</u> ruling, in 1969, the
American Civil Liberties Union could observe that:

> It seems that the extent of procedural rights re-
> quired by courts will depend on the severity of the
> possible punishment, the nature of the substantive
> issue presented, and the actual fairness of the pro-
> cedure adopted. It does not appear that any court
> has expressly disapproved <u>Dixon</u>..., however,
> some federal district courts have merely paid lip
> service to [its] authority. 23

The purpose of this study is to survey and synthesize
the more important court decisions and more conspicuous legal writing pertinent to procedural and substantive rights of
college students in the United States, with emphasis on the
years 1961-69, in effort to reflect the trend of judicial decisions on the subject. As a study in a nascent branch of
case law, this book reflects an interest in social conditions
only to the extent that they have had a direct influence on
the law.

The study is thematically presented in eight parts, or
chapters. Chapter I undertakes to explore the basic nature
of the college in the United States <u>vis-a-vis</u> liberties accorded
individual students, then examines six recent or current pressures on the student-college relationship which have altered
the basic nature of that relationship and caused students to be
more protective of their status as students--an increasingly
valuable status--against arbitrary threats. Chapter II examines seven legal theories which have been advanced from
time to time in efforts to describe the legal relationship between college and student. Chapter III explores the historical background of the student-college relationship by reviewing two of the more prominent cases heard in state courts.

Chapter IV attempts to develop the neglected Negro-
rights characteristics of <u>Dixon</u> and the new doctrine on constitutional right to due process in college dismissal cases.

It would be difficult to overemphasize the importance of Dixon in expanding the procedural and substantive rights of students in all state-supported colleges, regardless of the fact that the case and the Fifth Circuit's opinion were inspired by a small group of incidents in the Negro-rights revolution.

Chapter V examines Dixon and related federal court cases against a background of legal comment aimed at interpretation. It attempts to get at the meaning of "due process" as it applies to college students. Chapter VI presents a discussion of other procedural considerations pertinent to the student-college relationship, and is primarily concerned with fourth- and fifth-amendment considerations. Chapter VII undertakes to summarize the cases and writings dealing with substantive rights of college students, with emphasis on the first-amendment rights of speech and press. Chapter VIII represents an effort to draw logical conclusions from the study.

Unless otherwise indicated, the words, "college," "university," and "school" are used interchangeably throughout this study to denote any institution awarding degrees of the baccalaureate level or higher.

Notes

1. 294 F. 2d 150 (5th Cir.) cert denied, 368 U. S. 930 (1961).

2. "The Constitution on the Campus," 22 Vanderbilt Law Review 1027 (October, 1969).

3. Steier v. N. Y. State Ed. Cmm'r., 271 F. 2d (2d Cir. 1959) cert denied, 381 U. S. 966 (1960).

4. See Chapter VII, infra. The highly litigious state of student rights promptly gave birth to a monthly publication, the College Law Bulletin, issued monthly by the United States National Student Association.

5. See Chapter VII, infra.

6. See esp. Esteban v. Central Missouri State College, 277 F. Supp. 649 (W. D. Mo. 1967), in which the court prescribed ten days' notice and rights to legal counsel, cross-examination and hearing record.

7. Shepardizing <u>Dixon</u> establishes that no court has denied its authority.

8. The <u>Index to Legal Periodicals</u> reflects no interest in the subject of student rights by legal writers prior to the case of <u>Anthony</u> v. <u>Syracuse University</u> (1927), which attracted notes in the <u>University of Pennsylvania Law Review</u>, <u>New York University Law Review</u>, <u>Tennessee Law Review</u>, <u>Harvard Law Review</u>, and <u>Michigan Law Review</u>. Aside from case notes, it would appear that the first indexed scholarly treatment of the general subject was Warren A. Seavey's "Dismissal of Students: 'Due Process,'" 70 <u>Harvard Law Review</u> 1406 (1957). The <u>Columbia Law Review</u> did publish, in 1935, "Expulsion of Students from Private Educational Institutions" (35:898); and M. M. Chambers' "Legal Right of a Student to a Diploma or a Degree" appeared in <u>Educational Law and Administration</u> in January, 1936.

9. "University Purpose, Discipline and Due Process," 43 <u>North Dakota Law Review</u> 739, 742 (1967).

10. "Comment," 45 <u>Denver Law Journal</u> 582, 625 (Summer, 1968).

11. <u>Ibid.</u>, p. 640.

12. "The Student as University Resident," 45 <u>Denver Law Journal</u> 582, 605 (Summer, 1968).

13. "Developments in the Law--Academic Freedom," 81 <u>Harvard Law Review</u> 1045, 1150 (1968).

14. "Procedural Due Process and State University Students," 10 <u>UCLA Law Review</u> 368, 369-70 (1963).

15. <u>Ibid.</u>, p. 371.

16. For an able exploration of this doctrine, see Van Alstyne, "The Demise of the Right-Privilege Distinction in Constitutional Law," 81 <u>Harvard Law Review</u> 1439 (1968).

17. "Procedural Due Process and State University Students," <u>op. cit.</u>, p. 371.

18. See, e.g., Thomas F. Brady and Laverne F. Snoxell, Student Discipline in Higher Education (Washington, D.C.: The American College Personnel Association, 1965).

19. General Order on Judicial Standards of Procedure and Substance in Review of Student Discipline at Tax Supported Institutions of Higher Education 45 F.R.D. 133, 142.

20. Ibid., at 136.

21. "Comment," 45 Denver Law Journal, 643 at 672.

22. Tinker v. Des Moines, 393 U. S. 503. This is a free-speech case which involved the wearing of arm bands by public school students. The court ruled that public school students have a right to hearing before disciplinary dismissal.

23. Academic Freedom and Civil Liberties of Students in Colleges and Universities (New York: American Civil Liberties Union, 1969), Appendix B, p. 2.

Chapter I

HIGHER EDUCATION IN AMERICA:
THE GREAT CHANGE

Historian Henry Steele Commager has observed that
"academic freedom was born seven centuries ago as student
freedom." Professor Commager quickly adds that "It is not
the business of the university to go bustling around like some
Aunt Polly, censoring a student newspaper here, cutting out
indelicacies in a student play there, accepting this club or
that, accepting or rejecting speakers invited by students,
snooping...." "These matters," he declares, "are the responsibility of the students themselves."[1]

In these words Professor Commager addresses himself to an ideal--an ideal which he knows is far from realization in the American context. Or else he momentarily
succumbed to the sentimental inclination of some college
teachers to view themselves as the "Mr. Chips" of twentieth
century America. The "Mr. Chips" syndrome would seek to
project an image of the American college and university
campus as a sanctuary for scholarship--a sequestered community in which kindly gray-haired professors and their dedicated and inquisitive students work together in an atmosphere
of amity and co-operation in search of undiscovered truths,
protected in this quest by a public tolerance which places
scholarship, at least in some respects, above the law and
immune to the ravages of public opinion.

Evidence abounds to support an observation that this
is a view of higher education in America which has been
inapposite, with perhaps some minor exceptions, throughout
the nation's history. Jencks and Riesman, for example,
have described nineteenth-century American colleges as "extremely authoritarian,"[2] and student-college relationships in
twentiety-century America have been shrouded in a mantle
of paternalism denominated in loco parentis with its forth-
right attribution of a child-like status to the college student.

10

Authoritarian treatment of college students by administrators--usually with the quiet acquiescence of faculties--was the rule in campus relationships generally upheld by the courts prior to 1961 and the landmark decision of the Fifth Circuit in Dixon. Higher education was a privilege, not a right, and a number of rationalizations were employed to deny arbitrarily that privilege to some students in both public and private colleges and universities.

"American educators," observe Jencks and Riesman, "have seldom been able to give coherent explanations for what they were doing. Even when they did have a consistent theory, it often had little or no relationship to the actual results of their actions."[3] If one ties this observation to the same authors' statement that the nineteenth century "was a time when financial solvency was so precarious that colleges responded to even the smallest external pressures and had only the most limited ability to reshape the priorities established by their supporters,"[4] one begins to see an emerging picture of academic pragmatism inconsistent with the concept of the campus as a cloistered sanctuary for democratic cooperation and experimentation.

Apparently in general agreement with Professor Commager in his normative view of the status of students in a democratic society is Phillip Monypenny, Professor of Political Science at the University of Illinois. Says Monypenny, "Students are not only dependents in a paternalistic society. They are also citizens of a republic and as citizens have a fairly well defined and traditional role as critics of the social order and as activitsts in defending it or changing it."[5]

If the subordinate role of the college students has remained pretty much the same throughout a large part of American history, the role of the faculty in student discipline matters has nonetheless changed abruptly. Jencks and Riesman thus point out that there was a time when most college teachers saw themselves "as policemen whose job it was to keep recalcitrant and benighted undergraduates in line, exacting a certain amount of work and imposing a measure of discipline." More often trained as clergymen than as scholars, some saw themselves as both. They were naturally inclined to view their work more in terms of improving the social and moral character of the young than of their intellectual growth. This cast them in "a quasi-parental role." Today's college faculty, they added, seldom sees itself that way.[6] Pointing to the experience at Harvard, they report:

[D]uring the nineteenth century [student discipline] was handled by the full faculty and occupied most faculty meeting time. Eventually patience wore thin, and it was turned over to a committee, but this committee remained responsible to the full faculty. At Berkeley, on the other hand the Academic Senate decided before World War II that it wanted nothing to do with student discipline and handed the whole problem to the administration. [7]

In 1947, the President's Commission on Higher Education declared that, "... integration of democratic principles into the active life of a person and a people is not to be achieved merely by studying or discussing democracy. Classroom teaching of the American tradition, however excellent, will not weave its spirit into the innermost fiber of the students."[8] The commission report noted that, "Experience in the give and take of free men in a free society is equally necessary. Democracy must be lived to be understood."[9] Democracy, said the Commission, "must become an established attitude or activity, not just a body of remote and abstract doctrines--a way for men to live and work harmoniously together, not just words in a textbook or a series of slogans."[10]

This was the Commission's proposal as to the ideal ideological context of higher education in the United States. Democracy must be lived. But did the Commission find that higher education in the United States had lived up to this standard? Apparently not, for in its next breath the Commission observed.

To achieve such practice in democratic action the President's Commission recommends a careful review of administrative policies in institutions of higher education. Revision may be necessary to give students every possible experience in democratic processes within the college community. Young people cannot be expected to develop a firm allegiance to the democratic faith they are taught in the classroom if their campus life is carried on in an authoritarian atmosphere. [11]

In other words, the Commission did not think democratic processes were adequately observed in American higher education. "To achieve such practice," it recommended "careful review of administrative policies" in higher educa-

tion. In a broader sense, the Commission paid tribute to the
achievements of specialized education, but cautioned that the
modern college graduate too often is "educated" in the sense
that he has acquired competence in some particular occupa-
tion, "yet falls short of that human wholeness and civic conscience which the cooperative activities of citizenship require."[12] The Commission thus warns against the increasing
"trade school" trend in higher education, at least insofar as
it curtails "general education"--preparation for living life in
a democratic society. If this, then, is a major problem confronting higher education in twentieth-century America, what
is the solution? For a partial answer to this question, the
Commission returned to the topic of the ideological atmosphere on campus:

> To teach the meaning and processes of democracy,
> the college campus itself should be employed as a
> laboratory of the democratic way of life. Ideas
> and ideals become dynamic as they are lived, and
> the habit of cooperation in a common enterprise can
> be gained most surely in practice. But this learn-
> ing cannot take place in institutions of higher edu-
> cation that are operated on authoritarian princi-
> ples.[13]

In these words, the President's Commission stated the
goals, or at least some of the ideal characteristics of higher
education in a democratic society. Much similarity might be
detected between the Commission's normative standards for
student status in higher education and those expressed by
Thomas Jefferson twelve decades earlier. Jefferson, a devoted advocate of tax-supported higher education and a de-
fender of personal liberty, avid inspiration of the University
of Virginia, wrote this poignant reflection on that campus in
1825:

> Our University goes on well. We have passed the
> limit of 100 students some time since. As yet it
> has been a model of order and good behavior, hav-
> ing never yet had occasion for the exercise of a
> single act of authority. We studiously avoid too
> much government. We treat them as men and
> gentlemen, under the guidance mainly of their own
> discretion. They so consider themselves and make
> it their pride to acquire that character for their
> institution.[14]

However, for all his dedication to individual liberty,
and the foregoing statement would seem to indicate a large
degree of it, Jefferson was not incapable of appreciating the
value of order on a university campus. Less than two
months after he wrote the description quoted above, he was
constrained to write the same friend concerning the first
disciplinary action taken on the university campus. Fourteen
students, "animated with wine," he recorded, masked themselves and undertook a frolic which ended with their defying
and throwing stones at some of the faculty members. Since
their identities were unknown, they were asked to step for-
ward. However, they responded with defiance, raising a petition bearing the signatures of fifty other students. When
they were confronted by the Visitors, the culprits stepped
forth, but denied that they had committed any trespass. As
Jefferson recorded it:

> They were desired to appear before the Faculty,
> which they did. On the evidence resulting from
> this inquiry, three, the most culpable, were ex-
> pelled; one of them, moreover, presented by the
> grand jury for criminal punishment (for it happened
> that the district court was then about to meet).
> The eleven other maskers were sentenced to sus-
> pensions or reprimands, and the fifty who had so
> gratuitously obtruded their names into the offensive
> paper retracted them, and so the matter ended. [15]

A month later Jefferson wrote, in a letter to the same
personal friend, that, insofar as the goal of self-government
was concerned, "With about three-fifths of them this did well,
but there were about fifteen or twenty bad subjects who were
disposed to try whether our indulgence was without limit."
After the students had been confronted with a stern response
from the faculty and board, Jefferson observed:

> It gave a shock and struck a terror, the most se-
> vere as it was less expected. It determined the
> well-disposed among them to frown upon everything
> of the kind hereafter, and the ill-disposed returned
> to order with fear, if not from better motives. A
> perfect subordination has succeeded, entire respect
> toward their professors, and industry, order and
> quiet the most exemplary, has prevailed ever
> since. [16]

This anecdote from the life of Thomas Jefferson would

seem to be pregnant with points pertinent to the student-college relationship today. In the first place, it underscores a basic question confronting the head of any college administration: What is the optimum balance of liberty and authority on the college campus? Certainly it would be difficult to fault Thomas Jefferson as one committed to individual liberty and freedom from superfluous regulation. And yet, even he was driven to writing--seemingly with satisfaction--of the "shock" and the "terror" instilled in college students by a massive show of authority. If a man of Jefferson's libertarian convictions could so easily be driven to an authoritarian posture, can the often lesser men who head college administrations today be severally censured for eschewing campus democracy?

Secondly, even in the brief passages selected here from Jefferson's letters, one might infer that Jefferson was so utterly committed to the indispensable value of due process that he could conceive of no alternative. Perhaps this is reading too much into his words, but his casual mention in the second letter of the fact that the misbehavers appeared before the faculty for determination of their guilt and the nature of their punishment "On the evidence resulting from the enquiry," would seem to denote an impatience with arbitrariness or punishment without hearing. Significant, too, is the fact that three degrees of severity in penalty were meted out to the offending students: the most culpable was sent before the grand jury, the less culpable expelled, and the least culpable merely reprimanded.

The twentieth-century student of procedures might scoff at the nature of the "due process" afforded the Virginia students, but it would appear from Jefferson's account that some form of hearing was conducted, that the accused were permitted to confront their accusers, that punishment was based on the presentation of substantial evidence. One would not need to search long to discover instances of more summary treatment accorded students at American colleges in the twentieth century.

In the twentieth-century vernacular, one might observe that Jefferson's experience, as related in his letters, and his apparent retreat from a libertarian stance demonstrates "what it's all about" in the realm of college discipline today. The problem of authority versus freedom has apparently plagued the American campus throughout a large part of its history. The President's Commission of 1947, as has been shown,

elected to align itself with a quest for greater campus freedom in observing that, "learning cannot take place in institutions of higher education that are operated on authoritarian
principles." And yet, an impressive number of scholars
have reported in recent years that authoritarian principles
predominate in student-college relationships, as will be demonstrated in the following chapters. At least one university
president has added his voice to the scholarly chorus in so
declaiming. Martin Meyerson, President of the University
of New York and President-elect of the University of Pennsylvania, in 1965 reported that, "Most colleges are as authoritarian as high schools." President Meyerson elaborated
in these words:

> ...the college student is far less able to influence
> his relationships with teachers and administrators
> than he is able to retort and otherwise respond to
> his parents. Once the youth has made his choice
> of an institution of higher learning and of a field
> within it, he has few meaningful educational choices
> left. Students are on the fringe of the adult world,
> but not in it. They are in limbo. Many are grate-
> ful of the deferral because they can test themselves
> in different ways and so find their identity. Others
> are resentful of the deferral; they sense more keen-
> ly than they did in high school that students do not
> have inalienable rights, or, indeed, many rights at
> all.[17]

And what aspect of the authoritarian atmosphere on
campus disturbs college students the most? Meyerson has
an opinion on this subject, too. He writes:

> What many students quarrel with most are the rules
> that infringe, they think, upon their personal dig-
> nity. These may include rules relating to appear-
> ance; to personal behavior, including the use of
> liquor and drugs; to living arrangements and the
> access of persons of the opposite sex to them; to
> entertainment, including what society might con-
> sider obscene; and to political expression, includ-
> ing the right to listen to and advocate radical views.
> Certain students feel that regulations on these mat-
> ters are used only to control them, and are never
> used for their protection; some restrictions they
> regard as petty and inconsequential, and therefore
> completely unnecessary; others they regard as in-

fringements on their liberties, and therefore intolerable. [18]

Jencks and Riesman were quoted earlier in this chapter as describing nineteenth-century American colleges as
"extremely authoritarian." Among the scholars who decry
twentieth-century campus authoritarianism is Alvin L. Goldman, Assistant Professor of Law at the University of Kentucky. In 1966 Goldman wrote in an article for the Kentucky
Law Journal that, "The disciplinary power of a university is
a force which every student has cause to fear. The exercise,
or threat of exercise, of a school's disciplinary power is felt
in every area of campus life." Goldman decries the invoca-
tion of university disciplinary powers "in such ludicrous
cases as the failure of a co-ed to be a 'typical Syracuse
girl'." Nonetheless, he observes, "it is in the area of student expression and association that the university's disciplinary power poses its greatest potential threat to society,
to the university itself and possibly to the individual student."[19]

Professor Goldman, then, views the university not at
all as the sheltered sanctuary for the preservation and protection of fundamental freedoms from a philistine public, but
as a guardian which has turned upon those very values it was
assigned to protect. Its disciplinary standards are so "ludicrous" as to pose a "potential threat" to the society which
created it and maintains it. He cites an example of students
clearing a demonstration against racial segregation with the
police, only to have a university spokesman announce that
any student participant would be expelled. In another case,
he reports, "four students were suspended indefinitely for
publishing, in an off-campus magazine, an article which,
though admittedly not obscene, was found by a committee of
administrative personnel to be 'generally objectionable'."[20]

Repression of a more general nature is reflected in
Goldman's statement that, "On many campuses representatives of unpopular political philosophies are prohibited from
addressing student groups." He also notes that one of the
nation's leading universities confined the use of a course
book on Soviet diplomatic policy to students enrolled in a
course "in which the 'corrective influence' of a professor
may be brought to bear."[21]

In 1957, nine years before Goldman wrote the remarks
cited above, Warren A Seavey, Bussey Professor of Law

Emeritus at Harvard Law School, decried the lack of procedural safeguards for students involved in college disciplinary actions. In an assault on college discipline procedures
which was to become a classic, Professor Seavey wrote:

> ...our sense of justice should be outraged by de-
> nial to students of the normal safeguards. It is
> shocking that the officials of a state educational in-
> stitution, which can function properly only if our
> freedoms are preserved, should not understand the
> elementary principles of fair play. It is equally
> shocking to find that the court supports them in
> denying a student the protection given to a pick-
> pocket. [22]

Professor Seavey took particular exception to the fact
that students in disciplinary hearings were sometimes not allowed to cross-examine their accusers, indeed, on occasion
were not told who their accusers were. He concluded:

> The fiduciary obligation of a school to its students
> not only should prevent it from seeking to hide the
> source of its information, but demands that it af-
> ford the student every means of rehabilitation. If
> it has not done so, this opportunity should be given
> by the courts. [23]

But who had ever said that a school had a fiduciary
obligation to its students? Apparently this was Professor
Seavey's invention, and it was not to go overlooked by other
legal scholars or by the courts. Professor Seavey's "pick-
pocket" figure of speech was colorful enough to attract the
attention of the Fifth Circuit, which was to borrow it four
years later in Judge Rives' opinion in the Dixon case.

Thomas E. Buess, a student leader at Harvard Law
School, in 1968 presented a dismal picture of the historical
disciplinary relationship between colleges and students.
Writing for the Harvard Law Review, he pointed out that in
1897 a Massachusetts court refused to interfere with a college's expulsion of a student for visiting her parents on Sun-
day, when such conduct violated the school's regulations.
"Courts today," Buess points out, "will allow universities to
deal with students pretty much as they please, taking exceptions only when the action appears to be clearly arbitrary or
unreasonable." He pointed out that the student facing severe
disciplinary action may find "that the rights he can exert are

only those which the university has deigned to confer on
him. " And that may mean, Buess pointed out, that he is
not entitled to a hearing at all.   Evaluating this situation,
he remarked:

> This is anomalous when numerous steps are being
> taken to secure the rights of criminal defendants.
> Furthermore, the very institution which is prepar-
> ing students for entrance into a democratic society
> is exercising an arbitrary power, in flat denial of
> that society's liberties. [24]

Michael T. Johnson, Beaumont attorney who later
joined the faculty of the University of Oklahoma College of
Law, observed in a 1964 article for the Texas Law Review
that:

> One of the highest aims of colleges and universities
> must be to instill in their students the ideals of the
> democratic way of life.   It is indeed anomalous that
> many of these institutions accord the students ac-
> cused of breaches of discipline few, if any, of the
> judicial safeguards. [25]

Professor Van Alstyne is probably the most prolific
writer on the subject of student rights.   In 1963, Professor
Van Alstyne sketched a most undemocratic picture of the
American college:

> Judging from the autocratic fashion in which many
> students are disciplined for alleged offenses...
> more attention [to fair treatment of students] or a
> different kind is needed.   Many students who may
> be expelled from college and barred from their
> chosen profession frequently receive less protec-
> tion today than does the most petty offender on
> trial in a state court. [26]

Five years later, in 1968, Professor Van Alstyne
turned his attention from procedures to substantive rights of
college students.   He described many of the controversies
gripping the campuses as "too foolish for serious consideration, disputes where the complaint of the students seems
trivial and the concern of the college seems petty. " While
expressing no great sympathy for typical student causes,
Van Alstyne at the same time expressed disdain for the college regulation which "serves no discernible important pur-

pose and reduces the individual to another conforming card-
board cutout jigging up and down in a ticky-tacky college."27

       Roy Lucas, Assistant Professor of Law at the Univer-
sity of Alabama, commenting on Van Alstyne's remarks from
which the preceding quotation is taken, added this word about
substantive rights on campus: "There can be no doubt that
school officials would ask the state militia and national guard
to protect students from the theft of their property. Yet the
same officials are rarely outraged by the attempted 'theft' of
the liberty of expression."28 Noting the campus demonstrations and riots which have marked the present decade, Professor Lucas observed that, "where college officials themselves have contributed to disruptive conditions by system-
atically depriving students of their first amendment rights,
a court could refuse to uphold expulsion until the officials
have cleaned themselves of their own misconduct.29

       Listing some of the specifics of student grievances,
Robert S. Powell, Jr., University of North Carolina student
body president, wrote in 1968 that, "Students will take a
great many campus controversies into the courtroom, even
if they recognize the probable futility of their efforts. But
the merits of these issues can and will be actively and publicly debated as a result of the legal challenge." Listing
the campus issues he had in mind, Powell included: "the
right of the university to meddle in the private sex life of
the student; the use of the campus police to search indis-
criminately student dorm rooms without student consent; the
right of students to hold demonstrations on campus property;
the fairness of suspending students under vague and sweeping
prohibitions that are generally clarified after the fact; and
the whole area of procedural due process in disciplinary
matters."30

       Altogether, these commentaries--most of quite recent
vintage--would seem to constitute an indictment against those
who run America's colleges and universities or against the
social forces which influence them.

Colleges and College Students

       The tragic failures of our culture that can be
       traced to the educational institutions are so gigan-
       tic and so compelling that we simply cannot disre-
       gard the challenges of university reform and move

on to something less basic. [31]

Since the days of Jefferson and the 1825 student "riot" at the University of Virginia, many changes have come to pass on the college campus. Too many authoritative works have been published on the history of higher education in the United States to warrant a recapitulation of that history here. It should perhaps suffice to say that colleges and universities have changed, and changed radically, in their relationships with students during the past five, ten or fifteen decades.

Perhaps the key word to describe the major characteristic of that change is the word, impersonality. Impersonality on the college campus as elsewhere has been born of many factors--the primary one of which may be growth. Martin Meyerson in 1965 gave this capsulated picture of the growth in college enrollments:

> A century ago there were about fifty thousand students enrolled for degrees in American institutions of higher education. The Morrill Act, supporting land-grant colleges, had been passed in 1862; the egalitarian principle of the frontier and its emphasis on advanced practical education as the opening to opportunity had begun to be felt. As the American dream was sketched in, the number of students enrolled for degrees rose five times to almost a quarter of a million by the turn of the century. By the end of World War I the figure had more than doubled; it doubled again by 1929 and more than doubled once more by the end of World War II and again since then. [32]

With this growth came computerization and the resultant impersonality. In spite of this growth, as numerous writers have observed, unrelated events nudged bona fide college professors increasingly out of the classroom as they devoted more and more of their time to research activities. Classroom teaching was shuffled downward in the American educational value system. Teaching was a chore assigned ever more frequently to graduate assistants.

At the same time, the college and university institutional personality may have assumed corporate characteristics more than had previously been the case. The university became an entity of its own, possessed of its own drive for self-perpetuation and self-fulfillment. It has been noted that

both academic and disciplinary decisions are often made on
the American campus in terms of what is best for the institution, not necessarily what is best for the individual student.   Jencks and Riesman cite the example of a university
seeking endowment for a new chair: "...concern for the
students," they observe, "is seldom the reason for seeking
the chair.   Rather, the college wants such a chair to enhance its academic reputation vis-a-vis other colleges, and
to make local faculty feel their institution is 'with it'."33

    Promoting the corporate theme in 1968, Neal R.
Stamp, university counsel and secretary to the corporation,
Cornell University, used the description, "special purpose
corporation."   He wrote that, "The university is in fact a
corporation.   It has a charter from the state and a set of
by laws from which it draws its life and which, at the same
time, prescribe and limit its purposes, powers, and function."34

    In a similar sense, Jencks and Riesman acknowledged
the corporate self-interest of the college when they observed
that, "Despite the hopes of some of the best admissions officers, few colleges evaluate applicants in terms of what the
college might do for the student.   Almost all colleges with
which we are familiar ask, implicitly if not explicitly, what
the student is likely to do for the college."35

    In 1947, the President's Commission projected a col-
legiate image of specialization and auto-actuated self-perpetuation, when it reported that specialization, "in the more extreme instances...has made the liberal arts college little
more than another vocational school, in which the aim of
teaching is almost exclusively preparation for advanced study
in one or another specialty."36

    Robert B. McKay, Dean of the New York University
School of Law, while acknowledging the corporate image of
the university, has conceded that, "there is no entirely relevant model for the modern university."37

    At any rate, it is not too much to propose that the
assumption of a corporate image by the modern American
university has done some violence to the "alma mater" personality which once characterized higher education and the
relationship between the college and its students.   Vis-a-vis
this personality change, one might feel confident in inferring
that it was inevitable that higher education should have as-

sumed a more litigious posture.

The Litigious Students

Although, as will be seen in Chapter II, American
college students have been disadvantaged generally and often
discriminated against in a legal sense, several writers have
noted the relatively small number of student legal challenges
directed against campus authority.

Thus, William M. Beaney, Professor of Politics at
Princeton University, was able to note in 1968 that, "The
relatively small body of case law involving student challenges
to expulsions or to refusals to grant degrees represents a
very small number of isolated attacks on the system by offended individuals."[38]   Striking a similar theme, Goldman
wrote in 1966 that, "Although abuses of university power are
often suffered in silence, some have been carried to the
courts.   In the courts, results have seldom been favorable
to students...."[39]

Increasing litigation involving the exercise of campus
authority has been noted by numerous writers, as will be
seen in Chapter V.   If a change in the personality of the
university is accepted, as suggested above, as a reason for
the increase in litigation, one must at the same time consider two other factors of prime importance: the changes
in the law which have increased the justiciability of student
causes, which is examined in Chapter V; and the changes
which have taken place in the college clientele in the college
milieu.

Changes in the Clientele

Before the midpoint in the twentieth century, social
pressures were beginning to mount which help explain the
abrupt change in campus relationships.   Prominent among
these are six which can be tentatively identified: (1) the
Negro-rights revolution, which focused on the college campus; (2) increasing value and importance attached to the college degree and to the status of the student in good standing; (3) the resultant demand for student status and the rapid
growth of college enrolments; (4) court-enforced expansion of
civil liberties across the board during recent decades; (5)
increased maturity of college students; and (6) pressures of

the military draft for an unpopular war, with student exemption, which for many college men have increased the value attributed to student status. The Negro-rights revolution will be examined in some detail in Chapter IV. The other five pressures on college students vis-a-vis their student status command attention at this point.

Increasing Value of the Status

Much has been written on the question of whether a student attends a tax-supported college as a matter of "right" or as "privilege," and so far as the courts are concerned, the question is one which many judges would rather avoid. The Fifth Circuit boldly confronted the rights-privilege question and added to the erosion of the distinction which has progressed for many years.

The District Court's opinion had noted that, "The right to attend a public college or university is not in and of itself a constitutional right." For the Fifth Circuit, Judge Rives observed that this was "not enough to say." Then, in a telling blow at the rights-privilege distinction in the campus context, he wrote that, "the State cannot condition the granting of even a privilege upon the renunciation of the constitutional right to due process."[40] He quoted the Supreme Court's words in the case of Cafeteria and Restaurant Workers Union v. McElroy, "One may not have a constitutional right to go to Baghdad, but the Government may not prohibit one from going there unless by means consonant with due process of law." As in that case, notes Judge Rives, "so here, it is necessary to consider 'the nature both of the private interest which has been impaired and the governmental power which has been exercised'."[41]

In 1968, Van Alstyne noted that, "we may well conclude that the right-privilege distinction has lost most of its significance in constitutional litigation."[42] O'Leary found a discussion of the subject "unrewarding."[43]

Nonetheless, in Dixon, the Fifth Circuit obliquely declared that a student does have a property right in his status as a student. In dicta, Judge Rives declared: "The precise nature of the private interest involved in this case is the right to remain at a public institution of higher learning in which plaintiffs were students in good standing "[44] (emphasis added).

Thus the Fifth Circuit distinguished between the "right to attend" and the "right to remain," drawing an analogy with the legal status of aliens before and after entering the United States.

Acknowledging the increasing importance to the individual of higher education, the Fifth Circuit in Dixon stated its property-right concept in these words:

It requires no argument to demonstrate that education is vital and, indeed, basic to civilized society. Without sufficient education the plaintiffs would not be able to earn an adequate livelihood, to enjoy life to the fullest, or to fulfill as completely as possible the duties and responsibilities of good citizens.[45]

In the nineteenth century and early twentiety century, less stress and less value were placed on education. College entrance was available to practically any student who met the technical requirements. But with the progressively growing emphasis placed on higher education as a prerequisite for career opportunities, the United States Supreme Court was able to observe in 1954 that, "In these days, it is doubtful that any child may reasonably be expected to succeed in life if he is denied the opportunity of a public education."[46]

When Syracuse University in 1926 dismissed Beatrice O. Anthony, a fourth-year student, because she was not a "typical Syracuse girl," Justice Sears of the Appellate Division of the Supreme Court of the State of New York, rejected the student's appeal for reinstatement, as will be related in Chapter III, by declaring that attendance at the university was a privilege and not a right.[47] One might imagine that Miss Anthony met little difficulty in finding another New York university which would accept her. Three decades later, in Dixon, Judge Rives viewed the plight of dismissed students in these terms:

There is no offer to prove that other colleges are open to the plaintiffs. If so, the plaintiffs would nonetheless be injured by the interruption of their course of study in mid-term. It is most unlikely that a public college would accept a student expelled from another public college of the same state. Indeed, expulsion may well prejudice the student in completing his education at any other institution.[48]

The Crowded College Campus

In the United States an educational phenomenon of the twentieth century has been the rapid growth of college enrolments. The number of students enrolled for degree credit in American colleges in 1899-1900 was 237,000, a number which more than doubled to 597,000 in the first two decades of the century, and nearly doubled again in the next decade, which ended with 1929-30. From a 1929-30 enrolment of 1,100,000, campus population roughly trebled in the following three decades, to a total of 3,215,000 in 1959-60. By 1963, the figure had topped four million.[49] In the fall of 1967, enrolment in United States higher educational institutions passed 6.9 million.[50]

At the same time, the cost of higher education had risen so dramatically that some writers found it clumsy to continue speaking in terms of millions of dollars, preferring to speak in terms of percentage of the gross national product. Thus, Jencks and Riesman report that higher education today, "is a growth industry, consuming about 2 per cent of the GNP and exercising an indirect effect on the whole of the society."[51]

The impact which spiraling enrolments have had on college curricula, standards, and entrance requirements has been recorded by Hofstadter and other writers.[52] This is of no interest here. What is of interest here is the fact that this "democratization" of higher education did occur and the fact that it tended to change college admission of an individual student from a casual occurrence to an event weighted with much importance. Hofstadter and Hardy report that per capita enrolment in 1840 was only about one-tenth of what it was in 1952, adding that, "Although college training was an advantage, it was not necessary in the early nineteenth century to go to college to become a doctor, lawyer, or even a teacher, much less a successful politician or businessman...."[53]

In 1954, J. A. Perkins, President of the University of Delaware, wrote of the "crisis" posed by the "heavy load about to fall on public, state-supported higher education."[54] He pointed out that, "Every twenty years since 1900 has witnessed a doubling of the percentage of young people going to college."[55]

An upshot of the rapid growth of campus populations

has been a race by the public agencies of support--primarily
the states--to keep building programs abreast of increasing
demands for educational facilities.   The race has not always
been won by the states and the custodians of the campuses.

Consequently, many students have been unable to gain
admission to the colleges they would have preferred to attend.
As every admissions officer knows, many students apply for
admission to three or four colleges, hoping to gain admission
to at least one.   Thus, in the vernacular of business, the
law of supply and demand has converted higher education into
a seller's market.   At the same time, admission to college
has become a matter of grave concern to the students, and
loss of student status might mean that one has been crowded
out of higher education altogether.   This fact first received
judicial notice in the Fifth Circuit's Dixon opinion.

Expanding Civil Liberties

If American political historians should ever need a
convenient label for the first half of the twentiety-century, it
is not at all unlikely that they will name it "The Era of Expanding Liberties."   For, despite the fact that twentiety-century America has been largely dominated by an upsurgence
of militarism, including two global wars, a nebulous "Cold
War," a perennial state of "preparedness," and exceptional
exploits of demagoguery, procedural and substantive guarantees of individual rights nonetheless made significant gains
in the first five decades since the nineteenth century.

The exact time span to which these gains should be
ascribed is largely arbitrary.   Some would argue, not without reason, that the first two decades of the present century
constituted a civil liberties hiatus.   Melvin L. Wulf, Legal
Director for the American Civil Liberties Union, would join
some constitutional scholars in singling out "the era of the
Warren Court" as the decade and a half in which the great
strides were made toward expansion of civil liberties.   Thus,
Wulf could write in August, 1969:

> The end of the Warren Court marks the end of the
> most expansive period in judicial protection of
> First Amendment freedoms, defendants' rights in
> criminal cases and the rights of America's black
> minority.   Not that the Warren Court decided
> every case as the ACLU would have liked.   But

given the vagaries of the individual justices and
the self-imposed limitations on the Court as a political institution, one must acknowledge the Warren
Court's very substantial contribution to political
and civil rights.

Admirers and detractors agree that the Court's
most significant decisions were those extending the
protection of persons caught up in the criminal
process, particularly the decisions that attempted
to achieve some degree of equality between the
poor and the rich and those that were designed--
perhaps futilely--to end the worst kinds of illegal
police practices. [56]

It must be conceded that the years of the Warren
Court, 1954-1969, provided the high-water mark in the progression of civil liberties in all American history. Writing
in 1966, Milton R. Konovitz observed that, "In the United
States in the last twenty-five years, progress in civil liberties and civil rights has been made at an unprecedented
pace." He continued:

On numerous fronts--including the right of even
men and women in our prisons and our mental institutions, migrant laborers, Indians on reserva-
tions--those who are 'the least' among us--the
government and the nation have taken steps to im-
plement or broaden the reach of the Bill of Rights,
and even to go beyond the plain compulsions of the
Constitution to new ideals of freedom. [57]

Professor Konvitz, who describes himself as a civil
libertarian, but as a civil rights pessimist, observes that,
"The test of civilization will be... the degree to which any
group, no matter how small or weak, is excluded from full
participation in life, society, work, and ideals of a common
community." In spite of his enthusiasm, reflected above,
for the "unprecedented pace" of progress in civil liberties,
one must remember that he was writing even before the
Warren Court had rendered its landmark decisions in such
important criminal-justice cases as Miranda v. Arizona[58]
and In re Gault, [59] both of which substantially expanded procedural protections for "the least" in American society. By
1970 it would seem to be beyond dispute that civil liberties
as normally conceived have expanded--and expanded rather
rapidly--in the United States during the twentieth century.

Both procedural and substantive rights of the individual in the United States were considerably greater in 1940 than in 1920, in 1960 than in 1940, in 1970 than in 1960. The federal courts, and the United States Supreme Court in particular, have been the trailblazers in the discovery of new liberties for the individual.

Is it too much to propose that the entire federal court system felt the liberalizing effects of this trend? One might easily infer that the general spirit of expanded civil liberties touched every element of the American society and that college students, as well as union pickets and religious nonconformists, should have been expected to declare their rights in dealing with the Old Order.

Greater Maturity of Students

Van Alstyne has noted that the mean age of American college students is more than twenty-one years and that more college students in the United States are over the age of thirty than below the age of eighteen. [60] Comparing this fact with student data from an earlier era, Jencks and Riesman declare that, "Whether one looks at the books they read, their attitudes toward the opposite sex, their alergy to Mickey Mouse extra-curricular (or curricular) make-work, or their general coolness, today's entering freshmen seem older than those of the 1920s and 1930s."[61] Even high school students, they observe, "seem to feel that they are more on their own and that their fate depends more and more on what they do and less on what their parents do for them."[62] Extending this comparison farther back in time, Jencks and Riesman wrote that, "During the eighteenth and nineteenth centuries many students presented themselves for admission to college during early adolescence--though Cotton Mather was unusual in graduating from Harvard at fifteen."[63]

All this points to a possible explanation, or a partial explanation, of the widely heralded "generation gap" so commonly touted in the American tabloid, and to a plausible explanation, or partial explanation, of why mid-twentieth-century college students in the United States grew restive under the yoke of their in loco parentis legal status on campus. One might reasonably suspect that they refused to be retarded by their elders, who, perhaps like most elders, seek to delay the maturation of the younger generation.

Jencks and Riesman take this into account, too, when they observe that a "likely source of trouble for the academic imperium is generational conflict." They add that:

The first and less dangerous problem will be direct attacks on the universities by their students... many young people raised on television and permissiveness now enter college cynical about the adult world of business, politics, and expertise. [64]

They do not expect the generational revolt to achieve "victory" in the same sense that the Algerian revolt did, but believe that "Neither legislators nor trustees are ready to haul down the banner of adult responsibility and turn over regulation of student affairs to the students themselves."[65]

Within the educational community, Joseph F. Kauffman, consultant to the American Council on Education, a national alliance of more than one thousand educational organizations and institutions, has found a cause for students' insistence on their rights growing out of the family-social milieu in which many of today's college students are raised. Writing for the Educational Record in 1964, Kauffman proposed that:

A postwar period of general prosperity, mobility, and redefinition of values brings to the campus many young people who have been free of all but a minimum of family or community restraints. They are often beyond parental control and sophisticated in social experience far beyond their age group of two decades ago. [66]

Similarly, two educational researchers have described the mature approach followed by college students seeking campus reforms. Joseph Katz and Nevitt Sanford [67] in 1966 wrote of students as a new fourth power on campus.

Although it is well established that today's college students are advanced in maturity beyond those of the nineteenth century, Jencks and Riesman have noted an anomaly in the situation when they observed that, "many parents and professors are likely to share the conviction that a 16-year-old boy is too young for college, at least emotionally, even though he may be more mature in every relevant way than boys in an earlier generation were at 18."[68]

One might reasonably propose, then, that the increasing maturity of college students has contributed in an important way to their readiness to challenge authority, and especially arbitrary authority--whether it be the authority of their parents or of college administrators acting in the fictional role of their legal parents.

The Military Draft

Anyone who has spent even a few years on the college campus--whether as student or faculty member--cannot but be impressed with the great importance, the great threat, posed by the military draft to a significant number of male students. Idealism feeding on the unpopularity of the military commitment in Vietnam would seem to fuse with a fear of the unknown and a contempt for the military regimen to make civilian status a matter of extreme importance to many college men.

Student deferment has placed an extremely high worth on the student status of men. The more idealistic college men may consider the "2-S" classification as an inherently unfair class advantage, but most have demonstrated a willingness to accept the advantage and defend it with all reasonable exertions. In their dormitories, college men may joke about transferring to "Vietnam Community College," or about receiving a "McNamara scholarship," but the military draft is no joking matter to a majority of college men.

Many college professors have objected to the student deferment, and especially to the use of academic standing as a guide to validating student deferments, but the system persists. Harvard Sociologist David Riesman finds "something morally questionable" in student deferments, and Aaron Wildovsky, Associate Professor of Political Science at the University of California's Berkeley campus, spoke for many academics when he played a leading role in urging a random, lottery-like selection of draftees. [69] But The New York Times was able to report in 1966 that draft avoidance had become a fact of life for undergraduates. Not only did the student stand to lose his favored 2-S status if he ceased to be a student, but he stood to lose it if his grades lagged below an established level. This situation led to the bizarre spectacle of a full-page advertisement in The Michigan Daily, University of Michigan student newspaper, urging coeds to purposely make low grades and thereby raise the relative class standing of their 2-S male colleagues. [70]

It would of course be impossible to determine how
many, and to what extent, college men were using the campus as a haven from the military draft. But there can be
no doubt that draft deferment has increased the value and
importance of student status for thousands of male students.

This increased value and importance of the student
status, then, would naturally inspire a student to exert
greater efforts to avoid expulsion, loss of student status,
loss of deferment and, in the campus vernacular, compulsory transfer to "Vietnam Community College."

As for the unpopularity of military service in the
Vietnam conflict, some college students elected to go to
prison rather than go to the military service, and the American Civil Liberties Union felt constrained in 1968, after deferments for graduate students were discontinued, to issue
an appeal against academic reprisals against students who
are "moved to refuse induction into the armed forces and go
to prison rather than participate in a war they feel is morally indefensible."[71]

Notes

1.   "The Nature of Academic Freedom," Saturday Review,
     August 27, 1966, p. 14.

2.   Christopher Jencks and David Riesman, The Academic
     Revolution (Garden City, New York: Doubleday & Co.,
     Inc., 1968), pp. 29-30.

3.   Ibid., p. xi.

4.   Ibid., p. 6.

5.   "University Purpose, Discipline and Due Process," 43
     North Dakota Law Review 739, 746-47 (1967).

6.   The Academic Revolution, op. cit., p. 58.

7.   Ibid., p. 39.

8.   Higher Education for American Democracy (Washington,
     D.C.: U. S. Government Printing Office, 1947) Vol.

I, p. 14.

9. Ibid.

10. Ibid.

11. Ibid.

12. Ibid., p. 48.

13. Ibid., p. 51.

14. Letter to Ellen W. Coolidge, August 27, 1825, as quoted by "A Judicial Document on Student Discipline," in the United States District Court for the Western District of Missouri, en banc, 1968.

15. Letter to Joseph Coolidge, Jr., October 13, 1825, Ibid.

16. Letter to Ellen W. Coolidge, November 14, 1825, Ibid.

17. "The Ethos of the American College Student: Beyond the Protests," Higher Education and Modern Democracy, (Robert A. Goldwin, ed.) (Chicago: Rand-McNally & Company, 1965) p. 7.

18. Ibid., p. 12.

19. "The University and the Liberty of Its Students--A Fiduciary Theory," 54 Kentucky Law Journal 643 (1966).

20. Ibid., p. 644.

21. Ibid.

22. "Dismissal of Student; 'Due Process'," 70 Harvard Law Review 1406. 1407 (1957).

23. Ibid., p. 1410.

24. "A Step Toward Guaranteed Student Rights--The University as Agency," Student Lawyer Journal, May, 1968, p. 7.

25. "The Constitutional Rights of College Students," 42 Texas Law Journal 344 (1964).

26. "Procedural Due Process and State University Students,"
     10 UCLA Law Review 368 (1963).

27. "The Student as University Resident," 45 Denver Law
     Journal 582, 603-604 (1968).

28. "Comment," 45 Denver Law Journal 622, 631 (1968).

29. Ibid., p. 632.

30. "Comment," 45 Denver Law Journal 669, 672 (1968).

31. Robert S. Powell, "Comment," 45 Denver Law Journal
     669, 674 (1968).

32. "The Ethos of the American College Student," op. cit.,
     p. 3.

33. The Academic Revolution, op. cit., p. 127.

34. "Comment," 45 Denver Law Journal 663, 665 (1968).

35. The Academic Revolution, op. cit., p. 130.

36. Higher Education for American Democracy, op. cit.,
     p. 48.

37. "The Student as Private Citizen," 45 Denver Law Jour-
     nal 558, 559 (1968).

38. "Students, Higher Education, and the Law," 45 Denver
     Law Journal 511, 513-514 (1968).

39. Alvin L. Goldman, "The University and the Liberty of
     Its Students--A Fiduciary Theory," 54 Kentucky Law
     Journal 643, 647 (1966).

40. For a comprehensive discussion of this question, see
     William W. Van Alstyne, "The Demise of the Right-
     Privilege Distinction in Constitutional Law," 81 Har-
     vard Law Review 1439 (1968).

41. 294 F. 2d 150, 156.

42. Van Alstyne, "Right-Privilege Distinction," op. cit., p.
     1458.

43. Richard E. O'Leary, "The College Student and Due Process in Disciplinary Proceedings," 1962 University of Illinois Law Forum 438, 462 (1962).

44. 294 F. 2d 150, 157.

45. Ibid., p. 157.

46. Brown v. Board of Education, 347 U. S. 483, 493 (1954).

47. Anthony v. Syracuse University, 231 N. Y. Supp. 435, 438 (1928).

48. 294 F. 2d 150, 157.

49. Standard Education Almanac--1968 (Los Angeles, California: Academic Media, Inc., 1968).

50. The 1969 World Almanac and Book of Facts (Cleveland, Ohio: Newspaper Enterprise Association, Inc., 1968), p. 344.

51. The Academic Revolution, op. cit., p. 13.

52. See, e.g., Richard Hofstadter and C. DeWitt Hardy, The Development and Scope of Higher Education in the United States (New York: Columbia University Press, 1952).

53. Ibid., p. 21.

54. "Soaring College Enrollments: a Critical Problem for the States," State Government, October, 1954, p. 201.

55. Ibid., p. 200.

56. "The End of an Era: The Last Warren Court Term," Civil Liberties, August, 1969. p. 3.

57. Expanding Liberties (New York: The Viking Press, 1966), p. xiii.

58. 384 U. S. 436 (1966).

59. 387 U. S. 1 (1967).

60. "The Judicial Trend Toward Student Academic Freedom," 20 University of Florida Law Review 290, 292 (1963).

61. The Academic Revolution, op. cit., p. 28.

62. Ibid., p. 41.

63. Ibid., p. 28.

64. Ibid., p. 540.

65. Ibid., p. 57.

66. "The New Climate of Student Freedom and Rights," Educational Record, Fall, 1964, p. 360.

67. Sanford is director and Katz is research co-ordinator of the Stanford University Institute for the Study of Human Problems. Katz is directing a five-year study of students at Stanford and the University of California at Berkeley. Sanford was editor of the 1,000-page study, The American College, published in 1962.

68. "The Viability of the American College," Nevitt Sanford (ed.), The American College (New York: John Wiley & Sons, Inc., 1962), p. 126.

69. "Life & Death Grades," Time, March 25, 1966, p. 70.

70. Mitchel Levitas, "2-S--Too Smart to Fight?" New York Times Magazine, April 24, 1966, p. 27.

71. School & Society, October 12, 1968, p. 350.

Chapter II

STUDENTS AND INSTITUTIONS:
THE THEORETICAL CONTEXT

The great change which took place in the status relationship between college students and college administrations
in the first six decades of the twentieth century was not accompanied by a corresponding change in the legal relationship
between the colleges and their clientele. College student
bodies became older in years and more mature in learning
and behavior, but they were still often considered legal infants by the courts--and, all too often, by college administrators.

Predominant Theories Before Dixon

Before the Fifth Circuit utilized Dixon in 1961 to admit college disciplinary appeals to federal jurisdiction and to
assure college students that they were not without constitutional rights in disciplinary proceedings, the few challenges
to college disciplinary discretion were heard in state courts.
So it was from state courts that the predominant theories of
student-college relationships emerged. The two most broadly applied theories were heard in state courts. So it was
from courts that the predominant theories were the contract
concept and the in loco parentis rationale. Three lesser
theories identified and distinguished by legal scholars were
referred to as: (1) the status concept; (2) the trust theory;
and (3) the statutory rationale. The primary purpose of
this chapter is to explore these five concepts, with emphasis
on the contract and in loco parentis theories.

First, it must be observed that the two prevailing
theories, contract and in loco parentis, although occasionally
both relied on in one decision,[1] must be viewed logically to
constitute a legal nullity. Contract presumes that the student
enrolling at a college enters into a legally binding agreement

37

to abide by all the rules of the institution, while not exacting
any guarantee of minimal performance from the college; in
loco parentis presumes that the enrolling student is a legal
infant. It is quite likely that no court relying on both
theories has undertaken to explain how a legal infant may
enter into a binding contract on his own behalf.

In a word, the status theory presumes an inherent
role for both students and colleges, a status relationship
growing out of custom, tradition and usage.   The trust
theory views the student as a beneficiary of the trustee college or university.   The statutory theory holds that the relationship between college and student is implicit in the statutory provisions authorizing the founding and operation of a
college.

As indicated earlier, the most-often-applied of these
theories during the past half century has been the contract
theory, although in loco parentis overtones were sometimes
present.   These two theories--although logically incompatible--
existed side by side, and occasionally in the same opinion
one could find them interwoven.   Distinctive characteristics
of each of the five theories will bear examination.

The Contract Theory

The courts have often looked to contract law--or at
least a semblance of it--to rationalize decisions growing out
of campus conflicts.   The courts were disposed to find that
provisions of the student-college contract were to be found
in all statements contained in such documents as the student's
application for admission, the registration form, the college
catalogue and formal statements of college rules and regulations.   Professor Goldman has observed that, "The rather
obvious questions to be raised to this approach under the
Status of Frauds and parol evidence rule are ignored in the
decisions, probably because litigants failed to raise them."[2]

Inconspicuous in the catalogue or registration form or
student handbook of most universities is a blanket statement
to the effect that the school reserves the right to cancel the
student's registration, refuse to award academic credits or
deny a certificate or degree without having to state a reason
for the action.   Contract, with its broad implication of pro-
perty-like rights, falls within the ready comprehension of
any court.   The concept has often been seized, given broad

construction, and enforced by the courts to which it was addressed.

A bromide in the literature of college rights is the case of Anthony v. Syracuse University. [3] Symbolizing judicial application of the contract theory, Anthony represents a case in which a fourth-year home-economics student, Beatrice O. Anthony, signed a registration card which stated:

> I agree to honor and comply with the regulations and requirements of Syracuse University and to cooperate with the university authorities and my fellow students in maintaining high standards of conduct and scholarship and in promoting the general welfare of the university. It is understood that I accept registration as a student at Syracuse University subject to the rule as to continuance therein found... [on a specified page] of the university catalogue. [4]

The catalogue rule referred to on the registration card which Miss Anthony signed stated:

> Attendance at the University is a privilege and not a right. ... The University reserves the right and the student concedes to the University the right to require the withdrawal of any student at any time for any reason deemed sufficient to it, and no reason for requiring such withdrawal need be given. [5]

On October 6, 1926, Miss Anthony was dismissed from the university. Although she demanded to be told the reason for her dismissal and an opportunity to be heard, she was told only that university officials had heard rumors about her, that officials had discussed her with several coeds in her sorority house. She was told that although she had done nothing lately, she had caused considerable trouble in the past, and that officials did not think she was "a typical Syracuse girl."

Miss Anthony's suit to enjoin the university to reinstate her drew the expected response. University officials responded that because of the statement on the registration card and the waiver in the college catalogue, Miss Anthony was bound in a contractual relationship which authorized the university to dismiss her without a statement of cause. The trial judge rejected the university's argument and ordered

Miss Anthony's reinstatement, holding that the rule on which
the university based its case was contrary to public policy.
The university appealed, and the trial court was reversed in
a rhetoric which was to buttress the contract theory for a
period of more than three decades.

Justice Sears, who wrote the opinion for the appellate
court, reasoned that the parties had voluntarily entered into
the contract. A student is not required to enter the university, his rationale continued, and could withdraw without reason at any time. The university had been under no compulsion to admit the student in the first place. It could, therefore, "retain the position of contractual freedom in which it
stood before the student's course was entered upon." This
might be done by express agreement. There was no reason
why the student could not agree that the university may terminate the relationship. Although the university must have a
reason for the dismissal which relates to either scholarship
or moral atmosphere, it need not state this reason. On the
student, then, falls the burden of proof that dismissal was
not within terms of the regulation contractually accepted.
This places the student in the anomalous position of disprov-
ing an allegation which has not been revealed to him. Nevertheless, the judgment of the lower court was reversed because Miss Anthony had not sustained that improbable burden.

The sharp difference in findings of the trial court
from those of the appellate court is only partially explained
by the fact that the trial court relied on the status theory to
find the university had violated certain minimum rights inherent in the student status, and the appellate bench relied
on contract law to reverse. [6]

This should not, however, be interpreted to mean that
students have consistently fared better whenever courts have
applied the status theory than when they applied the contract
theory. The reverse was true in a 1902 New York case.
Here, a student was expelled from New York Law School for
denying that he had passed an innocuous note to a female
student. Drawing on the basic principle of contract law,
the trial court ridiculed the notion that the school, one party
to the contract for education, could constitute itself a tribu-
nal to decide when the student had breached the contract and
forfeited his right to education. The question of breach was
for the courts, it was held. On appeal, this decision was
reversed, with the appellate court holding that status, rather
than contract law, governed. It followed that the school's

inherent power to decide questions of student conduct and expulsion had been properly exercised.   The appellate decision
compelled denial of reinstatement. [7]

    In an angry and significant article for the Harvard
Law Review, Professor Seavey observed that, "...the courts
depart from the usual rule of contracts which requires one
terminating a contract for breach to justify his action." Embracing a subject which was to win him a following and establish a prop for the Dixon opinion four years later, Professor Seavey went on to say:

> Bearing in mind that a university and its instruc-
> tors are subject to fiduciary duties in dealing with
> their students, a university should at least be un-
> der a duty to explain to a student the sweeping na-
> ture of his waiver [of rights against the univer-
> sity]. [8]

    In 1963 the Yale Law Journal added its voice to Sea-
vey's by noting that the student's freedom to contract is in
fact "only freedom to adhere," and urging judicial evaluation
of school-student disputes, because:

> ...satisfactory legislative solutions are not to be
> expected.   Students have small political influence,
> because they may be out-of-staters, transients, or
> minors.   Universities, on the other hand, have es-
> tablished legislative channels of contact, and po-
> litical power as employers, landowners, and in-
> vestors.   Consequently the legislative process will
> probably reflect the imbalance of power and failure
> to establish protections for the weaker party, the
> non-voting students, whose weakness is the cause
> of their need for governmental protections.   There-
> fore, the courts may properly apply to the univer-
> sity-student situation the principle that the court's
> constituency consists of those not represented in
> the political branches--that it represents the other-
> wise helpless, an idea as old at the chancellor's
> equitable jurisdiction to protect minors. [9]

    On the same subject and in the same article, the
Yale Law Journal observed that, "...once the court has
seized upon the contract analogy, it acts as if it were driven
to finding for the college."[10]   The Harvard Law Review has
joined in with the observation that the contract theory, "as

it has heretofore been applied--unduly favors the institution
and is of limited effectiveness in conferring rights upon students. "[11]   Professor Goldman outlines circumstances which
put the student in a "weak bargaining position," and points
out that, "The law of contracts is not an appropriate basis
for deciding student-university disputes.   Contract rules
were made to deal with the hard bargains made by self-in-
terested persons operating in a commercial setting."   He
points out that courts have neglected to apply the multitude
of devices developed by the bench in recognition of the fact
that the farther a bargain is removed from the environment
of the open market, the more sensitive courts should be to
the demands of fair and honest conduct."[12]

Van Alstyne points out that, "The free market contract model of comparison is especially attractive because
it... provides an answer to those who would criticize the
fairness and not merely the legality of campus rules."   Rejecting the proposed validity of the contract theory, Van Alstyne wrote in 1968:

> The rules which a student 'contracts' to observe
> are altogether non-negotiable, and there is in fact
> an absence of bargaining.   The majority of 'sell-
> ers' uniformly employ a self-serving clause re-
> serving the right to terminate the relation at will
> according to standards they unilaterally determine
> pursuant to a vague 'good conduct' rule.   Thus
> the non-negotiability of terms is compounded by
> the real lack of shopping alternatives, the inequal-
> ity of the parties in fixing terms, parallel prac-
> tices among sellers, and the impotency of individual
> applicants to affect terms.   The contracts are
> purely on a take-it-or-leave-it basis.   Frequently
> the student has little idea of the terms of his con-
> tract in advance of matriculating, as he more of-
> ten than not becomes enrolled before being pre-
> sented with any sort of handbook at all.   Its pro-
> visions are typically subject to change at the sole
> pleasure of the college.   Moreover, the student
> may be a minor when he enrols, and while he thus
> may avoid the contract based on his own capacity,
> he may also be unable to enforce it until he be-
> comes of age. [13]

Although several writers have observed that assumption of the contract theory of student-college relationships

usually militates against the student, it has not always been
so. For example, the <u>Yale Law Journal</u> pointed out in 1963
that the New York Court of Appeals employed the "implied
contract" theory to provide relief to a medical student who
was excluded from final examinations after finishing his
course. [14] Responding to the college's claim that it had exercised legal discretion, the court said, "It is nothing but
a willful violation of the duties which they have assumed.
Such a position could never receive the sanction of a court
in which a semblance of justice was attempted to be administered. "[15]

In a more general sense, the Yale journal summed up
institutional responsibilities under the contract concept in
these terms:

> When the implied contractual terms of a student-
> school relationship are supplemented by specific
> documents, the contract analysis is no less a
> source of limits to the school's authority. Courts
> have rejected interpretations of the contract autho-
> rizing an absolute power to expel, in situations
> where the contract waiver clauses reserved the
> right to expel only for specific reasons. [16]

After surveying the literature, one cannot avoid the
conclusion that the contract theory is inapposite to student-
college relationships, and that it has been misused to distinguish between citizen and student, so as to deny the latter
the dignity and many rights routinely accorded the former.
In general agreement with this statement, the <u>Harvard Law
Review</u> in 1968 nonetheless held out some hope for applicability of <u>real</u> contract principles when it noted:

> A rigorously followed contract theory could pro-
> vide a means for creating and preserving student
> rights. For example, the burden of proof would
> always be on the institution. The putative mis-
> conduct of the student is, after all, an alleged
> breach of contract; the imposition of sanctions by
> the institution should, therefore, be regarded as
> attempted rescission or as a penalty set forth in
> the contract. Otherwise, putting the burden of
> proof on the student forces him to prove a nega-
> tive fact, that his conduct in no way violated the
> university's regulations. Likewise, since the
> terms of the contract are dictated, the law of con-
> tracts of adhesion would provide the proper stan-

dard for interpretation.   Accordingly the burden of
clarity as well as the burden of proof would be on
the institution. [17]

The "In Loco Parentis" Theory

In loco parentis identifies the theory that the college
or university stands in the position of the parent in its relationship with students.   It follows that the student is a legal infant, with no more "rights" against the school than he
has against his parents.   This relationship might be unob-
jectionable if the courts were to require that a school assuming to act in the place of a parent act as a wise and en-
lightened one.   But such would be beyond judicial determination.

While in loco parentis might be said to be improperly
applied to campus relationships today--and most legal writers
rejoiced in its demise as a legal doctrine affecting college
students--the Harvard Law Review has nonetheless suggested
an area of potential legitimacy for the concept when it observed:

> It can be argued that the ghetto school, especially,
> must assume a parental role to prevent the student
> from entrapment in a vicious circle created by the
> limited expectations of his actual parents.   In any
> case, the theory has the virtue of emphasizing the
> need for the school to participate in the process
> of rearing the child. [18]

However, the ghetto school is far removed from the
conventional American college scene.   In loco parentis would
at least have something to be said for it if it were consistently applied.   The fact that it has not been consistently
applied is well known.   In such instances as it has been applied, it has scarcely reflected the degree of familial at-
tachment which might be expected of a parent.   Like the
contract theory, it would seem to have been utilized in a
unilateral application scarcely characteristic of filial relationships.   The "parent" has been more stern than loving,
more vindictive than understanding.

It has been suggested that in loco parentis is significant more as the college administrator's view of his role
than as a judicial view of the student-college relationship.

To the extent that this is true, in loco parentis might be labeled more of an administrative theory than a legal theory of campus relationships. However, it is a theory which has won judicial acquiescence and espousal often enough to be viewed seriously in a study of student-college relations.

Since in loco parentis rests upon a traditional relationship between parent and child, its close relationship to the status theory of student-college relations has attracted occasional attention. Thus Professor Goldman has observed that, "Although the loco parentis theory is inapplicable to student-university cases, the fact that courts have on occasion turned to this concept for guidance suggests acknowledgement by the bench that these disputes involve the law of status, not the law of contracts."[19]

Perhaps as well as any other legal rationalization, the doctrine of in loco parentis exemplifies the extremities of distortion which can occur over a period of several decades in a legal system based on the principle of stare decisis. William M. Beaney, Professor of Politics at Princeton University, has pointed out that the doctrine developed from the judicial reaction in the nineteenth century to criminal and civil actions by parents against private tutors who were responsible for the imposition of physical punishment on their students.[20]

Gott v. Berea College[21] is often cited as the 1913 case which infused the college-oriented in loco parentis doctrine into American case law. Professor Beaney points out that "cases of an earlier vintage can be found,"[22] but nonetheless, Professor O'Leary views as "regrettable" the Kentucky court opinion in Berea that "college authorities stand in loco parentis concerning the physical and moral welfare, and mental training of the pupils." O'Leary adds that "this unfortunate characterization of the school-student relationship has been adopted by university administrators who seemingly lack any clear definition of their role, as well as by students who find themselves in need of a 'popular' whipping post."[23] Professor O'Leary places the doctrine in its proper legal perspective when he observes that "All cases discovered that defer to the phrase, three in number, cite only Gott v. Berea for authority."

Several facts would seem to distinguish Gott v. Berea. These facts have been lost to college administrators seeking to embrace in loco parentis as a means of exercising broad

powers over the academic and private lives of their students.
In the first place, Berea College was a private institution,
not a public-supported school falling within the limitations
exacted by the fourteenth amendment. Secondly, the action
itself was for damages allegedly suffered by a restauranteur
whose establishment had been placed off-limits by the college
administration which was intent on feeding its own students.
Coupled with this was an equity action to enjoin the college
from further enforcement of its rule. Further distinctions
lie in the fact that the college had a paternalistic goal,
clearly stated, of educating "inexperienced country, mountain
boys and girls of very little means at the lowest possible
cost...from rural districts and unused to the ways of even
a college the size of Berea." The court also takes note of
the public-health rationale involved in the college's restriction of places where students could eat. [24]

The Harvard Law Review in 1968 joined a chorus of
critics of the in loco parentis doctrine as unrealistic when
applied to college students. It observed:

> ...the courts, and too often the schools, have in-
> terpreted the in loco parentis doctrine as confer-
> ring upon the school the powers of the parent with-
> out accompanying responsibilities. Furthermore,
> the types of restraint on student behavior which
> the courts have sustained under this theory--rules
> seeking to inculcate the moral values of thrift and
> industriousness or regulations of dress and ap-
> pearance--bear little relation to the function of the
> school at the higher levels of education...[A]s a
> standard of review, it seems to condone excessive
> regulation. [25]

Major exceptions to the in loco parentis doctrine at
the college level include the argument that many students are
not juveniles and are not at all subject to the will of their
parents, with Professor Van Alstyne pointing out that "the
mean age of American college students is more than 21
years, and there are, in fact, more students over the age
of 30 than younger than the age of 18. Even in Blackstone's
time, the doctrine did not apply to persons over 21."[26]

Professor Goldman summarizes the commonest objection among legal writers when he writes:

> It does not explain the school's power to regulate

student conduct when the student acts with his
parent's consent. Nor does it explain the basis of
authority over an emancipated pupil or one who
has reached majority. Finally, it has been noted
that the parent may not lawfully do the very act
which the university frequently tries to accomplish
in asserting its purported loco parentis authority--
sever all ties. [27]

Ira Michael Heyman, University of California Professor of Law, finds in this doctrine that "the thrust of discipline is toward helping the offender become rule-abiding,
much as parents seek to channel the behavior of their children." He acknowledges that stiff penalties for major trans-
gressions, such as cheating, are imposed, and adds, "The
familial notion leads to nonspecific rules and informal procedures. Strict legalities are eschewed because they create
a wrong tone. Facts are to be determined by administrators' inquiries, not by courtroom combat."[28]

It must be conceded, however, that "informal procedures" constitute an open door to arbitrary conduct by
those vested with power. Informal procedures in juvenile
courts made it possible for a fifteen-year-old boy to be
sentenced to serve six years in a correctional institution
for an alleged telephone prank without ever having met his ac-
cuser. [29] On the campus scene, "informal procedures" were
to be used by the white establishment in Alabama to suspend
a group of Negro students from college without benefit of
the legal protections which formal procedures have made
manifest.

One might find good reason for maintaining that the
expression informal procedures can be equated with denial
of due process.

The Status Theory

While the contract theory and in loco parentis concept of student-college relationships have won predominant
consideration in state courts, the status concept has emerged
occasionally and, as the lone basis for the decision in a student-college disciplinary conflict, the status theory has attracted little attention, but it has been detected at times in
cases turning primarily on the contract theory.

The status theory is based on the concept that the
rights and duties of students and colleges are inherent in the
status of the parties and that they have developed through
custom, tradition, and usage. [30]

In the case of Anthony v. Syracuse University, discussed above, it was seen that the trial court relied on the
status theory to hold for Miss Anthony, only to be reversed
by an appellate court which relied on the contract rationale.
The trial court was free to select the doctrinal basis for its
decision and to hold for either party on the basis of that
assumption. It by no means ignored the contract theory or
the in loco parentis doctrine. But it felt the inherent role
of the university was being abandoned in quest of the "arbitrary power not only to destroy the career of a student, but
also to injure his reputation."[31]

The 1901 case of Koblitz v. Western Reserve University[32] showed how the contract and status theories are inter-
related. The case involved a law student who had not been
allowed to re-enter the school after he had been the subject
of criminal prosecutions. Notice and an opportunity for a
hearing had been provided by the school. His action to gain
readmittance was dismissed, with the court saying:

> Custom, again, has established the rule. That
> rule is so uniform that it has become a rule of
> law; and if the plaintiff had a contract with the uni-
> versity, he agreed to abide by that rule of law,
> and that rule of law is this: That in determining
> whether a student has been guilty of improper con-
> duct that will tend to demoralize the school, it is
> not necessary that the professors should go through
> the formality of a trial. They should give the stu-
> dent whose conduct is being investigated every fair
> opportunity of showing his innocence. They should
> be careful in receiving evidence against him; they
> should weigh it; determine whether it comes from
> a source freighted with prejudice; determine the
> likelihood of all surrounding circumstances as to
> who is right, and then act upon it as jurors with
> calmness. [33]

However, it is interesting to observe that the status
theory, like the contract theory, has reflected relatively
little concern with whether a student has received notice and
hearing. For example, in a 1924 Michigan case[34] a student

was denied mandamus to compel readmission, when the court
found that the school had not abused its discretion in denying
readmission after the student had been seen smoking in public and riding in a car on a young man's lap. The court
held that the college had the inherent power to regulate discipline in such manner as it deemed proper, so long as its
rules violated neither divine nor human law. As in this
case, the status theory often appears in the terminology of
"inherent" powers.

New York recognized the status theory in 1921. [35]
Here the court declined to compel the readmittance of an expelled law student because there had been an exercise of
discretion by the dean. It was held that he acted within the
scope of his authority in determining that a student's socialis-
tic views and offensive propaganda made him undesirable to
the school.

Knapp observes, however, that in at least one decision following the status theory, it has been pointed out that
notice and hearing are important to a finding of no abuse of
discretion. [36] His example is the Tennessee case of State
ex rel Sherman v. Hyman, [37] where it was held that mandamus would not lie to compel the readmittance of students expelled from the University of Tennessee for selling examination questions. In this case, it was apparent that expulsion
had been preceded by a fair hearing, hence no abuse of discretion by the university authorities. Indicating the shape of
things to come, the court said that the hearing required in
such circumstances did not require all the formalities of a
trial, but did require notice of charges, names of witnesses,
opportunity to make a defense, and information in the nature
of evidence against the student.

In 1963 the Yale Law Journal succinctly summarized
the applicability of the status theory in these words:

> When courts use status rather than contract rela-
> tionship as a source of authority...the only motive
> for punishment held proper is regard for the wel-
> fare of the child punished or, more broadly, the
> welfare of the children of the school. Painful
> punishment is authorized by law only when it is in
> the best interests of the child. [38]

The Trust Theory

A theory of student-college relationships which has been advanced in at least two cases, only to be rejected on both occasions, is the trust theory. But the dicta of these two decisions indicate a belief that the nature of the relationship is one of trust. One of these cases involved the refusal of the Ohio Supreme Court to grant mandamus to a petitioner seeking entrance to the university. The court suggested that, once enrolled, the student would be in the role of beneficiary to the trustee university. [39] Similarly the trial court in Anthony v. Syracuse University[40] described the dismissed student as the beneficiary of a trust.

In Koblitz v. Western Reserve University, [41] it was argued that the state could compel readmittance of a student, where his expulsion thwarted the purposes of an endowment. "Presumably," comments Knapp, "it is a breach of a fiduciary duty to deprive a beneficiary student of his interest arbitrarily." The court held that there had been no abuse of discretion and no arbitrary denial of readmittance which might have constituted a breach of trust.

The Statutory Theory

The statutory concept is another theory which has won limited judicial acceptance. It poses a potential judicial interest in situations where the source of the institution's disciplinary power is declared to be statutory. Knapp has pointed out that:

> For instance, in Matter of Lesser v. Board of Education, 18 A. D. 2d 388 (1963), a case involving Brooklyn College in New York City which is run by the Board of Education of the City of New York, it was held that the board's powers to prescribe conditions of admission were discretionary and as such they had to be exercised fairly, equally, and in accordance with reasonable standards. Such powers as the board possessed were not the product of status, contract, or trust, but were rather granted specifically by statute. [42]

The Constitutional Theory

Although a detailed discussion of the constitutional or
due process legal rationale describing the relationship between students and colleges is the substance of Chapter V,
it is of immediate interest to examine the relationship of
this new concept growing out of the federal courts with the
concepts described above which have issued from state
courts.

An arguable position would be that the new constitutional rationale supplants all other theoretical inventions in
describing the legal relationship between student and institution.   Certainly it is manifest in the opinion of Judge Rives
of the Fifth Circuit in Dixon that the student-college relationship is a citizen-state relationship in the case of tax-
supported colleges, with students entitled to procedural protections accorded other citizens in their relations with the
state.   In substantive rights, it would appear that the students have also achieved equality, with Wright, for example,
noting that "The first amendment applies with full vigor on
the campus of a public university"[43] and the United States
Supreme Court declaring that "it can hardly be argued that
either students or professors shed their constitutional rights
to freedom of speech or expression at the campus gate."[44]
The preponderance of legal opinion, as will be seen in Chapter V, is that the same rule will be made to apply to relations between students and private colleges.

If one should undertake to demonstrate that the constitutional rationale is an expansion of the status theory,
still the students would be no worse off for the effort.   But
the status accorded students under the new theory is the
status of citizens, rather than the anomalous status of students.

The contract theory of student-college relationships,
with its characteristic waiver of students' procedural rights,
would seem to be demolished by the Fifth Circuit's sweeping
dicta, when it observed that "the state cannot condition even
the granting of a privilege upon the renunciation of the constitutional right to due process."[45]

If this rationale demolishes the contract concept of
relationships between student and college in expulsion proceedings, it would seem to do no less damage to the in loco
parentis doctrine.   For certainly, in the familial context,

the child enjoys no constitutional rights in his relationship
with his parents. Insofar as procedural rights are concerned,
the statutory theory would seem to have been rendered inapposite by Dixon, since any statute must remain subordinate
to constitutional considerations. The trust theory would seem
to lose its limited pertinence in the dim shadow of the constitutional rationale. In short, Dixon has laid to rest all the
conventional, time-honored theories of how a student stands
in legal relationship to his university. One could probably
never establish with any certainty exactly how it came about
that students were denied constitutional rights in the very
first instance, but since Dixon it has been possible to observe, in the vernacular, that "It's a brand new ball game,"
insofar as the legal status of students is concerned. It remains to be seen what compatibility lies between the constitutional concept and another new-born, but untried, rationalization of campus relationships, the fiduciary theory.

The Fiduciary Theory

It was in 1957 that Professor Seavey wrote his article
for the Harvard Law Review in which he condemned the cus-
tomary denial to students of meaningful protection against arbitrary disciplinary treatment by college administrators.
Seavey's central complaint was the contract theory of student-
college relationships and its characteristic waiver by students
of the rights to notice and hearing. The remedy Professor
Seavey proposed was acceptance of a new theory of student-
college relations--the fiduciary theory.

Professor Seavey found the contract theory unacceptable because "the courts depart from the usual rule of contracts which requires one terminating a contract for breach
to justify his action."[46]

Ancillary to Professor Seavey's argument was his proposal that in college disciplinary actions students were being
penalized arbitrarily in the absence of procedural rights they
had waived at the time of enrolment without understanding the
waiver. "Bearing in mind," he said, "that a university and
its instructors are subject to fiduciary duties in dealing with
their students, a university should at least be under a duty
to explain to the student the sweeping nature of the waiver."[47]
He was also offended by the fact that in a university's disciplinary dismissal of a student, the burden of proof lay on
the student--and, even so, the student was denied "the op-

portunity for rebuttal by meeting the witnesses."

Professor Seavey was protesting against the apparent
injustice growing out of the case of Bluett v. Board of Trustees,[48] in which an Illinois appellate court refused mandamus
to a medical student who was dismissed without hearing for
allegedly submitting examination papers written by another
person. Seavey's espousal of the fiduciary theory was not
to go unheard. It was to be picked up and carried forth by
other legal writers--prominent among them his Kentucky col-
league, Alvin L. Goldman, Assistant Professor of Law at
the University of Kentucky.

Goldman, decrying the weak bargaining position of the
student within the context of the contract theory, as well as
other apparent weaknesses of that doctrine, views the fiduciary theory as a rationale providing a much-needed spring-
board from which to overcome the bench's usual deference
to the decisions of educators in areas within the academic
domain.

Describing the fiduciary theory as a status concept,
Professor Goldman observes that "a fiduciary is a person
having a duty, created by his undertaking, to act primarily
for the benefit of another in matters connected with his undertaking."[49] Quoting the Restatement of Torts, Goldman
observes that the fiduciary relationship is characterized by
the confidence existing between two parties. Confidence
lacking, he adds, a fiduciary relationship exists where one
party dominates another. "The fiduciary's dominance or influence gives him a high degree of effective control over the
entrusting or 'dominated' party's conduct. Actual inferiority
or weakness of the entrusting party is immaterial."[50] But
what would the fiduciary theory mean in the campus setting?
This can be read generally into Goldman's statement that:

> ...the courts hold that in a suit involving the bene-
> ficiary, the fiduciary has the burden of proving the
> validity of any transaction involving the subject
> matter of the confidence. The fiduciary also
> carries the burden of showing that the transaction
> was fair, just, open and reasonable...the fiduciary
> must show that the confidence was not betrayed,
> that he carried out his function conscientiously and
> in good faith and that he has not obtained any un-
> due advantage as a result of the relationship.[51]

Goldman claims the advantage for this theory that it
would be equally applicable to both private and public universities.   Three primary reasons, he says, explain why the
courts have failed to apply the law of fiduciary relations to
student-university disputes: (1) Lawyers have failed to pur-
sue this approach; (2) Case law in the area developed in
large part during the closing days of laissez faire jurispru-
dence--1900 to 1930--when courts were reluctant to interfere
with relationships based on contract; and (3) Only in recent
years has the need for higher education assumed the importance of other socially recognized needs.

Professor Seavey visualized the fiduciary relationship
on campus when he wrote that:

> A fiduciary is one whose function is to act for the
> benefit of another as to matters relevant to the re-
> lation between them.   Since schools exist primarily
> for the education of their students, it is obvious
> that professors and administrators act in a fiduci-
> ary capacity with reference to the students.   One
> of the duties of the fiduciary is to make full dis-
> closure of all relevant facts in the transaction be-
> tween them.... The dismissal of a student comes
> within this rule. 52

The fiduciary and constitutional concepts have in common a quest for greater procedural rights for college students and a sense of fair play which would necessarily come
with procedural guarantees.   Indeed, the fiduciary concept
would seem to be a concept devoted to procedures.   Judge
Rives, speaking for the Fifth Circuit in Dixon, acknowledged
the Seavey article and borrowed from it.

Since the constitutional and fiduciary concepts of student rights in disciplinary proceedings seemingly are aimed
at the same general objective, it would seem that the basic
pragmatic difference would be that the fiduciary concept could
seemingly be made applicable to private schools sooner than
the constitutional theory is likely to be stretched to that extent.   The fiduciary theory would elevate the role of the student through what might be considered a novel legal arrange-
ment, while the constitutional rationale would elevate the
status of the student to a par with the status of citizen or
person, in the language of the fourteenth amendment.

The Fifth Circuit in Dixon carefully limited the con-

stitutional rationalization to tax-supported colleges, whereas
the fiduciary theory, as Goldman points out, would be immediately applicable to both public and private colleges.

It must be remembered, of course, that application
of the constitutional principle to college disciplinary proceedings does not mean that all the other theories necessarily
will have run their course. Many non-disciplinary relationships persist between students and colleges. In the academic
realm these relationships presumably will still require some
theoretical rationalization which seems unlikely to grow out
of the constitutional assumption embracing major disciplinary
actions.

Summary

A study of student rights before the courts of justice
may lead one to the conclusion that the various theories advanced to describe the student-college relationship have
served as vehicles to rationalize the control or suppression
of college students, who perhaps are viewed as posing a
threat to the established order of society.

Where the college student was bound by contract, one
is hard put to understand why the institution was not also
uniformly bound by the same contract. If the college student was found to be a legal infant, one is similarly at a
loss to understand why the institution was not uniformly accorded the responsibilities inherent in parenthood. In any
case, it seems apparent that society has been motivated by
a strong determination to give short rein to the American
college student, and has utilized the courts with their various
theoretical rationalizations to enforce a tight social control.
How mysterious it is that the bar could remain silent in the
face of such legal logic!

With the state courts using the various legal theories
--of which five have been mentioned here--throughout the
years to establish the nature of the institutional powers and
the college-student relationship, the results have been only
slightly inconsistent. Generally speaking, those few students
who have approached the bench have fared poorly. Goldman
has summed it up in the passage:

> ...under the existing body of law governing stu-
> dent-university conflicts the courts have sanctioned

autocratic interference with, and suppression of,
the intellectual, social and political liberty of the
students. Academic freedom has been undermined
and fair process frequently denied. The responsibility for this lies, of course, primarily on university administrators for engaging in such conduct.
In addition, faculties, students and alumni groups
have often been guilty of callous disregard for the
cause of preserving the university as a citadel of
liberty, open mindedness and critical inquiry. But
the blame lies with the bar for failing to recognize
that student-university conflicts should be resolved
by the law of status rather than the law of contracts. [53]

It is well to remember that student-university litigation constitutes a small and immature body of case law.
Thomas E. Buess in 1968 wrote of the unsettled state of its
development:

As in any developing area of law, the cases are
confused, revealing no consistent characterization
of universities. But since the court's theory regarding the position the university should occupy in
relation to the student will naturally affect the
balancing of respective rights and liabilities, we
should examine the various theories which courts
have used as their bases for decision. We should
also examine these theories critically in order to
see if fact will justify them. [54]

In summary, it must be said that insofar as the
courts are concerned, Dixon and the constitutional theory
which it produced have in all probability laid to rest all
other legal theories of the student-college relationship, at
least insofar as tax-supported colleges are concerned. Only
time and experience can reveal whether the aegis of the
United States Constitution will be extended to protect students
in colleges which are not tax-supported.

Notes

1.   See, e. g., Anthony v. Syracuse University, 231 N. Y. S.
     435 (1928).

2. "The University and the Liberty of Its Students--A Fiduciary Theory," op. cit., pp. 651-652.

3. 224 App. Div. 487, 231 N.Y. Supp. 435 (1928).

4. Clark Byse, "Procedure in Student Dismissal Proceedings: Law and Policy," Journal of College Student Personnel, March, 1963, p. 134.

5. Seavey, op. cit., p. 1409n.

6. "Private Government on Campus--Judicial Review of University Expulsions," 72 Yale Law Journal 1362, 1376 (1963).

7. Goldstein v. New York University, 38 Misc. 93 (1902).

8. Seavey, op. cit., p. 1410.

9. "Private Government on Campus," op. cit., p. 1390.

10. Ibid., p. 1377.

11. "Developments in the Law--Academic Freedom," 81 Harvard Law Review 1048, 1146 (1968).

12. Goldman, op. cit., p. 653.

13. "The Student as University Resident," 45 Denver Law Journal 582, 584 (1968).

14. "Private Government on Campus," op. cit., p. 1371.

15. People ex rel Cecil v. Bellevue Hospital Medical College, 60 Hun 107, 14 N.Y. Supp. 490.

16. "Developments in the Law--Academic Freedom," op. cit., p. 1152.

17. "Developments in the Law--Academic Freedom," op. cit., p. 1156.

18. Ibid., p. 1144.

19. Goldman, op. cit., p. 651n.

20. "Students, Higher Education, and the Law," 45 Denver

Law Journal 511, 514 (1968).

21. 156 Ky. 376, 161 S. W. 204 (1913).

22. "Students, Higher Education, and the Law," 45 Denver
     Law Journal 511, 514 (1968).

23. "The College Student and Due Process in Disciplinary
     Proceedings," op. cit., p. 1145.

24. 161 S. W. 204, 206 (1913).

25. "Developments in the Law--Academic Freedom," op.
     cit., p. 1145.

26. "The Student as University Resident," op. cit., p. 591.

27. Goldman, op. cit., pp. 650-651.

28. "Some Thoughts on University Disciplinary Proceedings,"
     54 California Law Review 73, 75 (1966).

29. In re Gault, 378 U. S. 1 (1967).

30. Stephen R. Knapp, "The Nature of 'Procedural Due
     Process' as Between the University and the Student,"
     The College Counsel, 25 (No. 1, 1968).

31. Ibid.

32. 21 Ohio C. C. R. 144, 11 Ohio C. C. Dec. 515 (1901).

33. Ibid. at 157.

34. Tanton v. McKenney, 226 Mich. 245, 197 N. W. 510
     (Michigan 1924).

35. Goldenkoff v. Albany Law School, 198 A. D. 460, 191
     N. Y. S. 549 (New York 1921).

36. State ex rel Sherman v. Hyman, 180 Tenn. 99, 171 S.
     W. 2d 822 (Tennessee 1942), cert. denied 319 U. S.
     748 (1943).

37. Ibid.

38. "Developments in the Law--Academic Freedom," op.

cit., p. 1144.

39. Koblitz v. Western Reserve University, 21 Ohio C. C. R. 144, 11 Ohio C. C. Dec. 515 (1901).

40. 130 Misc. 249, 231 N. Y. Supp. 435 (1928).

41. Ibid.

42. Knapp, op. cit., p. 29.

43. Charles Alan Wright, "The Constitution on the Campus," 22 Vanderbilt Law Review 1027, 1037 (1969).

44. Tinker v. Des Moines Independent Community School District, 393 U. S. 503, 507 (1969).

45. 294 F. 2d 150, 156 (1961).

46. Seavey, op. cit., p. 1407.

47. Ibid., p. 1409.

48. 10 Ill. App. 2d 207, 134 N. E. 2d 634 (1956).

49. Goldman, op. cit., p. 668.

50. Goldman, op. cit., p. 670.

51. Ibid., pp. 670-671.

52. Seavey, op. cit., p. 1407.

53. Goldman, op. cit., p. 665.

54. "A Step Toward Guaranteed Student Rights--The University as Agency," op. cit., p. 9.

Chapter III

SCHOLARS IN COURT: SOME EARLY CASES

Clark Byse, Harvard Law Professor, has proposed
that two state-court decisions mark the polar extremities in
judicial efforts to define the procedural requirements in student dismissal proceedings. [1] These decisions are the 1887
case of Hill v. McCauley[2] and the 1928 case of Anthony v.
Syracuse University, which was discussed in Chapter II.
The purpose of this chapter is to examine Hill v. McCauley
and a number of other state-court decisions, along with one
King's Bench case often cited, for the purpose of providing
a backdrop and contrast against which the Dixon decision
might be compared. Other objectives are to explain how the
scholarly estate managed to get its views written into law
and to demonstrate the impact of the judicial process on the
institution.

In the 1887 case, a court of common pleas in Cumberland County, Pennsylvania, pointedly rejected Dickinson College's espousal of the in loco parentis rationale and invalidated the dismissal of a student who was not given "such a
trial as he was entitled to under the laws" of the state.
The Hill decision was to be largely ignored until resurrected
by the Fifth Circuit three-quarters of a century later in
Dixon. During this seventy-five year lapse, the contract
analogy of Anthony was to be utilized by state courts in
search of a rationalization in support of college disciplinary
actions.

Although the number of reported decisions growing
out of state-court challenges to college dismissals is relatively small, they reflect a broad range of judicial viewpoints concerning the law's requirements in student dismissal proceedings. It is necessary to turn to these decisions
to find a backdrop against which to project recent decisions
issued by federal courts.

Representatative State-Court Decisions

Hill v. McCauley

The state-court case often cited by Byse and other American legal writers as constituting one extreme in this judicial spectrum is Commonwealth ex rel. Hill v. McCauley, an early Pennsylvania case involving Dickinson College. Dickinson College was exempt from taxation and from time to time had received financial aid from the state. Its charter vested in the faculty the disciplinary authority, "giving them power to censure, suspend, dismiss, or expel students who shall be disobedient or refractory, or shall have violated any by-law of the institution, to whose violation such penalty is annexed, and forbids appeal to the trustees, except in the case of expulsion."[3]

John M. Hill enrolled in the college in September, 1885. He enrolled for his second and final year in September, 1886. On the evening of November 9, 1886, while the faculty was meeting, a disturbance occurred near the meeting room. President McCauley later was to describe the disturbance as characterized by "hooting, singing, making noises, throwing stones against the front window, and a large one through the back window with great force which passed through both rooms, and in close proximity to some of the faculty, and out the front one."

A witness testified he had seen Hill rushing from the scene of the disturbance under circumstances which made Hill highly suspect. Hill was called before the faculty, where President McCauley addressed him in a statement which had been agreed upon by the faculty: "Mr. Hill, the faculty are satisfied that you are connected with the riotous conduct of Tuesday night, the 9th of November, and they have asked you to come in that you might make any statement in regard to the matter you might wish, if any." Hill then asked what was meant by riotous conduct, and was told that "it was singing, hooting, and throwing stones." Hill denied throwing any stones. He said he had been studying in his room when he heard the noise and had come down to where it was. Asked if he had "anything further to say," he repeated the denial that he had thrown any stones. Hill testified that he had left the faculty thinking that he was clear in the matter.[4]

After Hill's withdrawal, the faculty discussed the matter and took action which was recorded in their minutes in these words: "The connection of Mr. Hill with the disorders of last Tuesday night was considered, and whereas he was found connected with the said disorder in different ways: Resolved, that his further continuance in the college would be prejudicial to the order of the college and to the best interests of the students, and that he therefore be dismissed from the college and required to leave Carlisle within twenty-four hours, mem. con. "[5]

Hill was advised of this action the following day. He applied to the college treasurer for a refund of a proportionate share of the fees he had paid for the semester. His fees were refunded. Five days later, Hill wrote to President McCauley, requesting reinstatement, adding, "I am fully prepared, if necessary, to prove my innocence in a court of law, but cannot imperil my case by a trial before a body already prejudiced to a certain course by their former action. "[6]

When he received no reply within the time limit expressed in the letter, Hill filed a petition for a writ of mandamus.

Judge Sadler of the Court of Common Pleas of Cumberland County apparently found a nightmare of procedural inadequacy in the circumstances of Hill's dismissal. He was sharply critical of the faculty's action against Hill. "This form of procedure, " he declared, "was condemned in England a hundred years ago. "[7] Elsewhere, he observed:

> Investigations such as this ought to be carried out in such a way as the experience of mankind has shown is most conducive to a just determination of the guilt or innocence of the party charged. Had the by-laws of the college indicated a method of procedure, not inconsistent with the principles of justice, they would have been followed on the trial of Hill, but, as no form of procedures was so fixed, then the proceedings on the trial should have been conducted in accordance with the principles of natural justice and the laws of the land. [8]

Procedural safeguards Hill was entitled to, but did not receive, according to Judge Sadler, included: (1) notice of the charge against him in such detail that he would have realized its gravity; (2) the testimony against him should have been given in his presence; (3) he should have had opportunity to question witnesses against him; and (4) he was entitled to call witnesses in his own defense.

Judge Sadler was also critical of the proceeding and thought it defective because when Hill was brought before the faculty he was informed that the faculty was satisfied or convinced of his connection with the riotous disturbance, thus depriving Hill of the "legal presumption in favor of innocence." This, he said, placed the burden of proof on Hill, rather than on his accusers.

The court firmly rejected the proposed in loco parentis concept urged upon it by the college, observing: "It can never be safely admitted that the rights of so large and mostly so worthy a body of our citizens, in whose welfare society has such a deep and abiding interest, shall be utterly deprived in this respect of the protection of the law through its ordinary tribunals."

Although Dickinson was not a state school in the purest sense, Judge Sadler declared that youths "have the right of admission to its halls when properly qualified and well behaved, and it would be absurd, therefore, to hold that they can be excluded except for due cause, properly determined."

The college argued that if the court overruled the faculty, it would end the faculty's disciplinary control of the students, and the courts would be overwhelmed by a new and innumerable class of suitors. Judge Sadler responded:

> There need be no apprehension of such direful results from the declaration of the doctrine that the dismissal of students from colleges should be in accordance with those principles of justice which existed even in Pagan times, before the dawn of Christianity...

Judge Sadler, of course, concluded that since Hill was not given an adequate trial his dismissal from the college was invalid.

Anthony v. Syracuse University

The appellate court decision of Judge Sears in the Anthony case was examined in Chapter II and need not be re-

peated here. Judge Sears' opinion is what Professor Byse
had in mind as constituting the other end of the spectrum,
opposed to Judge Sadler's opinion in Hill. However, the account of Anthony v. Syracuse University would be incomplete
if it failed to note the trial court opinion of Judge Smith.

In an exhaustive opinion for the trial court, Judge
Smith demolished most of the arguments advanced by the defendant, Syracuse University. He started off with an examination of the legal status of the university and concluded
that, "...it would be absurd to say that such an institution
does not at least take on a quasi-public character so as to
be affected by considerations of public policy."9 He arrived
at this conclusion from an examination of the university's
charter, granted by the New York State legislature. Fore-
shadowing the United States Supreme Court's opinion a quarter of a century later in Brown v. Board of Education10 and
the Fifth Circuit's opinion in Dixon, he noted that "...the
subject of public education has been, is, and of necessity
must remain to be a matter of the highest public concern."
He acknowledged that Syracuse was not supported directly by
taxation, but observed that it had received its charter by
special grant from the state, was exempt from taxation, was
subject to visitation by the State Regents, was endowed with
the power to confer degrees and had "the power during attendance at the university to regulate [students'] conduct and
their courses of study."11

In the reasoning reflected here, one might conclude
that Judge Smith was at least four decades ahead of his time.
He was to be vindicated by the Fifth Circuit in Dixon. As
will be seen in Chapter V, his reasoning parallels in many
respects that advanced by legal writers in the late 1960's.
He conceded the existence of a contract between Miss Anthony
and the university, but insisted that in such a contract:

> ...the university...agrees that, in the event stu-
> dent successfully pursues the course of study pre-
> scribed and complies during his attendance at the
> institution with the disciplinary rules and regula-
> tions of it, he will receive...a certificate or di-
> ploma. 12

Judge Smith attached to the experience of college life
"values which are very great and which cannot be measured
in dollars, " and concludes that "dismissal is pregnant with
consequences which may spell the ruination of a life."13

Here, again, he expressed values and reasoning which were to be paralleled thirty-four years later by Judge Rives for the Fifth Circuit in Dixon.

In support of his bilateral interpretation of the contract relationship between student and university, Judge Smith cites Ruling Case Law, infra; People ex rel. Cecil v. Bellevue Hospital, [14] infra; Corpus Jiris, [15] infra; and Goldstein v. New York University, [16] infra. From these sources he quoted convincing legal language. For example, from Ruling Case Law, he quotes, "One who is admitted to college and pays the fees for the first year's instruction has a contract right to be permitted to continue as a student until he, in regular course, attains the diploma and degree which he seeks...he cannot be arbitrarily dismissed...."[17]

Citing the 1891 opinion in the case of People ex rel Cecil v. Bellevue Medical College, Judge Smith quoted this language: "It seems clear that [a claimed right to discipline arbitrarily] cannot for a moment be entertained." With obvious approval, he quoted other language to the effect that arbitrary disciplinary discretion "is nothing but a willful violation of the duties" which the college had assumed. "Such a position," he further quoted, "could never receive the sanction of a court in which even the semblance of justice was attempted to be administered."[18]

Judge Smith cited the 1902 decision in the case of Goldstein v. New York University, [19] in which the court's opinion declared that "The relation existing between the university and a matriculated student thereof is contractual, and the law will protect the student against an unauthorized or unjustified expulsion."[20]

Authorities thus cited, Judge Smith declared, are sufficient "to show not only that the relationship between a student and a university is contractual, but also that the action of a university or college in arbitrarily dismissing a student is subject to review by the courts. It is obvious that the courts are loath to interfere with the exercise of discretion by the governing body of an institution of learning upon an established state of facts." Judge Smith added that, "wide latitude, indeed, of necessity, must be given; but that is far from saying that arbitrary action, or action motivated by prejudice or false information ought to be tolerated."[21]

Having thus affirmed the justiciability of the question

before his court, the judge then returned to considering the rights, in general, of the parties before the bench. Quoting Corpus Juris, he declared, "A college cannot arbitrarily and without cause refuse examination and degree to a student who has complied with all the conditions entitling him thereto,"22 and "A college cannot dismiss a student except on a hearing in accordance with a lawful form of procedure, giving him notice of the charge and an opportunity to hear the testimony against him, to question witnesses, and to rebut the evidence."23

Judge Smith then turned his attention to the in loco parentis concept:

> So far as infants are concerned, university and college authorities 'stand in loco parentis concerning the physical and moral welfare and mental training of the pupils, and to that end they may make any rule or regulation for the government or betterment of their pupils that a parent could for the same purpose. Whether the rules or regulations are wise or their aims worthy is a matter left solely to the discretion of the authorities, and in the exercise of that discretion the courts are not disposed to interfere unless the rules and aims are unlawful or against public policy."24

Judge Smith elected to say no more about in loco parentis, returning instead to the presumption of a contract between Miss Anthony and the university, concluding that, "the court has not only the power but it would be its duty, in view of the arbitrary character of the act of dismissal, to decree a reinstatement of the plaintiff."

After thus finding for Miss Anthony, Judge Smith devoted more than five additional pages of his opinion to discussing contractual relationships in general, the peculiar applicability of the contractual relationship to the student-university situation, and the specific nature of the contractual relationship between Miss Anthony and Syracuse University. He found especially inviting to attack the Syracuse statement that, "Attendance at the University is a privilege and not a right." If this be a valid provision, he observes, "Syracuse University has by its own declaration placed itself outside the realm of the law of contracts."25 The university clearly has a right to refuse matriculation to any applicant for admission. But this rule related to attendance after admission.

"Sound public policy is offended by this part of the rule," the judge reiterated. He added:

> The obvious effect of this rule is to reserve to this institution the arbitrary power not only to destroy the career of a student but also to injur his reputation, not by reason of anything which he may have done, but by the very act of the University itself, because the purpose of a dismissal under the rule is 'to safeguard those ideals of scholarship and that moral atmosphere,' etc. No arbitrary act can be taken under this provision which by force of the declared purpose does not cast a blight upon the reputation as to ideals of scholarship or as to moral standing, or both, of the student against whom its provisions are invoked. [26]

"The regulation," wrote Judge Smith, "as operative in the instant case creates an intolerable and unconscionable situation, and the action of the University under it is arbitrary, unreasonable, and in a high degree contravenes a true conception of sound public policy." He acknowledged that the rule "has in it salutary features" in that it might serve to protect the student from unfavorable publicity. But when a student demands to know the reason for his dismissal,

> that student is entitled to the elementary right of notice and opportunity to be heard. This element of notice lies at the very basis of the right of condemnation of property; and much more inherently does it lie at the basis of what is tantamount to an impairment of reputation. [27]

In the foregoing passage, Judge Smith once more implies a property characteristic in the status of the college student. As will be seen in Chapter V, the Fifth Circuit a quarter of a century later was to invent the property concept as a vehicle for including the student status within the penumbra of the Fourteenth Amendment's due process clause. A more apparent similarity between the Smith and Rives opinions, of course, is the finding in both cases that the student is entitled to notice and hearing before being subjected to severe disciplinary action.

Judge Smith observed that the state legislature "was itself without power" to grant Syracuse University the power

it sought to exercise against Miss Anthony. In another passage, he described the contested Syracuse rule as "a rule
which strikes the conscience as unjust, unrighteous and intolerable."

Judge Smith apparently viewed the contract as a bilateral obligation, for he returned to Ruling Case Law to
again quote:

> Where the contract contains an extraordinary pro-
> vision, one which, as a matter of law, renders
> the contract obnoxious to every sense of fairness,
> honesty and right, and is such as to make its en-
> forcement clearly unconscionable, the court is jus-
> tified in believing that the parties sought to be
> charged did not know of the presence of such pro-
> vision, or did not have any comprehension of its
> significance. [28]

However, the invalidity of the contract as the university sought to apply it "does not defeat the duty on the part
of the defendant to perform its part" of the agreement.

Judge Smith's opinion warranted a two-paragraph report in The New York Times, where it was particularly
noted that he had described a private college as a quasi-
public institution. [29]

Appeal and Reversal--As was noted in Chapter II,
Syracuse University carried its cause to the Appellate Division, where five judges heard it reargued. In spite of the
strong language and weighty argument advanced by Judge
Smith in finding for Miss Anthony, the Appellate Division,
fourth department, reversed the trial court and set an important precedent in the history of contract law which was
to bind college students. Judge Sears delivered the opinion
of the court. [30]

Judge Sears employed a tight system of logic to support the court's reversal. He dismissed Miss Anthony's
legal infancy as "not material." Then he continued:

> The regulation, in my judgment, does not reserve
> to the defendant an absolute right to dismiss the
> plaintiff for any cause whatever. Its right to dis-
> miss is limited, for the regulation must be read
> as a whole. The University may only dismiss a

> student for reasons falling within two classes, one
> in connection with safeguarding the University's
> ideals of scholarship, and the other in connection
> with safeguarding the University's moral atmos-
> phere. When dismissing a student, no reason for
> dismissing need be given. The University must,
> however, have a reason, and that reason must fall
> within one of the two classes mentioned above. Of
> course, the University authorities have wide dis-
> cretion in determining what situation does and what
> does not fall within the classes mentioned, and the
> courts would be slow indeed in disturbing any de-
> cision of the University authorities in this respect.
>
> When the plaintiff comes into court and alleges a
> breach of contract the burden rests upon her to
> establish such a breach. [31]

In other words, the burden of proof was on the student to disprove a charge which was being kept secret from
her. In essence, Judge Sears said: The parties had voluntarily entered into a binding contract. A student is not required to enter a university and could withdraw without reason at any time. A university is under no compulsion to
accept as a student one desiring to become one. "It may,
therefore, limit the effect of such acceptance by express
agreement and thus retain the position of contractual freedom in which it stood before the student's course was entered upon." Judge Sears saw no reason why a student
could not agree that the institution may terminate the relationship between them. "The contract between an institution
and a student does not differ in this respect from contracts
of employment." To Judge Sears, then, the only significant
question in the case was what were the terms of the contract.
He found the contract not to constitute "an absolute right to
dismiss...for any reason whatever." The university could
dismiss only for reasons relating to safeguarding the university's "ideals of scholarship" or "moral atmosphere." The
university, then, must have a reason for dismissal which
relates either to scholarship or atmosphere. But it need
not state the reason. The student was dealt the burden of
proving that the reason for her dismissal was not within the
terms of the regulation. Miss Anthony did not sustain that
burden. Her failure was fatal to her cause. To Judge
Sears it apparently was extraneous circumstance that Miss
Anthony was not notified by the university of the nature of
her infraction.

In all likelihood, a careful search would lead one to numerous cases reflecting a greater absence of equity, but Judge Sears' opinion must be recognized for what it is: the game of, "I'm thinking of a number between one and ten."

Significance--What is the significance of Hill and Anthony today? Byse approached an answer to this question when he observed:

> Judge Sadler's early clarion call has been muffled by a cacophony of opposing voices. Although no court seems to have followed the literal approach of Anthony v. Syracuse University, the case has not been overruled, nor has its reasoning been explicitly rejected by any court. Those courts that have ruled that the student should be given notice and opportunity to defend himself have not agreed with Judge Sadler concerning the nature of the hearing. Not even Judge Rives, whose opinion in the Dixon case is clearly the most able and impressive of all those written in this century, would require an opportunity for confrontation and cross-examination; in addition, Judge Rives was most explicit in confining his holding and opinion to "public" institutions which are subject to constraints of the Fourteenth Amendment....32

Other Cases

The "cacophony of opposing voices" which have come from the state courts have, indeed, muffled Judge Sadler's "clarion call." Since Hill and Anthony would seem to represent, as Byse noted, polar opinions in the area, it follows that all other opinions issuing from state courts have fallen between these two extremities. In this wide breach, they have fallen in no distinguishable pattern. However, the generalization by Goldman would seem justified when he observed that "...the overall impact of adjudication in student-university controversies has been characterized by judicial reluctance to interfere with the action of the university."33 The courts have occasionally given specific expression to this deferential attitude in their opinions.

Goldman believes the judicial self-restraint which has characterized cases in the area has sometimes been "unjustifiable." At the same time, he cites two areas of student-

university disputes which obviously warrant great deference
to the university's expertise: "(a) those involving the application of academic standards of performance, and (b) those
involving the design of curriculum." He cites as an example
of the former the case of a doctoral candidate who was dismissed from Columbia University because he refused to re-
vise his rejected dissertation. The student brought action
for reinstatement and lost. The New York court said that
the university had justifiable grounds for insisting on revision
of the dissertation, and the bench would not attempt to sub-
stitute its opinion of the merits of the work for that of the
educators. [34]

In 1917 a New York court declined to order reinstatement of a student expelled for academic reasons, holding
that the bench could not compose a competent examination of
the academic quality of the student's work. [35] Some courts,
however, have staked out limits to judicial deference to academic expertise. A California court, for example, ruled in
1902 that a pupil dismissed for mental incompetence should
be reinstated in the absence of firm evidence of incompetence, especially when the student had passed all his examinations. [36]

It might be noted here that at least one federal district court has proclaimed its own doctrine of deference in
student-college disputes. This came not in a formal opinion
resolving a particular case, but in a judicial document on
student discipline issued in 1969 by the United States District
Court for the Western District of Missouri, en banc. Two
years after it had handed down an important student-rights
decision, [37] the court seized upon an extraordinary publication to declare that "the courts should exercise caution when
importuned to intervene in the important processes and functions of education. A court should never intervene in the
processes of education without understanding the nature of
education." [38] This was not, however, the adoption of an
absolute hands-off policy toward higher education.

The court carefully distinguished its statement as applying to "tax-supported" higher education, declaring that,
"Only where the erroneous and unwise actions in the field of
education deprive students of federally protected rights or
privileges does a federal court have power to intervene in
the educational process." [39]

The U.S. District Court for the Western District of

Missouri would seem to have neutralized the right-privilege question surrounding tax-supported higher education. On this subject, which was broached in Chapter II, the court declared "The federal constitution protects the equality of opportunity of all qualified persons to attend [a public university]. Whether this protected opportunity be called a qualified 'right' or 'privilege' is unimportant. It is optional and voluntary." (emphasis added)40

"Reasonableness" creeps into the District Court's standard when the judges declare:

> So long as there is no invidious discrimination, no deprival of due process, no abridgement of a right protected in the circumstances and no capricious, clearly unreasonable or unlawful action employed, the institution may discipline students to secure compliance with these higher obligations [of students] as a teaching method or to sever the student from the academic community. 41

However, the due process accorded students in this statement is not the same as criminal due process, because, "The attempted analogy of student discipline to criminal proceedings against adults and juveniles is not sound."42

This statement of judicial standards will be examined further in Chapter VI, but its implications are so broad that it cannot be overlooked as a standard of comparison between what state courts have held in student-college disputes and what the law was to become four decades after Anthony.

Goldman cites an 1866 Illinois case in which the judge stated that the court can no more control a college's disciplinary actions than "control the domestic discipline of a father in his family."43

Probably the earliest instance of a court overturning an administrative decision of a university was in a 1732 mandamus action before the King's Bench. One Richard Bentley had been deprived of academic degrees without notice or hearing. The court condemned the procedure as being contrary to natural justice. 44

In 1908 the University of Minnesota was directed to reinstate a student because of abuse of administrative discretion and denial of notice and hearing. 45

More commonly, however, state courts have found
against petitioning students, while the federal courts have not
been open to them.   Of particular interest to some writers
because it is often cited as admitting the in loco parentis
concept into American case law concerning the student-college
relationship is the 1913 case of Gott v. Berea College.[46]
Although this decision by the Court of Appeals of Kentucky
had a profound influence on student-college relationships for
more than half a century, the case itself involved students
only indirectly.   Action was brought by one J. S. Gott, pro-
prietor of a restaurant across the street from the premises
of Berea College.   Gott claimed his business was damaged
after the Berea faculty adopted a rule which, in effect,
placed his restaurant off limits for Berea students.

Judge Nunn took judicial note of the fact that, "the institution aims to furnish an education to inexperienced country, mountain boys and girls of very little means at the lowest possible cost," that "there must be the fullest co-operation on the part of the students," and declared that the college stood in loco parentis to the students to justify the rule
"as a safeguard against disease infection...."[47]

Law students, as might be expected, have figured
disproportionately in student challenges of university authority.   An early such case was Koblitz v. Western Reserve
University[48] in 1901, heard by the Cuyahoga County, Ohio,
Circuit Court.   Involved was a student dismissed after his
first year in law school.   During the year he had been twice
arrested on criminal charges, had not been successful in
passing his examinations, and had been abusive toward other
students.   Judge Caldwell's opinion draws much of its importance from its discussion of distinctions between public
and private institutions.   But, of interest, too, is his concept of procedural fairness in the case of university expulsion.   After discussing the nature of the hearing to which
the student is entitled, the court generalized in these words:

> The only requirement necessary, so far as con-
> cerns a review of the matter in a court of justice,
> is that it shall not be so unreasonable as to leave
> the conclusion of unfairness on the part of the
> teachers.   It matters not whether we call this ar-
> rangement between the pupils and authorities over
> the school a contract or license.[49]

State courts have commonly restrained the power of

state universities to reject applicants for admission. [50] It is
well established that the state may not arbitrarily reject a
university applicant because of race, religion, or other unreasonable considerations. However, nothing exists to compel a state university to accept a student on his own terms,
as Professor O'Leary has pointed out. [51] If the relationship
between student and university is a contractual one, it remains nonetheless true that terms of the contract are not individually negotiated, but are established by state policy for
the education of the whole citizenry. But what terms may
the university, as agency of the state, establish in its contract with students? Different courts in different states have
supplied various answers to this question.

The Illinois Supreme Court has said that the university charter

> gives to the trustees and faculty the power 'to
> adopt and enforce such rules as may be deemed
> expedient for the government of the institution,' a
> power which they would have possessed without
> such express grant, because incident to the very
> object of their incorporation, and indispensible to
> the successful management of the college. [52]

In 1947 an Illinois appellate court took the questionable position that the "State through the legislature has no
power to take from or interfere with the power of the University to make such rules as are necessary to conduct the
University's business." [53] In 1924 the Michigan Supreme
Court, in Tanton v. McKenney, [54] took a sweeping view of
the authority of universities to set the terms of the student
contract when it said:

> Inherently the managing officers have the power to
> maintain such discipline as will effectuate the pur-
> poses of the institution. . . . That in the absence of
> an abuse shall prescribe the proper disciplinary
> measures. . . is settled by the text writers and the
> adjudicated cases.

As to the cases where the facts will prompt the
courts to interfere with administrative discretion, O'Leary
has compiled the following summation from state cases:

> . . . the courts have variously characterized them
> as 'palpably unreasonable,' Stetson Univ. [v.] Hunt,

88 Fla. 510, 102 So. 637 (1924); 'against the common right,' Stallard v. White, 82 Ind. 278 (1882);
'unauthorized,' ibid.; 'unreasonably oppressive,'
Koblitz v. Western Reserve Univ., 21 Ohio C. C.
R. 144 (1901); 'unlawful' and 'against the public
policy,' Gott v. Berea College, 156 Ky. 376, 161
S.W. 204 (1913); and, with reference to the acts of
officials charged with applying the regulations, 'arbitrary,' Booker v. Grand Rapids Medical Center,
156 Mich. 95, 120 N.W. 589 (1909); 'fraudulent,'
Stetson v. Hunt;...'without any cause whatsoever,'
Koblitz v. Western Reserve Univ., supra; 'lack of
impartiality,' Koblitz, supra; 'lack of good faith,'
Robinson v. Univ. of Miami, Fla., 100 So. 2d 442
(1958) cert denied, Fla. 104 So. 2d 595 (1958);
'with malice,' McCormick v. Burt, 95 Ill. 362
(1880); 'without sufficient reason,' Anthony v. Syracuse Univ. 224 App. Div. 487, 239 N.Y. Supp.
435 (1928); 'capriciously,' Frank v. Marquette
Univ., 209 Wisc. 372, 245 N.W. 125 (1932); 'no
exercise of discretion,' Goldenkoff v. Albany Law
School 198 App. Div. 460, 191 N.Y. Supp. 349
(1921); not 'within the scope of their jurisdiction,'
ibid.; and a 'clear abuse of discretion,' Ingersoll
v. Clapp, 81 Mont. 200, 263 Pac. 433 (1928).
But see Barker v. Bryn Mawr College, 278 Pa.
121, 122 Atl. 220 (1923), where the court went so
far as to declare itself without power to intercede.55

An expulsion opinion which was to prove of considerable significance was handed down by the Appellate Court of
Illinois, First Division, in the case of Bluett v. Trustees
of the University of Illinois.56 This 1956 case was a mandamus action brought by Patricia Bluett, a former medical
student at the University of Illinois, who sought to vacate
an order by the university trustees which expelled her from
the medical school.

Particulars of the case do not make it unique. Briefly, Miss Bluett was a student at the University of Illinois
Medical School from October 1, 1949 until May, 1953, when
she was suspended and prohibited from further continuing
her course at the university. She was not told of the cause
of her suspension until June 15, 1954. On the latter date,
she and her attorney appeared before a Committee on Policy
and Discipline and were advised by counsel for the university
that she had been suspended for attempting to turn in an ex-

amination paper which had been written by a Doctor Wong, and that she had previously submitted other examination papers which had been written by Doctor Wong.   Judge Niemeyer for the appellate court took note of the fact that "No witnesses were produced at the meeting to support the charges and no other evidence was heard than the testimony of the plaintiff, not under oath, denying the charges."[57]

The Committee, "after having given careful and thorough consideration to all the evidence before it..." unanimously found her guilty and changed her status as a student under suspension to that of one expelled from the medical college and recommended to the dean of the college that she be given failing grades in the three courses in which she had allegedly cheated.   Miss Bluett's appeal for reconsideration of the committee action was rejected, and her repeated demands for reinstatement were denied.

The plaintiff conceded the right of the committee to expel a student for cheating or attempting to cheat on examinations, and conceded further that the court should not attempt to control the exercise of that power unless it were substantially abused.   Miss Bluett's exception was based on the absence of notice and hearing at which she might have been confronted with accusing witnesses and have been given an opportunity to cross-examine them.   Her counsel based his case largely on the trial court's opinion in Anthony and on 11 Corpus Juris, "Colleges and Universities," to the effect that a student cannot be dismissed from a college "except on a hearing in accordance with a lawful form of procedure, giving him notice of the charge and an opportunity to hear the testimony against him, to question witnesses and to rebut the evidence."[58]

Judge Niemeyer was hearing a different drummer. He pointed out that the trial court in Anthony had been reversed and that the positive statement in 11 Corpus Juris "is not repeated in 14 C. J. S. Colleges and Universities, in treating of the same subject."[59]   He then utilized an assortment of state-court opinions which rejected the claimed right of notice and hearing.   He thus applied the coup de grace to Miss Bluett's contention.

The significance of Bluett, however, lies less in the particulars of the case than in the fact that the decision keenly disturbed the late Professor Seavey, driving him to compose at the age of seventy-seven a short article for the

<u>Harvard Law Review</u> which was to prove a landmark in the literature of college disciplinary proceedings for students. 60 Professor Seavey's article, previously cited, began with the opening summation of the procedural rights of college students before Illinois courts in dismissal proceedings:

> A woman student in a medical school of a state university was accused of cheating, which she denied. Though she was given a hearing prior to her dismissal, she was not told what evidence there was against her or the identity of her accusers; nor, in the proceeding for mandamus which she brought, was she permitted to give evidence of her innocence. Mandamus was denied on the authority of an earlier case in which the complainant had claimed to be ignorant of the evidence upon which dismissal had been based. Apparently all the Illinois courts require in proceedings resulting in the expulsion of a student, as was expressed in the earlier case, is that the institution's authorities should have heard 'some evidence.' The student is left with the impossible task of proving that the academic judges have acted wantonly or corruptly without having the information from which evidence to support his charges can be found. 61

How It Came To Be

One is confronted with a project involving considerable speculation when he undertakes to document an explanation of how the colleges were able to get their values so consistently written into the case law. From the viewpoint of the nineteenth century and its broad application of civil liberties concepts, one might easily view the pre-<u>Dixon</u> history of student-college relationships as a dark age of unconscionable repression of college students.

How did it come about in the first place that college students were denied individual rights which they would have retained outside the academic world? Why would the college, the symbol of democratic values in a democracy, undertake to deny democratic prerogatives to its student clientele? And why would the state courts go along with the peevishness of the academic community? Projected answers to these questions lie beyond the realm of conclusive proof. Indeed, the literature on higher education would seem to of-

fer little discussion on these seemingly basic questions.
However, some speculation would seem to be warranted.

Undoubtedly many possible reasons could be advanced
to help explain the paternalism which confronted college students prior to Dixon, and which confronts them even today
in many institutions. Four possible contributing causes of
the development of this paternalism and judicial support for
it are: (1) the ecclesiastical background of American higher
education and the consequent concern for the morality of college students; (2) political boards of control; (3) the pragmatic concerns of college presidents; and (4) the property
orientation of American judiciary until recent decades.

Ecclesiastical Background

Jencks and Riesman have pointed out that American
colleges prior to the twentieth century were "conceived and
operated as pillars of the locally established church, political order, and social conventions." The faculty were "more
often trained as clergymen than as scholars," and consequently were more interested in improving the moral character than the minds of their students. [62] This cast the instruc-
tor in a quasi-parental role with a natural concern for the
private life of the student and a parental interest in seeing
to it that the students did not depart from accepted conventions.

Political Boards of Control

Probably no more anachronistic agency plagues higher
education today than the lay board of control, commonly subject to political appointment. Jencks and Riesman describe
the nineteenth century as "an era when self-confident trustees tended to intervene in college affairs far more often
and more disastrously than is usual today." [63] The trustee's
most important job is to select a college president, and
choices of nineteenth century boards "tended to be far more
domineering than [college presidents] are today." [64] Early
in the twentieth century, Veblen could declare that the college boards of control "are of no material use in any connection," and that "they have ceased to exercise any function
other than a bootless meddling with academic matters which
they do not understand." [65] If this was the case in Veblen's
time, it is probably no less true today, as indicated by a

1969 survey by the Educational Testing Service of Princeton,
New Jersey. This survey of 5, 000 trustees at 536 colleges
and universities concluded that "trustees do not read--indeed
have generally never even heard of the more relevant higher
education books and journals."[66]

But the point to be made here is that the lay board
of control has throughout American academic history served
as an instrument to facilitate the imposition of non-academic
values on the academic community. One might propose a
priori that non-academic values directed toward the academy
are, and have long been, paternalistic values. This was
well and good before Dixon, but cannot stand the light of legal examination today.

College Presidents

Veblen refers to college and university presidents as
"captains of erudition, " and characterizes them as businessmen appointed by business-oriented boards for the purpose
of conducting an academic enterprise on a business-like basis.[67] If he is thus too harsh in his treatment of educational executives, his cynicism is perhaps more than compen-
sated for by Jencks and Riesman, who could declare that
"What is perhaps unusual about the academic world is the
extent to which top management, while nominally acting in
the interests of the board, actually represents the interests
of "middle management (i. e., the faculty) both to the board
and to the world."[68]

The point to be made here is a simple one. Con-
ceding, as Jencks and Riesman do, that college administrators serve well in their roles as scapegoats to the frustrated
faculty members, the commonest position of the tax-supported
college president is an impossible one, if democratic ideals
are to be preserved on campus. The college president is
caught in the middle of the impossible triangle constituted
by the faculty, students, and board. In the best academic
theory, he should serve all three of these publics. But he
serves at the pleasure of the board alone. Board members
"share the upper middle-class allergy to 'trouble' of whatever sort."[69] It is perhaps as sure as anything which cannot be proved that democracy and due process on campus
will create what appears to board members as "trouble."
Thus the college president, often a man of academic orientation, would seem to be cast in the either-or position of

being true to the board at the risk of offending the faculty
and the students. How often can a man be expected to be so
great as to represent principle in the face of personal sacri-
fice? It is reasonably certain that this caught-in-the-middle
posture of the college and university president has mitigated
against the concept of student rights on campus and will continue to do so until the president is given greater security.

An apparent solution to this dilemma would be power-
ful representation on the board to the two unrepresented pub-
lics--students and faculty--or else giving students and faculty
a veto over board decisions in the hiring and firing of college presidents.

Property Orientation of the Courts

Property and contract have always been two major
concerns of the law. An indication of this is evidenced in
the fact that when Morris R. and Felix S. Cohen compiled
a book of readings in jurisprudence, the first hundred pages
appeared under the heading, "Property," and the second hundred under the heading, "Contracts."[70] Bentham emphasized
the relationship between property and law when he wrote,
"The better to understand the advantages of law, let us en-
deavor to form a clear idea of property. We shall see that
there is no such thing as natural property, and that it is entirely the work of law."[71]

Whether one turns to Grotius in the seventeenth century or Blackstone in the nineteenth century, he will find
background for Cohen's statement in the twentieth century
that, "when we consider police power, its essence is the interpretation of property."[72] And the role of the judiciary in
the United States historically has been primarily the protection of property. Thus, in 1969, Abraham could write what
many other scholars have observed about the United States
Supreme Court, that "Even a cursory glance at the Court's
history proves that the economic-proprietarian sphere was
very much in the focus of the Court's work prior to the New
Deal, ... "[73]

Since institutions--including colleges--are historically
identified to some degree with property, and students--as legal infants--have scarcely been identified at all with property, one finds little difficulty in understanding how the scholarly estate was so successful in getting its value written into

the law. Indeed, the property concept would seem to be so
important to the American judicial scheme that the about-turn
in the law marked by Dixon involved the sudden discovery
that the student had property interests on his side, too, and
a serious weighing of equities ensued.

Further, the students were forced to await two historical developments before they could have their day in court
free of such myths as the unilateral contract obligation. They
were forced to await the development of a broad judicial interpretation of the fourteenth amendment's due process
clause--one aspect of what has been called "universalism,
that is, an increasing extension of principles like equality...
to all groups within the society...."[74]

Impact of Dixon on the Institution

The United States Supreme Court declared racial segregation in the public schools unconstitutional in 1954. After
sixteen years, this decree had not been fully complied with,
in the sense that racial integration in the public schools had
not been fully achieved. The school integration decision was
a 180-degree reversal in the law, just as Dixon amounted to
a 180-degree reversal in the law. One might assume that
more time will be required for full compliance with Dixon
than is being required for full compliance with the Brown
decision for the simple fact that the Fifth Circuit's opinion
attracted much less publicity than the Supreme Court's decision.

Probably the most ready compliance with the new
rationale of Dixon has been among the larger universities,
where legal staffs and law school faculty members could not
have missed the abundance of law-journal articles dealing
with the newly won constitutional status of college students.
For example, John P. Holloway, resident legal counsel for
the University of Colorado, has written extensively of that
university's rather extreme compliance with and beyond the
Dixon rationale. [75] Yet, judging by the number of cases
still entering the federal courts, where the facts indicate a
lack of understanding of the new student status, a period of
several decades might be expected to elapse before full compliance or even general compliance will be realized.

The Forces of Publicity

While the law journals perhaps reflected the greatest
interest in Dixon and its new direction of the law, educational
organizations and journals have by no means remained silent
or inactive. The Joint Statement on Rights and Freedoms of
Students, inspired by the American Association of University
Professors and adopted by numerous other professional organizations, will be discussed in subsequent chapters. But
it should be observed here that the Joint Statement is one of
the brighter developments in recent efforts to publicize the
fact that college students now enjoy a new legal status. As
will be shown later, the Joint Statement makes recommendations which go beyond what the courts have decreed as minimal student rights.

The United States National Student Association has
exerted an aggressive publicity force behind the new developments in student legal rights. A monthly newsletter, the
College Law Bulletin, issued by USNSA, reports latest case-
law developments without editorial comment. The USNSA
has also published a number of booklets on the subject of
student rights. [76] The American Civil Liberties Union has
given enthusiastic coverage to case-law developments in the
area in its monthly publication, Civil Liberties, and has
issued several booklets on the subject of student rights. A
private monthly newsletter, The Education Court Digest,
covers the same area, but extends beyond student-rights
considerations and embraces the public schools as well as
the colleges.

Relatively little notice of the new legal direction
broached by Dixon and subsequent cases is found in the standard indexed educational journals. What has appeared is
generally fair in tone. However, an unfortunate display of
editorial bias appeared in the summer, 1969, issue of the
Journal of Teacher Education. [77] Edward T. Ladd, Director
of the Division of Educational Studies, Emory University,
was author of an enthusiastic commentary on the ACLU's
publication, Academic Freedom in the Secondary Schools. [78]
Ladd points out that 20,000 copies of the new ACLU statement were bought in the first four months following its publication, and observes that, "One has only to read Frieden-
berg's Coming of Age in America, Herndon's The Way It
Spozed To Be, or even Jackson's Life in Classrooms to be
reminded how far removed is present school practice from
what the ACLU proposes. "[79] Ladd makes this further observation:

Alan Westin, the distinguished professor of public
law and government at Columbia, has offered some
summer institutes for teachers and administrators
dealing with American liberties and their bearing
on school practice. On a visit to the most recent
of these, I was struck with the naivete that some
of the participating teachers and other school personnel showed regarding relationships between freedom and order, liberty and authority, democracy
and leadership. But I was also struck by their enthusiasm for what they were studying, including a
firsthand experience in 'participatory democracy,'
by the rapidity with which they seemed to be learning.... 80

All in all, Ladd's article was an enthusiastic endorsement of the ACLU position on rights for students. The editor's values were revealed, however, in the title over the
article, "Civil Liberties: Yet Another Piece of Baggage for
Teacher Education?"

Joseph Katz and Nevitt Sanford of Stanford University
wrote in an article for the April, 1966, Phi Delta Kappan
that, "Perhaps administrators ought to relax and realize that
they simply cannot control much of the behavior they might
like to control," and, "Many deans seem to have an exag-
gerated conception of the amount of deviance that would result once rules were relaxed. Our own research, as well
as that of others, has shown that, in the matter of sex, for
instance, students exercise a high degree of responsibility."

Joseph F. Kauffman, Consultant for the American
Council on Education, wrote an article for the Fall, 1964,
issue of the Educational Record, endorsing the ACLU's statement on Academic Freedoms and Civil Liberties of Students
in Colleges and Universities, which will be discussed in later
chapters. Far from being antagonistic, he declares that,
"I do not mean to imply that colleges and universities are
innocent bystanders. We know all too well that arbitrary
punishment, invasion of privacy, and noneducational pressures have provided students in some institutions with legitimate cause for complaint."81

Ralph Thompson and Samuel P. Kelly of the education
faculty at Western Washington State College were able to
declare that "Men of reason must demand for students the
same range of civil rights as other citizens enjoy," in an

article for the Fall, 1969, Educational Record. [82]

Although a few articles[83] in the educational journals
have undertaken to clarify the meanings of some of the legal
precedents issuing from the courts, non-legal educational
writers in general seem more inclined to urge recognition
of student rights on moral grounds than to cite legal precedent.

Speaking of campus protest in 1969, Kenneth Keniston
wrote that, "Admittedly, a sudden increase in the administrative wisdom in college deans and presidents could reduce the
number of available 'on-campus' issues; but such a growth
in wisdom does not seem imminent."[84]

A report of the Illinois Legislative Council, February
18, 1969, prepared by James T. Mooney, Research Co-ordinator, closed with this admonition:

> There are those who would argue that a politics of
> confrontation, of violence and counter-violence can
> best be avoided by entrusting to college and uni-
> versity authorities the responsibility of keeping
> open to students the channels of legitimate protest
> and of introducing a greater measure of democracy
> into university affairs than now exists. [85]

Meanwhile members of college boards of control seem
to have remained relatively unmoved by the changed legal
status of the college student.   In the study referred to above,
the opinion survey of more than 5,000 trustees at 536 colleges and universities by Educational Testing Service, these
stark facts emerged:

> Most trustees feel that the administration should
> control the content of student newspapers; well
> over a third believe it reasonable to require loyal-
> ty oaths from faculty members, and a similar
> number hold that students punished for off-campus
> behavior should also be disciplined by the college.
>
> A fourth of the trustees would screen campus
> speakers, and deny to faculty members, 'the right
> to free expression of opinions.'[86]

Educational Testing Service concluded from its study
that:

> To the extent that ideological differences among
> [trustees, students, and faculty] remain (or in-
> crease), we might expect greater conflict and dis-
> ruption of academic programs, a deeper entrench-
> ment of the ideas of competing factions, and, worst
> of all, an aimless, confusing collegiate experience,
> where the student's program is a result of arbitra-
> tion rather than mutual determination of goals and
> purposes. [87]

Perhaps an opinion or a series of opinions from the
United States Supreme Court, broadly defining the constitutional rights of college students, would speed up the process
of nationwide acceptance of the new interpretation of student
legal status. Meanwhile, students who are arbitrarily denied
their constitutional rights by paternalistic administrators may
take some comfort from the fact that the weight of judicial
precedent has turned against autocracy on campus.

Notes

1. "Procedure in Student Dismissal Proceedings: Law and
    Policy," Journal of College Student Personnel, March,
    1963, pp. 140-143.

2. 3 Pa. C. C. Rep. 77 (C. P. Cumberland Cy. 1887).

3. Ibid., at 79.

4. Ibid., at 81.

5. Ibid., at 82.

6. Ibid., at 79.

7. Ibid., at 85.

8. Ibid., at 84.

9. 130 Misc. 249, 25.

10. 347 U. S. 483 (1954).

11. 130 Misc. 249, 251.

12. Ibid., at 253.

13. Ibid., citing 27 R. C. L. 144.

14. 60 Hun. 107, affd., 128 N. Y. 621. (1891).

15. 130 Misc. 249, 251, citing 11 Corpus Juris, 984, 997.

16. 76 App. Div. 80, 78 N. Y. Supp. 739 (1902).

17. 130 Misc. 249, 251, citing 76 App. Div. 80 (sic).

18. 130 Misc. 249, 254-255.

19. 60 Hun. 107, affd., 128 N. Y. 621 (1891).

20. Ibid., at 255.

21. Ibid.

22. 130 Misc. 249, 255, quoting "Colleges and Universities," 11 Corpus Juris 984.

23. 130 Misc. 249, 256, quoting "Colleges and Universities," 11 Corpus Juris 997.

24. 130 Misc. 249, 256, quoting 27 Ruling Case Law 141.

25. 130 Misc. 249, at 258.

26. Ibid.

27. Ibid., at 259.

28. Ibid., at 261, citing 6 Ruling Case Law 626.

29. August 20, 1927, p. 3.

30. 231 N. Y. S. 435.

31. Ibid., at 440.

32. "Procedure in Student Dismissal Proceedings," op. cit., pp. 311-312.

33. "The University and the Liberty of Its Students--A Fiduciary Theory," op. cit., p. 654.

34. Edde v. Columbia University, 8 Misc. 2d 795, 168 N.Y.
    S. 2d 643 (N. Y. Sup. Ct. 1957), aff'd mem., 5 N.Y.
    2d 777, 154 N.E. 2d 558, cert denied, 359 U. S. 956
    (1959), as cited by Goldman, op. cit., p. 655.

35. People ex rel Pacilla v. Bennett Medical College, 205
    Ill. App. 324 (1917); People ex rel Jones v. New York
    Homeopathic Medical College, 20 N.Y. Supp. 379
    (Super Ct. 1892), as cited by ibid.

36. Miller v. Dailery, 136 Cal. 212, 68 Pac. 1029 (1902),
    as cited by ibid.

37. Estaban v. Central Missouri State College, 277 F. Supp.
    649 (W. D. Mo. 1967).

38. "A Judicial Document on Student Discipline," Educa-
    tional Record, Winter, 1969, p. 2.

39. Ibid., p. 3.

40. Ibid., p. 4.

41. Ibid.

42. Ibid.

43. "The University and the Liberty of Its Students--A Fi-
    duciary Theory," op. cit., p. 655, citing People ex
    rel Pratt v. Wheaton College, 40 Ill. 186, 187 (1866).

44. The King v. Chancellor of the University of Cambridge,
    6 T.R. 89, 10 Eng. Rep. 451 (K.B. 1732).

45. Gleason v. University of Minnesota, 104 Minn. 359,
    116 N. W. 650 (1908).

46. 156 Ky. 376, 161 S.W. 204 (1913).

47. 161 S.W. 204, 207.

48. 21 Ohio C.C.R. 144, 157.

49. Ibid.

50. See, e.g., Stallard v. White, 82 Ind. 278 (1882).

51. Richard E. O'Leary, "The College Student and Due
     Process in Disciplinary Proceedings, " 1962 University
     of Illinois Law Forum 438, 441.

52. Pratt v. Wheaton College, 40 Ill. 186, 187 (1866), as
     quoted by O'Leary, ibid. , p. 441.

53. Turkioff v. Northwestern University, 333 Ill. App. 224,
     231, 77 N. E. 2d 345, 349 (1947), cert. denied, 335
     U. S. 829, 69 Sup. Ct. 37 (1948), as quoted by
     O'Leary, ibid.

54. 226 Mich. 245, 248, 197 N. W. 510, 511 (1924).

55. O'Leary, op. cit. , p. 433n82.

56. 134 N. E. 2d 635 (1956).

57. Ibid. , at 636.

58. Ibid. , at 637.

59. Ibid.

60. "Dismissal of Students: 'Due Process, ' " op. cit.

61. Ibid. , at 1406. The earlier case referred to by Seavey
     is Smith v. Board of Education, 182 Ill. App. 342
     (1913), which Seavey footnoted as a case in which a
     "student expelled from high school for membership in
     a fraternity had his claim dismissed even on the as-
     sumption that he had been denied the opportunity to
     prove that he had not joined the fraternity. "

62. The Academic Revolution, op. cit. , p. 1.

63. Ibid. , p. 6.

64. Ibid.

65. Thorstein Veblen, The Higher Learning in America
     (New York: Sagamore Press, Inc. , 1957), p. 48.

66. Commonweal, January 31, 1969, p. 544.

67. Veblen, op. cit. , esp. pp. 62-98.

68. The Academic Revolution, op. cit., p. 17.

69. Ibid., p. 16.

70. Readings in Jurisprudence and Legal Philosophy (New
     York: Prentice-Hall, Inc., 1951).

71. Ibid., p. 8, quoting "Principles of the Civil Code,"
     Part I ("Objects of the Civil Law"), pp. 111-113, Du-
     mont ed., Hildreth trans. (1864).

72. "Readings in Jurisprudence," op. cit., p. 15.

73. Henry J. Abraham, The Judiciary (Boston: Allyn and
     Bacon, 1969), p. 38.

74. Kenneth Keniston, "The Sources of Student Dissent,"
     Walt Anderson, (ed.) The Age of Protest (Pacific
     Palisades, Calif.:   Goodyear Publishing Co., 1969),
     p. 239.

75. See, e.g., "The School in Court," Grace W. Holmes,
     (ed.) Student Protest and the Law (Ann Arbor, Mich.:
     The Institute of Continuing Legal Education, 1969),
     p. 83.

76. The USNSA publications list includes: Elimination of
     Social Rules; Student Conduct and Social Freedom;
     Procedural Due Process and State University Students;
     Political Speakers at State Universities: Some Con-
     stitutional Considerations; Private Government on the
     Campus: Judicial Review of University Expulsions,
     and others.

77. XX, 2.

78. New York: ACLU, 1968.

79. Ibid., at p. 139.

80. "Civil Liberties: Yet Another Piece of Baggage for
     Teacher Education?" Journal of Teacher Education,
     Summer, 1969, XX 2, p. 139.

81. p. 360.

82. "In Loco Parentis and the Academic Enclave," p. 449.

83.   E.g., Richard D. Strahan, "School Board Authority and
      Behavioral Codes for Students," Texas School Board
      Journal, March, 1970, p. 9 (although Strahan, Presi-
      dent of Lee College, is a member of the Texas Bar);
      and "What the Courts Are Saying About Student Rights,"
      NEA Research Bulletin, October, 1969, p. 86.

84.   "The Sources of Student Dissent," Walt Anderson (ed.),
      The Age of Protest, op. cit., p. 242.

85.   Student Protest and the Law, op. cit., p. 66.

86.   Commonweal, January 31, 1969, p. 544.

87.   Ibid.

Chapter IV

NEGRO RIGHTS AND PRESSURE ON THE COURTS

To those civil libertarians who take the view that liberties cannot be neatly compartmentalized along group lines, that no subculture can gain rights without expanding the liberties of the general culture of which it is a part, the Dixon case provides a strong supportive argument. For Dixon presents a case of Negro students, discriminated against as Negroes, suing as Negroes, but winning their cause as students.

It is quite likely that long after the Negro passive-resistance movement of the 1960's has passed from the topical American scene into the quiet pages of modern history, students of any race will still be upheld in the quest of procedural fairness by the Fifth Circuit's decision in Dixon, a decision growing out of the heat of the Negro rights revolution of its time. True, the Dixon precedent was to be used by other groups of southern Negroes to fend off efforts at official reprisal for their participation in Negro-rights demonstrations, [1] but when the Negro-rights movement appeared to be waning in 1969, the Fifth Circuit's 1961 decision had become of less importance as a bulwark against racial discrimination. Elaborating opinions from the trial courts, however, had increased the importance of Judge Rives' opinion as a barrier against arbitrary treatment of college students.

The purpose of this chapter is to trace the major judicial victories for the Negro cause in the past two decades, sketch the beginning of the Negro movement of passive protest, and place Dixon within this context.

The Judicial Background

Milton R. Konvitz draws a contrasting comparison between the means utilized by American Negroes in pressing

91

their long-range campaign for civil rights and those employed earlier by organized labor to win the rights of self-organization and collective bargaining.[2] Briefly put, labor followed the legislative route in the face of a hostile judiciary, whereas the Negroes followed the executive and judicial routes in the face of an unresponsive national legislature.[3]

Because of the reams of literature which have been written on the subject, it is unnecessary to repeat here the story of the long judicial trek which led Negro rights advocates to the ultimate judicial victory represented by the United States Supreme Court's decision in the case of Brown v. Board of Education.[4] For the same reason, it is unnecessary to undertake a detailed account of the counter measures employed by southern whites in efforts to nullify the legal victory won by the blacks in Brown or the story of the passive resistance movement adopted by American Negroes, primarily in the South, under the leadership of the late Dr. Martin Luther King, Jr.

Rather, it will suffice to note that the Negroes did win what might be denominated "ultimate" victory in their judicial quest for equal status in education, and that in the face of white harrassment they did undertake numerous displays of passive resistance characterized by economic boycotts of white merchants and "sit-ins" at segregated lunch counters. Such demonstrations form an important background for the development of the Dixon case. The demonstrations were indigenous student affairs. The organizations were to take over later. But it was in the setting of the indigenous demonstration that the opening scene of Dixon v. Alabama was to be staged.

Dixon v. Alabama

In 1963, Van Alstyne observed that "Virtually every significant change affecting student prerogatives and college powers made within the past ten years has resulted from an authoritative interpretation of the fourteenth amendment." Thus, any effort to review the trends in the law of student prerogatives and college powers must of necessity show considerable deference to the fourteenth amendment and the Bill of Rights of the United States Constitution. Negro judicial victories which led eventually to Brown were victories based primarily on the equal protection clause. And, since the fourteenth amendment inhibits states, but not the District of

Columbia, the Court looked to the due process clause of the fifth amendment for a basis of its rationale to end public school segregation in the nation's capital.

Since, as was observed in Chapters II and III, students fared so poorly in state courts, the question might well be asked: What was the open sesame which admitted expulsion cases to the jurisdiction of the federal courts?   Central to the answer is the fact that the Civil Rights Act (28 U.S. C. 1343) provides that:

> The district courts shall have original jurisdiction of any civil action authorized by law to be commenced by any person... (3) To redress the deprivation, under color of any state law... of any right, privilege or immunity secured by the Constitution of the United States or by any Act of Congress providing for equal rights of citizens or of all persons within the jurisdiction of the United States.

However, Van Alstyne points out that Section 1343 requires that the "civil action" testing a due process claim in the federal courts--at least where a matter of intangible value is concerned--be "authorized by law."[5]   In other words, the cause of action must be otherwise described by federal statute.   Authorization for such an action would seem to lie in 42 U.S.C. 1983, which provides:

> Every person who, under color of any statute... of any state... subjects... any... other person within the jurisdiction thereof to the deprivation of any rights, privileges, or immunities secured by the Constitution and laws, shall be liable to the party injured in an action at law, suits in equity, or other proper proceeding for redress.

These two federal statutes, then, might be understood to admit to the federal district courts actions growing out of official state denials of constitutional rights.   However, prior to 1961 the federal courts interpreted Section 1983 as authorizing a cause of action only where the unconstitutional practice was directed against a readily isolated minority group on a systematic basis.   Thus, in June, 1960, the Seventh Circuit could observe:

> It might be argued that this case arises under the Civil Rights Acts, 42 U.S.C.A. S 1981 et seq.

However, our Court has held contra in the case of
Stift v. Lynch, 7 Cir. , 267 F. 2d 237. There we
held that the Civil Rights Acts do not create a
cause of action for false imprisonment unless such
imprisonment is in pursuance of a systematic policy of discrimination against a class or group of
persons. 6

Citing this language in November, 1960, the United
States District Court for the Northern District of Illinois apparently felt no discomfort in observing that "The Civil
Rights Act must be interpreted in light of delicate state-
federal relationships, " and at the same time expressed a
fear of flooding the federal courts with civil rights suits. 7

In 1961 the Supreme Court delivered a weighty opinion
undertaking to construe the applicability of Section 1983. Mr.
Justice Douglas wrote the opinion in Monroe v. Pape, 8 which
held, inter alia, that the victim of an unreasonable search
had cause for action against the Chicago police under Section 1983.   Thus the Seventh Circuit's restrictive interpretation in Truitt v. Illinois was superceded by the rationale
that individuals can find cause for action under 42 U. S. C.
1343 and 1983 against officers of a state acting under color
of state law in such a manner as to deprive the individuals
of their rights.   Monroe v. Pape was decided February 20,
1961.   The Fifth Circuit was to deliver its Dixon decision
eight months later.

Dixon had its inception on February 25, 1960, when a
group of twenty-nine students at Alabama State College, a
state-supported institution for Negroes, entered a publicly
owned lunch grill in the basement of the county courthouse
in Montgomery, and asked to be served.   Service was refused, and the lunchroom was closed.   After the Negroes
had refused to leave, police officers were summoned.   The
Negroes were ordered outside the lunchroom, where they
remained in the corridor of the courthouse for approximately
one hour.

On the same day, Alabama Governor John Patterson,
who served as ex-officio chairman of the state board of education, conferred with Dr. H. Councill Trenholm, president
of the college, requesting that the incident be investigated.
Governor Patterson advised the college president that if he
(Patterson) were in the president's position, he would consider expulsion or other appropriate disciplinary action.

The following day several hundred Negro students from
the college staged a mass attendance at a trial in the Montgomery County courthouse involving the perjury prosecution
of a fellow student. After the trial, these students filed two
by two from the courthouse and marched through the city approximately two miles back to the college campus.

On the third day, February 27, 1960, several hundred
Negro students from Alabama State College staged mass
demonstrations in Montgomery and in Tuskegee, Alabama.
Also on February 27, President Trenholm told the student
body that the demonstrations and meetings were disrupting
the orderly conduct of the college's business and affecting
the work of the other students, as well as the work of the
participating students. Dr. Trenholm personally warned
three students who were later to become plaintiffs in the
federal court action which was to ensue--these three being
Bernard Lee, Joseph Paterson and Elroy Embrey--to cease
the disruptive demonstrations immediately, and advised members of the student body to "behave themselves and return to
their classes."[9] However, on this same day, one of the
students, Bernard Lee, filed a petition with Governor Patterson, protesting statements attributed to the Governor by the
press.

The innocuous petition addressed the Governor formal-
ly and politely, stating the cause of the students in a simple
language, more moral than legal in appeal. Pointing out
that the students had violated no law, it described the courthouse snack bar as "a symbol of injustice to a part of the
citizens of Montgomery," and a "contradiction of the Christian
and democratic ideals of our nation." The language, at the
same time, however, clearly indicated that a struggle of
principle, not just an isolated demonstration, had been
launched at the courthouse snack bar. How strange it must
have seemed to the Governor of Alabama in 1960 to read a
petition from Negro students which could say, "We have no
desire for a prolonged and bitter struggle. But we shall
not yield our rights and student-destiny without an extreme
effort to retain them."[10]

Before a week had passed, approximately six hundred
Alabama State College students held a meeting on the steps
of the state capitol, where they sang hymns and heard a
speech by Bernard Lee. Lee called on his fellow students
to strike and boycott the college if any students were expelled because of the demonstrations.

On the day following the state capitol demonstration, the state board of education met and received reports on the demonstrations from Governor Patterson. These reports included the results of investigations conducted respectively by the college president, the state director of public safety, and the office of the state attorney-general. These reports identified the six students who were to become plaintiffs in Dixon and several others as the "ring leaders" in the demonstrations. President Trenholm reported to the board that the demonstrations were having a disruptive influence on the work of other students and on orderly operation of the college. He declared that, in his opinion, he could not control future demonstrations. Twenty-nine Negro students were identified as the core of the organization responsible for the demonstrations. After hearing these reports and recommendations, the board voted unanimously on the Governor's recommendation to expel nine students and place twenty others on probation.

Accordingly, President Trenholm, himself caught in the middle by the racial demonstrations, notified the nine students of their expulsion during the first week of March, 1960. No formal charges were placed against the students and no hearing was granted any of them prior to the expulsion.

On or about March 3, approximately two thousand Negro students staged a meeting at a church near the campus. At this meeting, attended by a number of those who were to become plaintiffs in Dixon, the state school board and the college administration were denounced.

Of interest in the proceedings which were to follow is the text of the letter received by each of the nine expelled students, notifying him of his expulsion. As printed in the margin of the district court's opinion, President Trenholm's letter of March 4, 1960, read as follows:

Dear Sir:

This communication is the official notification of your expulsion from Alabama State College as of the end of the 1960 Winter quarter.

As reported through the various news media, The State Board of Education considered this problem of Alabama State College at its meeting on this

97

past Wednesday afternoon. You were one of the
students involved in this expulsion-directive by the
State Board of Education. I was directed to proceed accordingly.

On Friday of last week, I had made the recommendation that any subsequently-confirmed action would
not be effective until the close of this 1960 Winter
Quarter.

The State Board of Education, which is made responsible for the supervision of the six higher institutions in Montgomery, Normal, Florence, Jack-
sonville, Livingston, and Troy (each of the other
three institutions at Tuscaloosa, Auburn and Monte-
vallo having separate boards) includes the following
in its regulations (as carried on page 32 of the
1958-59 Registration-Announcement of Alabama
State College).

'Pupils may be expelled from any of the Colleges:

'a.   For willful disobedience of the rules and regulations established for the conduct of the schools.

'b.   For the willful and continued neglect of studies
and continued failure to maintain the standards of
efficiency required by the rules and regulations.

'c.   For Conduct Prejudicial to the School and for
Conduct Unbecoming a Student and Future Teacher
in Schools of Alabama, for Insubordination and In-
surrection, or for Inciting Other Pupils to Like
Conduct.

'd.   For any conduct involving moral turpitude.'

    Since so few student expulsion cases had been heard
in the federal courts prior to 1960, it is interesting to note
that U. S. District Judge Frank M. Johnson found no difficulty in accepting jurisdiction of the case. "The law is now
too well settled," he said, "and the authorities are now too
numerous for this Court to spend any considerable time on
the various defenses herein raised by these defendants challenging the jurisdiction of this Court to hear and decide this
type of controversy." Citing Title 28 U. S. C. S 1331 and
S 1343(3), the court summarily dismissed defendants' claim

that the action was prohibited by the eleventh amendment.

From this point on, however, the trial court proceeding for an injunction against the college ran against the student plaintiffs, who were six of the nine expelled students. Raising the specter of the contract relationship, the court observed that "The right to attend and matriculate in a public college or university is conditioned upon an individual student's compliance with the rules and regulations of the institution." Then, after quoting a long passage from the state board's rules published in the college catalogue, the court proposed that:

> The courts have consistently upheld the validity of regulations that have the effect of reserving to the college the right to dismiss students at any time and for any reason without divulging the reason other than its being for the general benefit of the institution. This is true as long as the dismissal is not arbitrary and falls within the classes specified for preserving ideals of scholarship or moral atmosphere. [11]

U.S. District Judge Frank M. Johnson, an Alabama Republican who went to college with George Wallace and who had written the order outlawing city bus segregation in Montgomery, [12] presided at the hearing. Judge Johnson stated in his opinion that nothing "stated or concluded herein [is] to be construed as an approval or condonation of publicly owned and maintained lunchrooms where there is practiced discrimination solely on the basis of race in violation of the settled law...." At the same time, he observed, conclusions of the court were "not to be construed as either an approval or disapproval of the so-called sit-in demonstrations; the legality of such actions is not here involved."

But one might conclude from even a casual reading of Judge Johnson's opinion that he had little difficulty in relegating students to a role of inferior citizenship. His words would seem to imply that attendance at a state-supported college was a privilege which could be earned by abandonment of conventional constitutional rights. Such would seem to be implied by this passage:

> ...this Court reaches the firm conclusion that these several plaintiffs in organizing their group and then presenting themselves at the public eating

establishment and others in this area, had as their
aim the intention of focusing public attention upon
themselves and upon that discrimination. The obtaining of service was only incidental to those objectives. This Court is of the further opinion that
the series of demonstrations, speeches, news re-
leases, petitions, and resolutions that followed the
initial demonstration... was for the same purpose
... these plaintiffs, considered to be illegal discrimination as to the members of their race by certain
public officials in this area, acted without regard
to their status as students at the Alabama State
College and acted without considering the damage
they were doing to the orderly operation of the
Alabama State College during this period.

It might be inferred that Judge Johnson was assuming
an in loco parentis status for the petitioning students. In
finding that their conduct was "unbecoming a student or future teacher in the schools," Judge Johnson further observed
that:

... the expulsion of these plaintiffs was in good
faith... and was not an arbitrary action. It necessarily follows that such action did not operate to
deprive any of these plaintiffs of their constitutional rights guaranteed them by the Constitution of
the United States.

Reversal by the Fifth Circuit

Judge Richard Taylor Rives, speaking for a 2-1 majority of the Fifth Circuit, stated the question and the decision of the appellate court tersely in the first paragraph of
his August 4, 1961, opinion:

The question presented by the pleadings and evidence, and decisive of this appeal, is whether due
process requires notice and some opportunity for
hearing before students at a tax-supported college
are expelled for misconduct. We answer that
question in the affirmative.[13]

What concerned the Fifth Circuit in its review of
Dixon was not the substantive values involved, but specifically the procedures. Judge Rives followed his opening syn-

opsis with a telling blow at the procedures ignored in the
expulsion of the Alabama State College students:

> The misconduct for which the students were ex-
> pelled has never been definitely specified. Defen-
> dant Trenholm, the President of the College, testi-
> fied that he did not know why the plaintiffs and
> three additional students were expelled and twenty
> other students were placed on probation. The no-
> tice of expulsion which Dr. Trenholm mailed to
> each of the plaintiffs assigned no specific ground
> for expulsion, but referred in general terms to
> 'this problem of Alabama State College. '

Judge Rives cited the findings of the district court as
establishing that "the only demonstration which the evidence
showed that all of the expelled students took part in was that
in the lunch grill located in the basement of the Montgomery
County Courthouse."

It was not established that the other demonstrations
were attended by all of the plaintiffs. And yet, only one
member of the board of education had said this was the sole
basis for his vote to expel the students. The question did
not involve sufficiency of notice or adequacy of hearing, the
opinion holds. Rather, the question was "whether the students had a right to any notice or hearing whatever before
being expelled. "

Judge Rives described the court as in frontal dis-
agreement with the district court's holding that no notice or
opportunity for any kind of hearing was required before the
students were expelled.

> Whenever a governmental body acts so as to injure
> an individual, the Constitution requires that the act
> be consonant with due process of law. The mini-
> mum procedural requirements necessary to satisfy
> due process depend upon the circumstances and the
> interests of the parties involved. 14

Reviewing the Alabama Board of Education's exculpa-
tory provision which applies to college expulsions, the Fifth
Circuit took issue again:

> We do not read this provision to clearly indicate
> an intent on the part of the student to waive notice

and a hearing before expulsion. If, however, we
should so assume, it nonetheless remains true that
the State cannot condition the granting of even a
privilege upon the renunciation of the constitutional
right to due process.

Only private associations may obtain a waiver of notice and hearing before depriving a member of a valuable
right. "And even here, the right to notice and hearing is so
fundamental to the conduct of our society that the waiver
must be clear and explicit."

The court then constructed a property rationale for
the nature of student status:

It requires no argument to demonstrate that education is vital and, indeed, basic to civilized society.
Without sufficient education the plaintiffs would not
be able to earn an adequate livelihood, to enjoy
life to the fullest, or to fulfill as completely as
possible the duties and responsibilities of good
citizens.

There was no effort to prove that other colleges
are open to the plaintiffs. If so, the plaintiffs
would nonetheless be injured by the interruption of
their course of studies in mid-term. It is most
unlikely that a public college would accept a student expelled from another public college of the
same state. Indeed, expulsion may well prejudice
the student in completing his education at any other
institution. [15]

Then came Judge Rives' clincher on the vestment of
the status of college students: "Surely no one can question
that the right to remain at the college in which the plaintiffs
were students in good standing is an interest of extremely
great value."

Turning then to the nature of the governmental power
to expel students from public colleges, the Fifth Circuit observed, "that power is not unlimited and cannot be arbitrarily exercised." Judge Rives then takes off on perhaps his
most creative adventure by observing:

Admittedly, there must be some reasonable and
constitutional ground for expulsion or the courts

would have a duty to require reinstatement. The
possibility of arbitrary action is not excluded by
the existence of reasonable regulations. There
may be arbitrary application of the rule to the
facts of a particular case. Indeed, that result is
well nigh inevitable when the Board hears only one
side of the issue. In the disciplining of college
students there are no considerations of immediate
danger or of peril to the national security, which
should prevent the Board from exercising at least
the fundamental principles of fairness by giving
the accused students notice of the charges and an
opportunity to be heard in their own defense. Indeed, the example set by the Board in failing to
do so, if not corrected by the courts, can well
break the spirits of the students and of others
familiar with the injustice, and do inestimable
harm to their education. 16

Turning to the error of the trial court, the Fifth Circuit found that it lay largely on the fact that the district
court "simply misinterpreted the precedents." Specifically,
Judge Johnson had held that, "the courts have consistently
upheld the validity of regulations that have the effect of reserving to the college the right to dismiss students at any
time for any reason without divulging its reason other than
its being for the general benefit of the institution." Judge
Rives points out that this statement is based on language
found in 14 C.J.S. Colleges and Universities, S 26, p. 1360,
which, in turn, is paraphrased from Judge Sears' opinion in
the case of Anthony v. Syracuse, supra. Then follows Judge
Rives' strongest language in pursuit of his effort to distinguish between public and private colleges.

Anthony v. Syracuse, he says, "concerns a private
university and follows the well-settled rule that the relations
between a student and a private university are a matter of
contract. The Anthony case held that the plaintiffs had
specifically waived their rights to notice and hearing." In
college expulsion cases involving the sufficiency of hearings
given students, he concedes, the courts have commonly upheld sufficiency of the hearings. He then reached back into
the nineteenth century to dredge up Hill v. McCauley, supra.
and Gleason v. University of Minnesota, 17 a 1908 state case,
to advance two state court decisions holding that some form
of hearing is required. Judge Rives points out that it was
not a case denying any hearing whatsoever, but one "passing

upon the adequacy of the hearing, which provoked from Professor Warren A. Seavey of Harvard the eloquent comment, "
and he quoted a long paragraph from Professor Seavey's an-
gry assault on the practice of denying procedural rights to
college students. 18

The Fifth Circuit then concluded: "We are confident
that precedent as well as a most fundamental constitutional
principle support our holding that due process requires notice and some opportunity for hearing before a student at a
tax-supported college is expelled for misconduct. "

The court then undertook to outline its views on the
nature of the notice and hearing required by due process considerations before a student at a tax-supported college may
be justly expelled:

> The notice should contain a statement of the speci-
> fic charges and grounds which, if proven, would
> justify expulsion under the Regulations of the
> Board of Education. The nature of the hearing
> should vary depending upon the circumstances of
> the particular case. The case before us requires
> something more than an informal interview with
> an administrative authority of the college. By its
> nature, a charge of misconduct, as opposed to a
> failure to meet the scholastic standards of the col-
> lege, depends upon a collection of the facts con-
> cerning the charged misconduct, easily colored by
> the point of view of the witnesses in such circum-
> stances; a hearing which gives the Board or the
> administrative authorities of the college an oppor-
> tunity to hear both sides in considerable detail is
> best suited to protect the rights of all involved.
> This is not to imply that a full-dress judicial
> hearing, with the right to cross-examine witnesses,
> is required. Such a hearing, with the attending
> publicity and disturbance of college activities,
> might be detrimental to the college's educational
> atmosphere and impractical to carry out. Never-
> theless, the rudiment of an adversary proceeding
> may be preserved without encroaching upon the in-
> terests of the college. 19

Turning to the case before the court, Judge Rives
spelled out the procedural rights of the students dismissed
from Alabama State College:

In the instant case, the student should be given the
names of the witnesses against him and an oral or
written report on the facts to which each witness
testifies.   He should also be given the opportunity
to present to the Board, or at least to an administrative official of the college, his own defense
against the charges and to produce either oral testimony or written affidavits of witnesses in his behalf.   If the hearing is not before the Board directly, the results and findings of the hearing
should be presented in a report open to the student's inspection.   If these rudimentary elements
of fair play are followed in a case of misconduct
of this particular type, we feel that the requirements of due process of law will have been fulfilled.

Judge Cameron's Dissent

Judge Ben F. Cameron dissented strongly, describing
the district court's opinion as "so lucid, literate and mode-
rate that I cannot forego expressing surprise that my breth-
ren of the majority can find fault with it."[20]   In large part,
his dissent is based on dicta from four tangential precedents,
the Second Circuit precedent in a college-expulsion case, two
authoritative commentaries and his deference to the expertise of educators.

Whereas the majority opinion had quoted the dicta of
the Supreme Court in California Cafeteria and Restaurant
Workers Union v. McElroy[21] to make a minor, almost whim-
sical, point, Judge Cameron turns to the same opinion to
quote this language:

It is the petitioner's claim that due process in this
case required that Rachel Brawner be advised of
the specific grounds for her exclusion and be accorded a hearing at which she might refute them.
We are satisfied, however, that under the circumstances of this case such a procedure is not constitutionally required.

The Fifth Amendment does not require a trial-type
hearing in every conceivable case of government im-
pairment of private interests....   The very nature
of due process negates any concept of inflexible

procedures universally applicable to every imagin-
able situation. . .

Then turning to 1951 dicta of the Supreme Court in
Joint Anti-Fascist Refugee Committee v. McGrath, [22] Judge
Cameron quoted this paragraph:

As these and other cases make clear, consideration what procedure due process may require under
any given set of circumstances must begin with a
determination of the precise nature of the government function involved as well as the private interest that has been affected by the governmental action. Where it has been possible to characterize
that private interest (perhaps in oversimplification)
as a mere privilege subject to the Executive's
plenary power, it has traditionally been held that
notice and hearing are not constitutionally required.
[Emphasis added by Judge Cameron]

Just as the majority opinion quoted 14 C.J.S., Colleges and Universities, Judge Cameron, too, borrowed from
that source:

Broadly speaking, the right of a student to attend
a public or private college or university is subject
to the condition that he comply with its scholastic
and disciplinary requirements, and the proper college authorities may in the exercise of a broad
discretion formulate and enforce reasonable rules
and regulations in both respects. The courts will
not interfere in the absence of an abuse of such
discretion. [23]

Judge Cameron's dissent also draws support from
American Jurisprudence[24] in its quotation of this language:

Where the conduct of a student is such that his
continued presence in the school will be disastrous
to its proper discipline and to the morals of the
other pupils, his expulsion is justifiable. Only
where it is clear that such an action with respect
to a student has not been an honest exercise of
discretion, or has arisen from some motive extraneous to the purposes committed to that discretion, may the courts be called upon for relief.

Turning to college-expulsion precedents, Judge Cameron observes that:

> A sane approach to a problem whose facts are closely related to the one before us was made by the United States Court of Appeals for the Second Circuit in Steier v. New York State Education Commission et al., 1959, 271 F.2d 13. Its attitude is thus epitomized on page 18:
>
> 'Education is a field of life reserved to the individual states. The only restriction the Federal Government imposes is that in their education program no state may discriminate against an individual because of race, color or creed.
>
> 'As so well stated by Judge Wyzanski in Cranney v. Trustees of Boston University, D.C., 139 F. Supp. 130, to expand the Civil Rights Statute so as to embrace every constitutional claim such as here made would in fact bring within the initial jurisdiction of the United States District Courts that vast array of controversies which have heretofore been raised in state tribunals by challenges founded upon the 14th Amendment to the United States Constitution. It would be arrogating to (the) United States District Courts that which is a purely State Court function. Conceivably every State College student, upon dismissal from such college, could rush to a Federal Judge seeking review of the dismissal.'[25]

One recurring rationale in state court cases which has militated against students seeking to overthrow administrative expulsions, as was previously indicated, has been the factor of judicial deference to the expertise of the educator. Judge Cameron's dissent would seem to be clinging to this deference, when it observes that:

> Everyone who has dealt with schools knows that it is necessary to make many rules governing the conduct of those who attend them, which do not reach the concept of criminality but which are designed to regulate the relationship between school management and the student based upon practical and ethical considerations which the courts know very little about and with which they are not equipped to deal.[26]

Some insight into Judge Cameron's values vis-a-vis campus relationships might be read into his observations that plaintiffs "were accused and convicted by competent proof, ... of
public boorishness, of defying the authority of the officials
of their school and state, of blatant insubordination, of en-
deavoring to disrupt the school they had agreed to support
with loyalty, as well as break up other schools, and had
openly incited to riot." "We are trying here," he said, "the
actions of state officials, which actions we are bound to in-
vest with every presumption of fairness and correctness,"
and stated his concept that "each college should make its own
rules and should apply them to the facts of the case before
it, and...the function of a court would be to test their validity if challenged in a proper court proceeding."

Further, Judge Cameron asserted:

> Certainly I think that the filing of charges, the dis-
> closure of names of proposed witnesses, and such
> procedures as the majority discusses are wholly un-
> realistic and impractical and would result in a ma-
> jor blow to our institutions of learning. Every at-
> tempt at discipline would probably lead to a cause
> celebre, in connection with which federal function-
> aries would be rushed in to investigate whether a
> federal law had been violated. [27]

Other Federal Cases

Although Dixon marks an important milestone in the
development of procedural rights for students in expulsion
cases, it was not the first federal court case dealing with
those rights. Dixon is considered the controlling precedent
today, but in 1959 the Second Circuit set a precedent which
can sharply contrary to Dixon in the case of Steier v. New
York State Education Commissioner. [28]

The Steier Case

Steier was apparently the first student-college action
brought in federal court under the Civil Rights Act, 28 U.S.
C.A. Section 1343(3), the same jurisdictional avenue to be
subsequently followed by Dixon. Steier may be sharply dif-
ferentiated from Dixon in that it questioned the adequacy of
procedures employed before a student was dismissed, whereas Dixon was to challenge the absence of notice and hearing.

Distinction may be drawn, too, from the sharply differing opinions which the two cases produced.

After entering Brooklyn College, a state-supported institution, in the fall of 1952, Arthur Steier apparently decided that some of the student organizations were unduly dominated by the college administration. In November, 1954, and again in February, 1955, he wrote bitter letters to the college president, in one of which intemperate language was directed at the college's office of student administration. On March 3, 1955, the dean of students, acting as a result of the two letters, suspended Steier for the remainder of the term. In his letter of suspension, the dean quoted a by-law of the governing board which dealt with student discipline.

Steier appealed his suspension to the college president, but without success. He subsequently applied for readmission in the fall of 1955 and was readmitted subject to his written promise to abide by the rules and to generally show a change of attitude. The terms of his probationary status provided that he could not participate as an officer in any student activity organization. Steier was subsequently warned that he was not adequately keeping his agreement. In June, 1956, after the academic year was ended, the dean wrote Steier that he still showed some deficiencies, but that he had made certain gains. The dean advised him that during the 1956 fall term he would not be permitted to hold office or membership in any student organization.

In September Steier caused to be published in the first issue of the college newspaper the story of his latest probation--claiming that it was caused by discriminatory and vindictive policies of the college administration. On the day following publication of this letter, Steier was suspended for the second time, as of three days later, because of his "continued disregard of the rules and regulations."

Steier and his parents promptly appealed the second suspension to the college president--again without success. In December, Steier applied for reinstatement, and was asked to appear before the faculty committee on orientation and guidance. He did appear, and the committee unanimously recommended his dismissal for these four reasons: (1) Although one provision of his suspension was that he was not to appear on campus, he had been seen on campus placing leaflets in mailboxes and had attended a meeting which he refused to leave until escorted out by a policeman; (2) He

had used abusive language in letters addressed to college officials; (3) In spite of college restrictions on his non-academic activities, he had been in attendance at the Students for
Campus Democracy booth of the Club Fair on September 19,
1956; and (4) "There is no indication that Mr. Steier under-
stands that his behavior is inappropriate."[29]   On December
20, Steier was notified that the faculty council had approved
the recommendation of the faculty committee and that he was
dismissed.

        Steier then appealed--in accordance with state law and
rules of the board of education--to the board of education.
After a hearing, his appeal was denied and he then appealed
to the New York State Commissioner of Education.   After
another hearing, this appeal was denied.   Steier then brought
action in the United States District Court for the Eastern District of New York, claiming jurisdiction under Title 28 U.S.
C.A., Section 1343(3).   In the words of Judge Gibson for
the Second Circuit, he alleged:

> that plaintiff was maliciously suspended by the Dean
> of Students of Brooklyn College, that on appeal the
> President of the College arbitrarily sustained the
> suspension and that later the Faculty Council of the
> College, acting upon the recommendation of the
> Faculty Committee on Orientation and Guidance,
> unlawfully dismissed plaintiff permanently; that
> thereafter on appeal for reinstatement to the Board
> of Higher Education, that Board illegally denied
> plaintiff's request for a fair hearing and that the
> State Commissioner of Education refused to reverse
> the action of the Board and the College, rendering
> unconstitutional decisions in so doing.[30]

        The District Court dismissed Steier's action, basing
its ruling on Steier's failure to exhaust state remedies.[31]
The Second Circuit's decision is interesting in that it was
apparently the first federal appellate decision ever rendered
in a college expulsion case, and for the fact that each of the
three judges wrote opinions, including one concurrent and
one dissent.   Gibson, district judge, writing for the court,
based dismissal of the action "squarely on the ground that
the complaint and uncontroverted facts clearly demonstrate
there was no jurisdiction in the United States District
Court."[32]   Circuit Judge Moore, concurring in the result,
disagreed with both the district court and Judge Gibson, except in the result.   He favored dismissal of the action, "not

because the district court lacked jurisdiction, nor because plaintiff had not exhausted state remedies, but because the pleadings and other documents... revealed no material issue of fact which required a trial."[33] Chief Judge Clark dissented, because: "I believe the plaintiff has presented claims which can be legally adjudicated only upon a full dress trial in the district court."

Judge Clark scoffs at the "details selected to show misconduct (which of course stand unproven) [and which] really only demonstrate the more that Steier's vice is non-conformity, rather than crime or misdemeanor." In response to the majority's position that the only restriction the federal government imposes on the purely state function of education is to bar discrimination based on race, color or creed, he raises a finger with these words:

> This indeed is a novel doctrine. No court, ever before to my knowledge, has suggested that the Fourteenth Amendment to the United States Constitution is a paltry piece of class legislation limited, it seems, to according protection to the Negroes in the South and Jehovah's Witnesses in other areas. Surely the noble privileges therein embodied are not to be thus denigrated.[34]

In sum, Steier, apparently the first college expulsion case taken to the federal courts on the basis of the Civil Rights Act, Title 28 U.S.C.A. 1343(3), found acceptance of jurisdiction at the trial court level and two of three circuit judges agreeable to jurisdiction in the Second Circuit. The disappointment felt by civil rights advocates over Steier most certainly was lessened by the fact that the case was not one which many plaintiff's lawyers would describe as a "good" case, as was suggested by Judge Moore's finding of "no material issue of fact which required a trial." Steier obviously was not the ideal case to usher student-college expulsion disputes into the realm of federal jurisdiction. Nor, one might suspect, was the Second Circuit the ideal court.

Dixon was to prove the ideal case, the conscience-searching South the ideal environment, the Fifth Circuit the ideal court, and 1960-61 the ideal year in American history.

The Dixon Judges

The Trial Court

A casual reading of the trial court's opinion in Dixon could easily lead one to the conclusion that its author, United States District Judge Frank Minis Johnson, like many another federal judge in the South, was drawing his $30,000 a year and writing his prejudices into case law. For the opinion was not devoid of a tone of condescension, as was noted earlier.

But such a conclusion would seem unwarranted. Judge Johnson made his contribution to the final outcome in Dixon, it would seem, by his sweeping acceptance of the case into federal jurisdiction. Less hesitation than aggressiveness can be read into his offhand declaration that "The law is now too well settled and the authorities are now too numerous for this Court to spend any considerable time on the various defenses herein raised by these defendants challenging the jurisdiction of this Court to hear and decide this type of controversy."[35] This is a strong statement, especially in view of Judge Gibson's opinion in Steier twenty months earlier that the district court for the eastern district of New York lacked jurisdiction in a college dismissal action brought under the same statute. Moreover, Johnson was able to rule that, "The various objections raised by these defendants as to the insufficiency of process and that this action is prohibited by the Eleventh Amendment to the Constitution of the United States are frivolous and merit no discussion." "The only real question in this case," he wrote, "is whether these plaintiffs were accorded 'due process' within the meaning of the Constitution of the United States in their expulsion from the Alabama State College by the Alabama State Board of Education."

Johnson is reputedly one of that rare genre of federal district judges in the South who have remained relatively immune to the pressures of their environment. An Eisenhower appointee from "The Free State of Winston,"[36] he has, according to Time, "probably faced more tough segregation cases than any other Southern judge."[37] Former Alabama Governor George Wallace, a Johnson classmate at the University of Alabama Law School, has called Johnson rash, headstrong, vindictive, unstable and erratic, and once demanded his impeachment.[38] In a 1965 Summary of civil rights demonstrations in Alabama, Johnson was thus described as "the man central to them all," and "one of the most important men in America."[39]

Disowning such labels as "liberal" or "conservative," Johnson claims to be what is popularly called a "constructionist," explaining, "I don't make the law. I don't create the facts. I interpret the law."[40] Nonetheless, he played a role in the finding of "liberal" law in such noted cases as Reynolds v. Sims[41] and Gomillion v. Lightfoot.[42] It was Judge Johnson, too, who in 1967 "mustered the three-judge court that ordered desegregation of all of Alabama's 118 school districts."[43]

The Appellate Court

Of the three Fifth Circuit judges who constituted the court which overruled Judge Johnson in the Dixon case, two--Ben F. Cameron and Minor Wisdom--were Eisenhower appointees. One--Presiding Judge Richard Taylor Rives--was a Truman appointee.

The dissent in Dixon was written by Judge Cameron, a "vigorous segregationist," 70 years old at the time and destined to die in his home state of Mississippi three years later. The New York Times described him as "the most dedicated segregationist on the Federal bench" after he attempted to block the admission to the University of Mississippi of George Meredith, first Negro student ever to win court-ordered admission to that school.[44]

Concurring on the majority opinion were Richard Taylor Rives, presiding judge for the Fifth Circuit and a Truman Democrat, and John Minor Wisdom, New Orleans attorney appointed to the Fifth Circuit by President Eisenhower. Rives (pronounced Reeves) has been described as "a conservative, tradition-minded Democrat," who has "invariably decided for liberalism, but not always without a twinge of regret."[45] Time credits him with establishing "the far-reaching principle that Negroes cannot be convicted of crime in counties that bar them from jury service. Of Judge Wisdom, The New York Times could report that he carried "the burden of the Republican fight" in Louisiana for Eisenhower in 1956.[46] Eisenhower carried Louisiana. Time described Wisdom as one of President Eisenhower's "first-rate Southern Republican judges."[47]

The Fifth Circuit itself has been described as both

"trail blazing"[48] and "the most significant Federal bench for
the South."[49] It handles appeals from all the federal district courts in six of the eleven states of the old Confede-
racy--Alabama, Florida, Georgia, Louisiana, Mississippi
and Texas.

Commentary on Dixon

Beginning almost immediately after the Fifth Circuit
handed down its opinion in Dixon and continuing through 1968,
the nation's law journals--perhaps largely because of their
normal campus orientation--have proclaimed the significance
of the decision. Professor Seavey, who had decried the lack
of procedural protections for students, [50] and who had been
quoted by the Fifth Circuit in Dixon, soon became widely
quoted by other writers and reviewers. From the very beginning, the great preponderance of commentary on Dixon has
ranged from favorable to outright laudatory. An illustration
of the degree of the favor with which the Fifth Circuit's decision was received may be gained by a brief synopsis of
some of the early reviews.

Harvard Law Review

Under its heading, "Recent Cases," in 1962, the Harvard Law Review published an unsigned three-page summary
and analysis of Judge Rives' opinion. "The court's result
seems eminently desirable," the writer observes, and, "under the balancing test adopted by the Supreme Court, ines-
capable." Again, "the court's decision to remand for a
hearing may be justified by the Board's failure to specify
the misconduct for which plaintiffs were expelled, which
made it impossible to say with assurance that no adjudica-
tive facts remained at issue."[51]

Alabama Law Review

Nearer to the scene of action which spawned the Dixon case, the Alabama Law Review in its fall, 1961, issue
noted that Corpus Juris maintained that a college could not
dismiss a student without giving him notice and a fair hearing; however, Corpus Juris Secundum dropped this statement
and premised court interference on arbitrary action or abuse
of discretion by college officials. Ben Leader Erdreich, who
signed the comment, observed that these and other authorities "add to the confusion by failing to distinguish clearly be-

tween cases involving public schools and those involving private schools." "It would seem," observes Erdreich, "that fairness and justice can best be assured if the student is given notice and hearing."[52] The author believed that:

> little difficulty will arise from this decision. If the courts extend themselves further into what must be an area within which school officials act with a great degree of discretion, real problems will develop. However, the instant case should not create difficulty. It has set out objective procedure by which the school must act.[53]

Temple Law Quarterly

Stanley S. Cohen, writing for the Temple Law Quarterly, observed that under the Fifth Circuit's procedural formula in Dixon, "it is not too farfetched to suggest that cross-examination may be allowed if the facts sufficiently warrant it." He doubted that the decision will "open the floodgate to spurious claims, and concluded his comment by observing that, "The court by including this case within the limits of the due process clause has reaffirmed the protection of individual liberties and provided an adequate safeguard which is 'appropriate to the case and just to the parties to be affected.' "[54]

North Dakota Law Review

Writing for the North Dakota Law Review, Dennis L. Thomte remarks that, "The majority opinion...seems to adhere to the minority rule and cites only two cases. Proposing that, "The dissenting judge presents somewhat more authority for his opinion, all of which appears to deny this is due process," he nonetheless concludes by stating, "It is the writer's opinion that the [North Dakota] courts should follow the decision reached in the instant case in an effort to preserve fair play and justice."[55]

Notes

1. E.g., Knight v. State Board of Education, 200 F. Supp. 174 (USDC MD Tenn. 1961) and Due v. Florida A & M University, 233 F. Supp. 196 (USDC Fla. 1963).

2. Expanding Liberties (New York: The Viking Press,

1966).   See esp. Ch. VI.

3.   Ibid., p. 266.

4.   347 U.S. 483, 74 S. Ct. 686, 98 L. Ed. 873 (1956).

5.   "Procedural Due Process and State University Students,"
     Reprinted in Student Rights & Responsibilities (Univer-
     sity of Cincinnati: The Associated Student Govern-
     ments, 1968), note 24, p. 262.

6.   Truitt v. Illinois, 278 F. 2d 819 (7th Circ. 1960).

7.   Swanson v. McGuire, 188 F. Supp. 112 (N.D. Ill. 1960).

8.   365 U.S. 167 (1961).

9.   Words here and chronology generally are from 186 F.
     Supp. 945, 948 (N.D. Ala. 1960).

10. Ibid., at 948n3.

11. 186 F. Supp. 945, 951 (1960).

12. "The Jinxed Seat: Who's Next?" Newsweek, Dec. 1,
     1969. p. 24.

13. 294 F. 2d 150, 151 (1961).

14. Ibid., at 155.

15. Ibid., at 157.

16. Ibid.

17. 104 Minn. 359, 116 N.W. 650 (1908).

18. "Dismissal of Students: Due Process," op. cit.

19. 294 F. 2d 150, 158-159 (1961).

20. Ibid., at 159.

21. 81 S. Ct. 1743 (1961).

22. 341 U.S. 123 (1951).

23. Section 26, p. 1360 cited.

24. Judge Cameron cites Section 22, p. 16.

25. As Judge Cameron knew, the facts of this case may be
     "closely related" to Dixon, but in central issue the
     two cases are radically different. Steier dealt with
     a total absence of notice and hearing.

26. 294 F. 2d 150, 160.

27. 294 F. 2d 150, 165.

28. 271 F. 2d 13 (1959).

29. 271 F. 2d 13, at 15-16.

30. Ibid., at 13.

31. 161 F. Supp. 549.

32. 271 F. 2d 13, 18.

33. Ibid., at 21.

34. Ibid., at 23.

35. 186 F. Supp. 945, 950 (1960).

36. Winston County in the northern hill country of Alabama,
     described by Time (Feb. 21, 1964, p. 76) as "a
     staunchly Republican island in a Democratic sea."

37. "Trail Blazers on the Bench," Dec. 5, 1960, p. 14.

38. Ibid.

39. "Interpreter in the Front Line," Time, May 12, 1967,
     p. 72.

40. Ibid.

41. Sims v. Frink, 208 F. Supp. 431 (M. D. Ala. 1962).

42. Gomillion v. Lightfoot, 167 F. Supp. 405. However,
     his ruling in this case was understandably in support
     of the contested Alabama statute.

43.   The New York Times, April 14, 1964, p. 27.

44.   Ibid.

45.   "Trail Blazers on the Bench, " op. cit.

46.   March 15, 1957, p. 15:1.

47.   "Interpreter in the Front Line, " May 12, 1967, p. 73.

48.   Ibid.

49.   The New York Times, April 14, 1964, p. 27.

50.   "Dismissal of Students: 'Due Process'," op. cit.

51.   75 Harvard Law Review 1429 (1962).

52.   14 Ala. L. Rev. 126 (Fall, 1961).

53.   Ibid., at 131.

54.   35 Temple L. Q. 437, 440-441, (Summer, 1962).

55.   58 North Dakota Law Review, 348 (April, 1962).

Chapter V

DISMISSAL AND SUSPENSION:
A MANDATE FOR DUE PROCESS

Exactly what does Dixon mean to the college student
who is faced with disciplinary action? Many pages of commentary have been published in efforts to answer this question. As with any newly developing area of case law, Dixon
invites speculation. It invites, too, subsequent elaboration
by trial courts and appellate courts confronted with challenges
to college expulsion proceedings. Narrow distinctions must
be drawn. Until they are drawn by courts of competent jurisdiction, they remain fair subjects for legal speculation.
One purpose of this chapter is to examine representative
speculation which has followed the 1961 decision by the Fifth
Circuit. Attention must be paid, too, to some of the leading judicial decisions which have helped amplify the meaning
of the Fifth Circuit's important precedent. Beyond this
Richard E. O'Leary, Assistant Legal Counsel at the University of Illinois, has noted that, "There seems to be sufficient
conflict between the language of Steier and Dixon on this question [of federal court jurisdiction] to warrant review by the
United States Supreme Court."[1] And, speaking of the broad
subject of constitutional rights of college students, Van Alstyne confessed in February, 1969, "I have not thought it
appropriate to compose a book length treatment of the subject as yet, because the field is in such a state of flux that
it seems better to watch the judicial trends for at least an
additional year or so...."[2] Added to this is the fact that
the American Civil Liberties Union in 1969 reported that
"some federal district courts have merely paid lip service"
to Dixon.[3] From the emerging picture of judicial uncertainty, one might conclude that commentaries by legal writers
and a study of subsequent cases would be of especially great
value.

During the period that state courts were using the
contract and in loco parentis concepts to justify a hands-off
policy, it has been observed that a judicial attitude prevailed

118

that higher education was a privilege, not a right. Some
writers have been willing to recognize the existence of extensive federal questions involved in education, especially
since Brown v. Board of Education, [4] but it was Dixon which
first recognized a federal question involved in a college expulsion case. It was Dixon which first resoundingly abandoned the concept of higher education as a privilege--at
least in tax-supported institutions. The case still represents
the authoritative precedent on due process in student disciplinary proceedings, although new facets have since been
added. In order to reach the conclusions which Judge Rives
formulated in Dixon, it was thus necessary to hold that
state-supported higher education was no longer a question of
mere privilege, but a question of right for a student who
had matriculated and been accepted by an institution. It follows that a student could be separated from the institution
for disciplinary reasons only if he were afforded the funda-
mentals of due process, as provided by the fourteenth amendment.

The fourteenth amendment says that no state shall deprive any person of life, liberty or property without due
process of law. Expulsion from college scarcely constitutes
a deprivation of life. Nor is it a denial of liberty, since
the student may not be incarcerated. The Dixon case held,
in effect, that the right to a higher education--or at least
the right not to arbitrarily be denied the status of student
in good standing--was a property right. Since the student
has a property vestment in his status as a student, he accordingly cannot be denied this status in the absence of "due
process." It remains for the courts to spell out exactly what
procedural considerations come within the meaning of due
process in any particular situation.

In the Dixon case the court said that the student
should have notice and that the nature of the hearing could
vary, depending upon the circumstances of the case. Not
every discipline case requires a full-dress hearing. But
the court stated that in every case the rudiments of an adversary hearing may be preserved without disturbing the interests of the college. The court then proceeded to outline
procedural safeguards which would meet the requirements of
due process in the case at hand. Judge Rives wrote:

> In the instant case, the student should be given
> the names of the witnesses against him and an
> oral or written report on the facts to which each

witness testifies. He should be given the opportunity to present to the Board, or at least to an
administrative official of the college, his own defense against the charges and to produce either
oral testimony or written affidavits of witnesses
in his behalf. If the hearing is not before the
Board directly, the results and findings of the
hearing should be presented in a report open to
the student's inspection. If these rudimentary elements of fair play are followed in a case of misconduct of this particular type, we feel that the
requirements of due process of law will have been
fulfilled. [5]

The foregoing standards were addressed to "the instant case." Elsewhere in the opinion, however, Judge Rives
would appear to be addressing himself to a general posterity
when he declared that:

...we state our views on the nature of the notice
and hearing required by due process prior to expulsion from a state college or university. They
should, we think, comply with the following standards. The notice should contain a statement of
specific charges and grounds which, if proven,
would justify expulsion under the regulations of the
Board of Education. The nature of the hearing
should vary depending upon the circumstances of
the particular case. [6]

The case before the court, he declared, "as opposed
to a failure to meet the scholastic standards of the college,"
requires a collection of facts concerning the alleged misconduct. Such facts are easily colored by subjectivity of witnesses. He continues:

In such circumstances, a hearing which gives the
Board or the administrative authorities of the college an opportunity to hear both sides in considerable detail is best suited to protect the rights of
all involved. This is not to imply that full-dress
judicial hearing, with the right to cross-examine
witnesses is required. [7]

Dixon, then, held that notice and hearing were required in college disciplinary expulsion proceedings, but left
open the question of how much process was due. This ques-

tion was to be partially answered in subsequent decisions by college administrative authorities and by the U. S. District Courts. An examination of representative cases is required for insight into subsequent developments.

Subsequent Expulsion Cases

Dixon authoritatively opened the federal courts to review of college expulsion proceedings. The purpose of this section is to review briefly a selection of some of the more widely publicized decisions in subsequent judicial actions.

The Knight Case

Less than five months after the Fifth Circuit delivered its opinion in the Dixon case, the Nashville Division of the U. S. District Court for the Middle District of Tennessee decided the case of Knight v. State Board of Education, 8 a case similar to Dixon in that it was colored by a backdrop of apparent political reprisal against students involved in the then-current civil rights protest movement. Knight has been widely reviewed in the legal journals, its greatest significance perhaps resting in the court's deference to Dixon.

The Knight case involved thirteen students at Tennessee A & I State University who were suspended following an ex parte hearing by the discipline committee of the university. At the time of their suspension, all thirteen students were being held in a Mississippi jail as an outgrowth of their efforts to undermine segregation in a Mississippi bus terminal.

District Judge William E. Miller performed a feat of semantical wizardry in reaching his finding that the students were due "injunctive relief to enforce their rights to procedural due process with respect to any disciplinary action on the part of Tennessee A & I State University...."9 Enroute to this finding, Judge Miller was able to describe Dixon as "an elaborate and carefully reasoned opinion...." and to observe that "...the principles so clearly enunciated therein are not necessarily determinative of this case, [but] they are entitled to considerable weight insofar as the question of procedural due process is concerned."

The Due Case

Providing perhaps the second test for the strength of
Dixon in the U. S. District Courts was Due v. Florida A &
M University, 10 decided two years after Dixon by the Talla-
hassee Division of the U. S. District Court for the Northern
District of Florida. This is the court presided over by
President Nixon's third nominee to the United States Supreme
Court, G. Harrold Carswell. 11

The facts in Due are similar to those in Knight.
Plaintiffs had been found guilty of contempt of court and
fined $1, 000 each for leading student demonstrations in vio-
lation of a restraining order. Due can be nominally distinguished from Knight on the basis that the Florida students
received at least rudimentary notice and hearing, whereas
the Tennessee students had received none. Unlike Judge
Miller in the Knight case, Judge Carswell did not summon
the legerdemain required to find for the students. According to a later note on the case by the ACLU, he paid "lip
service" to Dixon. 12 He noted that "this court concludes
that Dixon is, indeed, the most current, explicit and applicable statement of the law governing the disposition of this
case. "

But he then selected from Judge Rives' language in
Dixon a line to support his conditioned response to Negro
demonstrators and wrote:

> A fair reading of the Dixon case shows that it is
> not necessary to due process requirements that a
> full scale judicial trial be conducted by a univer-
> sity discipline committee with qualified attorneys
> present or formally waived as in a felonious charge
> under the criminal law. There need be no steno-
> graphic or mechanical recording of the proceed-
> ings. 13

It might be contended that judicial precedent firmly
dictated only one finding in the Due case--that the district
court had legal jurisdiction. Judge Carswell so determined.
Beyond that he was on his own. He ruled against the students. As to the dispensable status of a hearing transcript
volunteered by Judge Carswell, one writer has remarked,
"one wonders how the case can be reviewed in a judicial
proceeding if no transcript of the administrative proceeding
is made. "14

The Esteban Case

The ACLU has cited as "the most encouraging post-Dixon case (if not the most authoritative)" the 1967 case of Esteban v. Central Missouri State College. [15] The opinion in Esteban, written by Judge Elmo B. Hunter for the U. S. District Court, Western District of Missouri, constitutes what the ACLU may consider the first significant expansion of the Dixon doctrine. If Esteban did, indeed, "extend" the Dixon doctrine, this was because Esteban held that plaintiff students should be permitted to have counsel with them at a disciplinary hearing and that plaintiffs themselves might question at the hearing any witness who gave evidence against them. The Fifth Circuit had specifically eschewed both these undertakings by plaintiffs under the circumstances pertaining to Dixon.

In Esteban, Judge Hunter set forth what he viewed as the essential elements of due process: (1) written charges, (2) ten days' notice of hearing, (3) hearing before the college president, (4) student's right to advance inspection of the college's affidavits or exhibits, (5) student's right to counsel, (6) student's right to call witnesses, or introduce affidavits and exhibits, (7) right to confront and cross-examine witnesses, (8) determination solely on evidence in the record, (9) written findings and disposition, (10) either party may make a record of the disciplinary hearing at its own expense.

Jones v. Tennessee

The nearest a college expulsion case has come to being resolved by the United States Supreme Court was in the case of Jones v. State Board of Education of Tennessee.[16] The Supreme Court granted certiorari "primarily to consider issues raised by claim of one of the students that he had been suspended because of distribution of leaflets."[17] But the Court heard arguments, then ruled on February 24, 1970, that the fact that indefinite suspension of the plaintiff had been based in part on the fact that he allegedly lied at a college hearing on charges against him, was a fact which had not emerged on the record of the case.

Finding that the lying aspect "sufficiently clouds the record to render the case an inappropriate vehicle for this Court's first decision on the extent of First Amendment restrictions on the power of state universities to expel... students for the expression of views...," the Court dismissed

the case.   Justice Black dissented in part, saying he would
affirm the judgment below, which was against the students.
Justices Douglas and Brennan dissented, saying, "Our failure
to reverse is a serious setback for First Amendment rights
in a trouble (sic) field."18

        Briefly stated, the facts of the case are as follows.
Plaintiffs were students at Tennessee A and I State University, a predominantly Negro school.   They were indefinitely
suspended and given notice of nearly three months of their
suspension.   After they obtained counsel and requested a
hearing, they were given two days' notice of the specific
charges facing them, an assemblage of charges which ranged
from distributing subversive literature to the allegation that
one of them had been discovered in bed with a woman.   Apparently a basic cause of the action was the allegation that
the students had been disrespectful toward college officials.
Apparently the case can thus be distinguished from Dixon in
that it pitted the administration against the students, rather
than the state against the students, as was the case in Dixon.

        The suit was brought as a class action, and the court
ruled that it did not technically qualify as a class action.
More important, the trial court, sustained by the Sixth Circuit, held that two days' notice of specific charges was adequate to meet due process requirements.   This was after
the United States District Court in the first Esteban case
stipulated ten days' notice in such cases.   Concerning the
administrative hearings in the Jones case, three noteworthy
procedural facts stand out: (1) the students were represented by counsel; (2) students' counsel was permitted to
cross-examine hostile witnesses; and (3) a verbatim transcript of the proceedings was made (apparently at the expense of the school).   Thus, in the Jones decision, District
Judge William E. Miller followed or exceeded the precedent
of the first Esteban decision, with the qualified exception of
the provision for ten days' notice.   One might view this as
remarkable, since Esteban dealt with denial of notice and
hearing, while Jones dealt merely with the adequacy of notice and
hearing.   However, the penalties assessed in both cases amounted
to expulsion.   In effect, the trial court's dismissal of the action
was sustained when the Supreme Court dismissed certiorari.

Soglin v. Kauffman

        For several years, one of the burning issues sur-
rounding the subject of college discipline, especially in ex-

pulsion cases, has been the vagueness of college regulations
and the vagueness of charges used as bases for college expulsions. Students have been expelled for "misbehavior, "
"behavior unbecoming a student...," and for similarly vague
reasons. As was previously mentioned, the United States
District Court for the Western District of Missouri, in its
second Esteban opinion, followed the guidelines set by the
Missouri District, en banc, when it held that the legal doctrine of vagueness and overbreadth in criminal statutes "does
not, in the absence of exceptional circumstances, apply to
standards of student conduct."[19] In Soglin v. Kauffman, the
Seventh Circuit rejected this rationale pointedly and said
that, "in the present case, the disciplinary proceedings must
fail to the extent that defendant... did not base those proceedings on students' disregard of university standards of
conduct expressed in reasonably clear and narrow rules."[20]

More pointedly, the court ruled that "expulsion and
prolonged suspension may not be imposed on students simply
on the basis of allegations of "misconduct." Further, "The
use of 'misconduct' as a standard in imposing the penalties
threatened here must... fall for vagueness. The inadequacy
of the rule is apparent on its face."

Two other statements by the Seventh Circuit in this
opinion would seem to be pregnant with portent: (1) "It is...
immaterial that this controversy involves a disciplinary rule
rather than a criminal statute"; and (2) "Criminal laws carry
their own definitions and penalties and are not enacted to enable a university to suspend or expel the wrongdoer absent a
breach of the university's own rule." The first statement
might be suspected as signaling the demise of a distinction
which has barred students from enjoyment of complete procedural protections which are manifest in criminal cases.
The second statement could be interpreted as an undermining
of the standard college sanctions against students prosecuted
in the regular judicial system for off-campus behavior.

The Question of Counsel

Commenting on counsel representing students in disciplinary hearings, Van Alstyne has observed that, "The
presence of counsel in an advisory role is an emerging
trend. To the best of my knowledge, those universities
that have permitted counsel to participate in hearings have
not found it unduly awkward, time-consuming or expensive."[21]

As to the practical consequence of student representation by counsel, Van Alstyne observed:

> ...the university will ordinarily have to put counsel on the other side as well. The informality of proceedings in which the commission both hears and adjudicates and really informally prosecutes by asking the questions and bringing in the witnesses, probably cannot long endure once retained counsel represents the students. 22

Van Alstyne also discusses the possibility of "an intermediate position" at those universities having law schools, the appointment of a senior law student as counsel for a student charged with an offense. A reading of the cases would indicate that this would be acceptable to most, if not all, district courts and would be compatible with the Fifth Circuit's opinion in the Dixon case. But, the Dixon case is no longer the most extensive precedent in the matter of counsel. Dixon eschewed legal counsel for students in disciplinary proceedings. Esteban I stipulated counsel and cross-examination, but the cross-examination was not to be done by counsel. In Jones the court took note of the fact that the students had counsel at the administrative hearing and that the counsel cross-examined hostile witnesses.

On the subject of the makeup of the panel or "jury" hearing a college disciplinary action within the meaning of due process, Van Alstyne said:

> In regard to the question of trial by one's peers, it is suggested that the sixth amendment notion of trial by jury in that sense is unlikely to be important. The students have a calm and rational policy claim for some representation of their own peers on the hearing boards, but I do not anticipate a federal court decision to that effect. 23

Makeup of the Hearing Board

On the subject of student representation on disciplinary hearing boards, both the American Association of University Professors and the American Civil Liberties Union have taken policy positions. The AAUP has proposed that, "The hearing committee should include faculty members or students, or, if regularly included or requested by the ac-

cused, both faculty and student members. "24 The ACLU
statement is similar, stating that, "a hearing should be held
by a faculty-student committee, or if the student prefers, by
a faculty committee. "25

An Extraordinary Judicial Document

Mention was made in Chapter IV of the extraordinary
document issued in 1968 by the United States District Court
for the Western District of Missouri, en banc, on the subject of student discipline under the heading of, "General Order on Judicial Standards of Procedure and Substance in Review of Student Discipline in Tax-Supported Institutions of
Higher Education. " Judge Elmo B. Hunter, who wrote two
decisions in the Esteban case, was one of the four judges
issuing this statement of guidelines. It might be assumed
that the court's statement will prove weighty in other judicial districts, since it reflects a respectable amount of research by a court which had been confronted with three stu-
dent-expulsion cases. Although the document does not rule
out requests for "a decision de novo inconsistent with these
standards, " it would nonetheless seem to mark a noteworthy
departure from the American system of case law.

"The following memorandum, " the document asserts,
"represents a statement of judicial standards of procedure
and substance applicable, in the absence of exceptional circumstances, to actions concerning discipline of students in
tax-supported educational institutions of higher learning. "26

Under the subheading, "Relation of Courts and Education, " the judges pointed out that "The courts should exercise caution when importuned to intervene in the important
processes and functions of education. A court should never
intervene in the processes of education without understanding
the nature of education. "27

Adknowledging that human errors are likely to be
committed by "those invested with powers of management
and teaching in the academic community, " the court declares that "Only where the erroneous and unwise actions in
the field of education deprive students of federally protected
rights or privileges does a federal court have power to intervene in the educational process. "

Under the subheading, "Lawful missions of tax-sup-

ported higher education, " the court stated in general terms
sixteen goals of higher learning which would be difficult to
fault on any account. 28   It then observes that "If it is true,
as it well may be, that man is in a race between education
and catastrophe, it is imperative that educational institutions
not be limited in the performance of their lawful missions
by unwarranted judicial interference. "

On the question of whether attendance at a tax-supported college is a right or a privilege, the court offers the
opinion that the issue is unimportant, but, "The federal constitution protects the equality of opportunity of all qualified
persons to attend. " However, the student assumes "obligations of performance and behavior reasonably imposed... generally much higher than those imposed on all citizens by the
civil and criminal law. "

> So long as there be no invidious discrimination, no
> deprival of due process, no abridgment of a right
> protected in the circumstances and no capricious,
> clearly unreasonable or unlawful action employed,
> the institution may discipline students to secure
> the compliance with these higher obligations as a
> teaching method or to sever the student from the
> academic community.

> No student may, without liability to lawful disci-
> pline, intentionally act to impair or prevent the
> accomplishment of any lawful mission or function
> of an educational institution. 29

The Analogy to Criminal Law

Except in the case of irrevocable expulsion, the discipline of students in the academic community is a part of
the teaching process, the court declared, then continued:

> In the case of irrevocable expulsion for misconduct,
> the process is not punitive or deterrent in the crim-
> inal law sense, but the process is rather the de-
> termination that the student is unqualified to con-
> tinue as a member of the educational community.
> Even then, the disciplinary process is not equiva-
> lent to the criminal law processes of federal and
> state criminal law.   For, while the expelled stu-
> dent may suffer damaging effects, sometimes ir-
> reparable, to his educational, social, and economic

future, he or she may not be imprisoned, fined, disenfranchised, or subjected to probationary supervision. The attempted analogy of student discipline to criminal proceedings against adults and juveniles is not sound.   (emphasis added)30

A federal court should not intervene in college disciplinary matters, the judges thought, unless there appears one of the following:

(1) a deprival of due process, that is, fundamental concepts of fair play;
(2) invidious discrimination, for example, on account of race or religion;
(3) denial of federal rights, constitutional or statutory, protected in the academic community; or
(4) clearly unreasonable, arbitrary or capricious action. 31

Procedural and Jurisdictional Standards

The Missouri judges expressed no doubt about federal jurisdiction in college expulsion cases.   "... United States District Courts, " they declared, "have jurisdiction to entertain and determine actions by students who claim unreasonably discriminatory, arbitrary or capricious actions lacking in due process and depriving a student of admission to or continued attendance at tax-supported institutions of higher education. "32

As to the legal action which may be brought in a federal court by an aggrieved student, the judges state that "The action may be (a) Under Section 1983, [Title 42, U. S. C.] an action at law for damages triable by a jury; (b) Under Section 1983, a suit in equity; or (c) Under Section 1893 and Section 2201 [Title 28, U. S. C.] a declaratory judgment action, which may be legal or equitable in nature depending on the issues therein. "33   This statement would seem actually to represent no more than the Missouri court's interpretation of jurisdictional aspects of federal civil rights statutes.   But the interpretation is harmonious with that of the Fifth Circuit in Dixon.   One might well take note of the possibility presented here for a tort action against college administrators guilty of arbitrary action in dismissal proceedings.

On the subject of exhaustion of remedies, the court tersely states that, "... the doctrine of exhaustion of state

judicial remedies is not applicable. The fact that there is
an existing state judicial remedy for the alleged wrong is no
ground for stay or dismissal. [34] However, administrative
remedies must be exhausted, for, "Ordinarily until the currently available adequate and effective institutional processes
have been exhausted, the disciplinary action is not final and
the controversy is not ripe for determination." The judges
add that, "In an action at law under Section 1983, the issues
are triable by jury and equitable defenses are not available."

     College administrations in discipline litigation have
often advanced the claim of mootness because, for example,
of the lapse of time, progression of school year, dispersion
of involved students, etc. The Missouri federal judges followed precedent in their statement by observing that, "In an
action at law or equity under Section 1983, Title 42, U.S.C.,
to review severe student disciplinary action the doctrine of
mootness is not applicable when the action is timely filed."

     The court offered the opinion that legally acceptable
standards "may apply to student behavior on and off the campus when relevant to any lawful mission, process, or function of the institution." The burden of proof is placed on
the institution which undertakes to limit or forbid the exercise of a right guaranteed by the Constitution or a law of the
United States. However, the institution must merely demonstrate that a practice "is recognized as reasonable by some
reputable authority or school of thought in the field of higher
education." Unanimity of expert opinion is not necessary.

     In what is perhaps the most controversial aspect of
its advisory, the court proposes that:

> Outstanding educational authorities in the field of
> higher education believe, on the basis of exper-
> ience, that detailed codes of prohibited conduct are
> provocative and should not be employed in higher
> education.
>
> For this reason, general affirmative statements of
> what is expected of a student may in some areas be
> preferable in higher education. Such affirmative
> standards may be employed, and discipline of stu-
> dents based thereon.
>
> The legal doctrine that a prohibitory statute is
> void if it is overly broad or unconstitutionally

broad does not, in the absence of exceptional circumstances, apply to standards of student conduct. ... 35

Three minimal requirements, the judges declare, "apply in cases of severe discipline, growing out of fundamental
conceptions of fairness implicit in procedural due process."
These three requirements are notice, hearing, and the re-
quirement that such disciplinary actions be supported by "substantial evidence." As to the specifics of due process, the
judges declare that:

> There is no general requirement that procedural
> due process in student disciplinary cases provide
> for legal representation, a public hearing, confron-
> tation and cross-examination of witnesses, warnings
> about privileges, self-incrimination, application of
> principles of former or double jeopardy, compul-
> sory production of witnesses, or any of the re-
> maining features in a particular case to guarantee
> the fundamental concepts of fair play. [emphasis
> added]

In conclusion, the court pays tribute to "the current
unusual efforts of the institutions and the interested organizations which are devising and recommending procedures and
policies in student discipline which are based on standards,
in many features, far higher than the requirements of due
process." Here the court cites the Joint Statement of Rights
and Freedoms of Students and the University of Missouri's
Provisional Rules of Procedure in Student Disciplinary Matters.

The Document and Esteban II

One might well argue that the Missouri federal judges,
in the advisory discussed above, took a backward step in the
matter of procedural rights for college students in dismissal
actions. Most of what they said had been said before in
college-dismissal cases. Their major innovation, then, was
their statement waiving for college students the legal principles against "overly broad or unconstitutionally broad" standards of student conduct. One might well contend that this
position marks a retrogression toward the in loco parentis
doctrine--an acknowledgment that college students are, after
all, legal infants.

Irving Achtenberg, ACLU legal counsel in Kansas City who pleaded the Esteban case, believes that the document, which he describes as an "advisory opinion," adopts "both the good and the bad parts of the Esteban opinion."[36] Achtenberg is doubtful of the legal significance of the judicial document, but is aware that it has been cited at least twice by federal courts, once in the second Esteban case[37] and once disapprovingly by the Seventh Circuit.[38] Since its earliest use was in the second Esteban case, attention might well be turned here to that application.

The suspension case of Esteban v. Central Missouri State College was discussed elsewhere in this chapter. Although Judge Elmo B. Hunter's opinion in that case was hailed as an important precedent in expanding procedural rights of dismissed college students, the victory was a hollow one for the students involved. Esteban was originally suspended for two semesters following his alleged participation in campus disorders. Judge Hunter found that his suspension had been attended by inadequate procedural safeguards: a lack of adequate notice and hearing. Following this decision, the college gave Esteban notice and hearing generally in conformity with standards prescribed by the District Court, at the conclusion of which it, in effect, dismissed him, according to his plea before the court in the second Esteban case. He returned to Judge Hunter's court, claiming that:

(1) The college regulation with regard to mass gatherings violates the first amendment guarantee of freedom of speech and assembly.

(2) The college regulation with regard to participating in mass demonstrations violates the first and fifth amendments in that its language is vague, uncertain and overbroad, providing plaintiffs with no reasonable standard for observance and no notice of illegal conduct.

(3) The enforcement of the mentioned regulation as to offcampus conduct is beyond the powers of the college and is a denial of due process.

(4) The charge as originally made did not contain the words 'contributing to' which quoted language is not a part of the regulation and hence is unenforceable.

(5) The hearing before Dr. Lovinger [the college
president] lacked procedural due process as required by the fourteenth amendment in that there
was no evidence to support a charge of participating in an unruly or unlawful mass demonstration. [39]

Judge Hunter was one of the four district judges who
issued the judicial directive discussed above. At the time
the directive was formulated, the second Esteban case, referred to by Achtenberg as "Esteban II, " was before his
court. It can hardly be viewed as surprising, then, that his
opinion in the second Esteban case closely parallels the
Western District's broad policy statement on the subject of
student discipline. Jurisdictional challenges were decided in
favor of the plaintiff, but the central question was determined
in favor of the college.

The question of exhaustion of state judicial remedies
was ruled not applicable; administrative remedies need not
be exhausted before a controversy is "ripe for determination";
the doctrine of mootness was held not applicable; deference
to educational expertise was expressed; the earlier Esteban
litigation did not bar the students by the doctrine of res
judicata; the question was limited to whether the students had
been denied by the state any rights, privileges or immunities
secured by the Constitution and laws of the United States.

However, the court ruled that the disciplinary process
of a college is not equivalent to the criminal-law process of
federal or state criminal law; it is relevant to the mission
of a college to prohibit participation in unruly gatherings; the
legal doctrine that a prohibitory statute is void if it is overly
broad or unconstitutionally broad does not apply to standards
of student conduct; a student who engages in forbidden conduct
is in no position to invoke equity relief; college attendance is
voluntary and the student assumes obligations to observe
reasonable regulations.

Of particular interest in the second Esteban decision
are two points expounded by the court--dealing respectively
with (1) the nature or extent of "criminal law" procedures to
which students are entitled; and (2) the nonapplicability of the
legal ban against overly broad or unconstitutionally broad
prohibitory statutes.

Since the 1967 decision of the United States Supreme

Court in the case of In re Gault, [40] many civil rights enthu-
siasts had hoped that the principle of that decision--that juveniles were entitled to the procedural protection granted in
criminal law in actions which might deprive them of their
liberty--would broaden the rights afforded students in expulsion cases.   Paralleling the rationale of the Western District's advisory, Judge Hunter laid to rest this hope.   His
comment:

> ...the disciplinary process is not equivalent to the
> criminal law process of federal or state criminal
> law.   For, while the expelled student may suffer
> damaging effects, sometimes irreparable, to his
> educational, social, and economic future, he or
> she may not be imprisoned, fined, disenfranchised,
> or subjected to probationary supervision.   The at-
> tempted analogy of student discipline to criminal
> proceedings against adults and juveniles is not
> sound.   Such cited cases as In re Gault, 387 U. S.
> 1, 87 S. Ct. 1428, 18 L. Ed. 2d 527 (1967), Kent
> v. United States, 383 U. S. 541, 86 S. Ct. 1045,
> 16 L. Ed. 2d 84 (1966), and Cox v. State of Louis-
> iana, 379 U. S. 536, 85 S. Ct. 453, 13 L Ed. 2d
> 471 (1965) are not applicable. [41]

On the subject of specificity of regulations, the court
stated an opinion consistent with the judicial document which
perhaps most dismayed the ACLU counsel.   Judge Hunter
declared:

> The legal doctrine that a prohibitory statute is void
> if it is overly broad or unconstitutionally broad
> does not, in the absence of exceptional circum-
> stances, apply to standards of student conduct.
> [emphasis in original]
>
> Judicial notice is taken that outstanding educational
> authorities in the field of higher education believe,
> on the basis of experience, that detailed codes of
> prohibited student conduct are provocative and
> should not be employed in higher education.   See,
> Brady and Snoxell, Student Personnel Work in
> Higher Education, p. 378 (Houghton Mifflin, Boston,
> 1961).   For this reason, general affirmative state-
> ments of what is expected of a student may be
> preferable in higher education.   Such affirmative
> statements should, of course, be reasonably con-

strued and applied in individual cases. [42]

The AAUP and ACLU Statements

It must be remembered that all the preceding discussion has dealt with judicial views of the minimal procedural protections to which a college student is entitled under the fourteenth amendment due process clause before he may be suspended or expelled from a tax-supported college. The four federal judges for the Western District of Missouri pointed out in the judicial document discussed elsewhere in this chapter that efforts are being made by non-judicial interest groups toward "devising and recommending procedures and policies in student discipline which are based on standards, in many features, far higher than the requirements of due process." The judges specifically cited the Joint Statement on Rights and Freedoms of Students. Attention is now directed to procedural rights recommendations proposed in the Joint Statement and in a comparable publication by the ACLU. (See Appendices A and B.)

The Joint Statement

In June, 1967, a joint committee, composed of representatives of the American Association of University Professors, U. S. National Student Association, Association of American Colleges, National Association of Student Personnel Administrators, and National Association of Women Deans and Counselors, met in Washington, D. C., and drafted the Joint Statement on the Rights and Freedoms of Students. This meeting was held six years after the Fifth Circuit's decision in the Dixon case, and one might well argue that it is unimportant whether the five associations responsible for originating the document acted out of a response to pressure from the courts or out of a sense of recognition of the demands of "justice."

At any rate, this group originated what has become the much-publicized Joint Statement on Rights and Freedoms of Students. [43] The statement won prompt endorsement by the five groups whose members had created it, and by six other college-related organizations as well. Newcomers to the ranks of endorsers included the American Association for Higher Education, Jesuit Education Association, American College Personnel Association; Executive Committee, College and University Department, National Catholic Education Association; and the Commission on Student Personnel, American Association of Junior Colleges. [44]

Under the heading, "Procedural Standards in Disciplinary Proceedings," the Joint Statement asserts that the institution has "an obligation to clarify those standards of behavior it considers essential to its educational mission and its community life." Students should be as free as possible from regulations that have no direct relevance to education. Offenses should be defined as clearly as possible. Regulations should be formulated with student participation and published by the institution.

As to the hearing procedures, the statement proposes that the student who questions the fairness of disciplinary action against him should have the privilege of a hearing before a regularly constituted hearing committee. This committee should include faculty members or students or both faculty members and students. The committee should exclude persons otherwise interested in the action. The student should receive from the committee written notice of the reasons for the disciplinary action "with sufficient particularity and in sufficient time" to afford opportunity to prepare for the hearing. He should have a right to an advisor of his choice in his defense. The burden of proof should rest on the accusers.

The student should be given opportunity to testify and to present evidence and witnesses. He should have an opportunity to hear and cross-examine adverse witnesses. The committee should not consider statements against the student unless he has been advised of their content and has had opportunity to rebut unfavorable inferences. The committee's decision should be based on evidence introduced at the hearing. Improperly acquired evidence should not be considered, a provision which raises the question of unwarranted search of the student's quarters. In the absence of a transcript, both a digest and a verbatim record of the hearing should be made. The committee decision should be final, subject to the student's right to appeal to the college president or ultimately the governing board. [45]

The ACLU Statement

Probably no organization in the United States has displayed a greater interest in protecting the rights of students than the American Civil Liberties Union. Therefore, an

examination of the ACLU position on student procedural
rights might well be expected to be informative. In a working paper for a forthcoming edition of its publication, Academic Freedom and Civil Liberties of Students in Colleges and
Universities, the ACLU outlined its views on the subject.
The ACLU statement is parallel in most respects to the
Joint Statement, differing primarily in that it achieves greater specificity in places. For example, under the subtitle,
"A. Enacting and Promulgating Regulations," the ACLU
statement eschews generalizations to declare that "Regulations should be clear and unambiguous. Phrases such as
'conduct unbecoming a student,' or 'actions against the best
interests of the college,' should be avoided because they allow too much latitude for interpretation." The ACLU declaration adds that the range of penalties for the violation of
regulations should be clearly stated. Minor infractions may
be dealt with summarily, but the student should retain the
recourse to appeal. In the case of infractions punishable by
suspension, expulsion or notation on a student's permanent
record, the student is entitled to notice and hearing. At a
disciplinary hearing, the student should have the right to
remain silent, and the college should assist him in requiring the presence of witnesses and production of documents
at the hearing, at least to the extent that this is possible.

In other respects, the ACLU statement is closely
parallel with the Joint Statement. 46

Summary

It must be noted that all the cases of student discipline discussed in this chapter involved either expulsions or
suspensions, with the courts on occasion yielding to the inclination to use the two terms interchangeably. Expulsion
would seem to be the ultimate sanction available to the college administrator, against a student. Suspension would seem
to be the second ultimate sanction only by a matter of degree.

At the present stage of development of case law in
the area, judicial review in the federal courts would seem
to be limited to cases of expulsion or suspension. The
Fifth Circuit's opinion in the Dixon case embraced the matter of student expulsion. However, the district court opinion in the Knight case closely followed the Dixon precedent,
although Knight involved suspensions rather than expulsions.

Referring to the Knight case, O'Leary has observed that "Although reference was made to the fact that suspension here was tantamount to dismissal, the claim of denial of due process was directed against a university suspension, raising the question of whether all college and university actions, however minimal, may now be said to be open to review in the courts."[47]

On the other hand, the Harvard Law Review seemingly took the opposite view in 1968, when it noted that:

> The seriousness of the plaintiff's injury seems often to have influenced the court's decision to provide relief. At present, for the student to prevail, his injury must be severe and usually must be to an interest which the courts are accustomed to protect. The farther advanced the student in his program at a given institution and the more his reliance on successful completion is justified, the greater the likelihood of the court's intervening on his behalf.
>
> . . . .
>
> ...the student dismissed from professional school tends to have greater judicial protection than do others, including nonprofessional graduate students.
>
> . . . .
>
> The legitimate expectation of receiving such a degree may be regarded as a property interest, which the judiciary, of course, is accustomed to protect and an injury to which is traditionally necessary for the granting of specific performance, the remedy many students seek.[48]

Conclusions

From what has been observed in this chapter, one might feel justified in drawing a number of conclusions which would seem to be at least tentatively acceptable:

1. Federal court review is now available without prior resort to state courts for students who have been disciplined by expulsion or suspension by college officials in the absence of procedural safeguards adequate to satisfy fourteenth amendment due process requirements.

2.   The extent of procedures required at the administrative level to satisfy due process considerations is a flexi-
ble matter.   Pending an opinion from the United States Supreme Court, Dixon is the authoritative precedent, with its
provision for notice and a rudimentary hearing of an adversary nature.   The student's right to counsel, cross-examination of adverse witnesses and a record of the administrative
hearing at his own expense would seem to have been tentatively established by the first Esteban decision, but would
seem to be inadequately stable.

3.   Although it is the sort of proposition which hardly
lends itself to proving, one might feel secure in surmising
that acceptance of disciplinary cases into the federal courts
has led, and will continue to lead, to a greater procedural
awareness on the part of college administrators.

4.   Dixon is being followed by the district courts,
perhaps more than the literature would lead one to believe.
This would seem to be especially true when it is remembered
that Dixon dealt with an absence of notice and hearing, not
with inadequate notice and hearing.   Knight and the first Esteban case would seem to support this proposal.   Due and
the second Esteban case would seem to support a contention
that courts will hesitate to interfere where any rudiments of
a hearing can be demonstrated.

Notes

1.   "The College Student and Due Process in Disciplinary
     Proceedings, " op. cit. , p. 448, n82.

2.   Letter from William Van Alstyne, dated Feb. 27, 1969.

3.   Excerpt from a draft of an ACLU pamphlet, Academic
     Freedom and Civil Liberties of Students in Colleges
     and Universities, while that work was in preparation,
     Appendix B, p. 2.

4.   See, e.g. , O'Leary, op. cit. , p. 441, n33.

5.   294 F. 2d 150, 159 (1961).

6.   Ibid. at 158.

7.   Ibid. at 159.

8.   200 F. Supp. 174 (1961).

9.   Ibid. at 182.

10.   233 F. Supp. 396 (1963).

11.   Undoubtedly, Judge Carswell's ruling in this case constituted one of the reasons for the tenacious opposition by the N. A. A. C. P. to Senate confirmation of his appointment to the Supreme Court, an opposition which was to prove successful. This case was the second federal court test of the authority of Dixon. Judge Carswell faced the dilemma of finding for the plaintiff students and thus stretching the meaning of Dixon to include inadequate hearing, or else finding against the students and tending to minimize the authority of Dixon. One might well speculate that, had he opted the former course of action, he might have ingratiated himself sufficiently with the N. A. A. C. P. to have neutralized their attitude toward him, and might then have become an Associate Justice of the United States Supreme Court.

12.   Excerpt from a draft of the ACLU pamphlet, "Academic Freedom and Civil Liberties of Students in Colleges and Universities, " a work in preparation (n. d.) Appendix B, p. 2.

13.   233 F. Supp. 396, 403 (1963).

14.   John P. Holloway, "The School in Court, " (Ch. 3) Grace W. Holmes (ed.). Student Protest and the Law (Ann Arbor, Michigan: The Institute of Continuing Legal Education, 1969), p. 93.

15.   Excerpt from a draft of the ACLU pamphlet, op. cit. , p. 3.

16.   279 F. Supp. 190, 407 F. 2d 834, 90 S. Ct. 779 (1970).

17.   90 S. Ct. 779.

18.   90 S. Ct. 779, 781 (1970).

19.   290 F. Supp. 622, 630 (1968).

20.   418 F. 2d 163, 167 (7th Cir. 1969).

21. William W. Van Alstyne, "The Constitutional Protection of Protest on Campus," (Ch. 8) Grace W. Holmes (ed.), Student Protest and the Law, op. cit., pp. 194-195.

22. Ibid., p. 195.

23. Ibid.

24. Joint Statement on Rights and Freedoms of Students, infra.

25. Academic Freedom and Civil Liberties of Students in Colleges and Universities (New York: American Civil Liberties Union, 1961 (rev'd. ed.), p. 7.

26. General Order on Judicial Standards, op. cit., at 134.

27. Ibid. at 136.

28. In addition to standard encyclopedic writings, the court draws on the writings of Jefferson and an impressive number of government documents and works by noted authors.

29. General Order on Judicial Standards, op. cit., at 141.

30. Ibid., p. 4. The concept of discipline as an integral part of the educational process is supported by Brady and Snoxell, Student Discipline in Higher Education (Washington, D.C.: The American College Personnel Association, 1965), which the court acknowledges as a source.

31. General Order on Judicial Standards, op. cit., at 143.

32. Ibid., p. 5.

33. Ibid.

34. For authority, the court cites Monroe v. Pape, 365 U. S. 167, 81 S. Ct. 473, 5 L. Ed. 2d 492; Damico v. California, 389 U. S. 416, 88 S. Ct. 526, 19 L. Ed. 2d 647; and McNeese v. Board of Education, 373 U. S. 668, 83 S. Ct. 1433, 10 L. Ed. 2d 622.

35. Ibid. This standard of vagueness and overbreadth was

expressed in the second Esteban opinion by Judge Hunter, Esteban v. Central Missouri State College, 290
F. Supp. 622, 630, but was deliberately spurned by
the Seventh Circuit in Soglin v. Kauffman, 418 F. 2d
163 (1969), and was obliquely disowned by the Supreme
Court in Tinker v. Des Moines School District, 393
U. S. 503, 513.

36.   Telephone conversation with Irving Achtenberg, Feb. 22,
       1970. Achtenberg uses the term, "advisory opinion,"
       because the court then had before it two college-ex-
       pulsion cases.

37.   290 F. Supp. 622 (W. D. Mo. 1868).

38.   Soglin v. Kauffman, 418 F. 2d 163, 168 (1969).

39.   290 F. Supp. 622, 625 (1968).

40.   387 U. S. 1, 87 S. Ct. 1428, 18 L. Ed. 2d 527 (1967).

41.   290 F. Supp. 622 (1968) at 628.

42.   Ibid., at 630.

43.   54 A. A. U. P. Bulletin No. 2, Summer 1968, 258.

44.   Ibid.

45.   Ibid.

46.   Academic Freedom and Civil Liberties of Students in
       Colleges and Universities (working draft) (New York:
       American Civil Liberties Union, 1969), pp. 9-10.

47.   Richard E. O'Leary, "The College Student and Due
       Process in Disciplinary Proceedings," op. cit., pp.
       450-51.

48.   "Developments in the Law--Academic Freedom," 81
       Harvard Law Review 1134, taken here from reprint
       in Student Rights & Responsibilities, op. cit., pp.
       65-66.

Chapter VI

OTHER PROCEDURAL CONSIDERATIONS:
SEARCH AND SEIZURE, SELF-INCRIMINATION

What are a student's rights to privacy in his quarters
when he lives in a college-controlled residence hall? And,
for that matter, what are his rights to remain silent in a
disciplinary proceeding against him without attracting prejudice against his cause? These questions cannot be answered
categorically in terms of judicial precedent. Nonetheless,
both questions form bases for heated discussion in student
gatherings on many college campuses.

Although commentary on these particular aspects of
student rights has been less common than commentary on
due process in dismissal proceedings, what commentary has
appeared in legal journals would seem to indicate a conviction that the death of the in loco parentis doctrine will lead
to a greater acknowledgment of fourth amendment and perhaps fifth amendment protections due students in state-supported colleges. The first of the two questions--dealing with
the student's right to privacy in his dormitory room--would
seem to be the more compelling, since on most campuses it
would have direct application to a vastly larger number of
students than the question of procedural protections for students which may grow out of the fifth amendment. These
two constitutional questions will be treated separately.

The Student's Right to Privacy in Quarters

The college student's assertion of the right of privacy
challenges most directly the college administrator's view that
the college stands in loco parentis to its students and that
the administrator is vested with broad discretionary powers
to adopt and enforce any regulations thought reasonably necessary to exercise effective supervision and discipline over the
students. At least one writer has proposed that this view of
the university's role vis-a-vis its students has its antecedent

in the apprentice system and "reflects the Renaissance notion
that the university is responsible for educating the whole
man. "[1]

Consequently, many college catalogues contain statements essentially the same as the following one in the Troy
State College bulletin: "The college reserves the right to
enter rooms for inspection purposes. If the administration
deems it necessary the room may be searched and the occupant required to open his personal luggage and any other
personal material which is sealed. "[2]

The Moore Case: Protection Denied

Has the dormitory resident, then, no protection of his
quarters under the fourth amendment's injunction against unwarranted searches and seizures? Obviously, conflicting interests of the student and the institution must be reconciled
when a student's right of privacy in a dormitory room is involved. In spite of a preponderence of opinion by legal
writers that dormitory students either should have or will
have protection of their privacy under the fourth amendment,
the most-quoted precedent on the subject is Moore v. Student
Affairs Committee of Troy State University, [3] in which Judge
Johnson of the United States District Court, Middle District
of Alabama, eschewed the applicability of the fourth amendment to the college-dormitory situation.

In this case, police of Troy, Alabama, accompanied
by the dean of men at the college, acting on information
from informants, searched six dormitory rooms in two separate residence halls. Moore's room was searched in his
presence, but without his permission. It was later stipulated:

> That no search warrant was obtained in this case,
> that no consent to search was given by the defen-
> dant, that the search was not incidental to a legal
> arrest, that no other offense was committed by the
> defendant in the arresting officers' presence, that
> Troy State College had in force and effect at the
> time of the search and subsequent arrest of the
> defendant [the catalogue statement on room searches
> quoted above]. [4]

The search yielded from Moore's room a matchbox
containing marijuana. Moore objected that the evidence was

seized as a result of a search in violation of the fourth
amendment.   He also challenged the constitutionality of the
catalogue regulation under which the search was conducted.

Following a hearing before the student affairs committee, Moore was indefinitely suspended from the college.
He appealed to the United States District Court on the ground
that he had been denied due process in the administrative
hearing.   Judge Johnson determined that Moore had been denied his right to procedural due process and retained jurisdiction of the case pending remand to the college's student
affairs committee "for the purpose of conducting a hearing
comporting with procedural due process of law."   Following
a second hearing before the student affairs committee,
Moore was again indefinitely suspended.   He entered the
district court again, requesting readmission to the college
and a declaratory judgment that none of the evidence seized
in the search of his room "may be admitted in any criminal
proceedings..."   He also alleged that the admission in the
administrative hearing of evidence seized in the search of
his dormitory room violated his fourth amendment rights prohibiting illegal search and seizure.   Judge Johnson's dicta
are enlightening.   As to the relationship between the institution and the dormitory resident, he declared:

> College students who reside in dormitories have a
> special relationship with the college involved.   In-
> sofar as the Fourth Amendment affects that rela-
> tionship, it does not depend on either a general
> theory of the right of privacy or on traditional
> property concepts.   The college does not stand,
> strictly speaking, in loco parentis to its students,
> nor is their relationship purely contractual in the
> traditional sense.   The relationship grows out of
> the peculiar and sometimes the seemingly compet-
> ing interests of college and student.   A student
> naturally has the right to be free of unreasonable
> search and seizures, and a tax-supported public
> college may not compel a 'waiver' of that right as
> a condition precedent to admission.   The college,
> on the other hand, has an 'affirmative obligation'
> to promulgate and enforce reasonable regulations
> designed to protect campus order and discipline
> and to promote an environment consistent with the
> educational process.   The validity of the regulation
> authorizing search of dormitories thus does not
> depend on whether a student 'waives' his right to

Fourth Amendment protection or whether he has
'contracted' it away; rather its validity is determined by whether the regulation is a reasonable
exercise of the college's supervisory duty. 5

If the regulation or action of college authorities is
necessary in aid of the basic responsibility of the institution
regarding discipline and the maintenance of an "educational
atmosphere, " Judge Johnson wrote, "then it will be presumed
facially reasonable despite the fact that it may infringe to
some extent on the outer bounds of the Fourth Amendment
rights of students. " [Emphasis added]

Judge Johnson then reached back four decades to a
Supreme Court of Missouri decision to quote the following
statement about a dormitory resident: "When appellant took
up residence there, he impliedly agreed to conform to all
reasonable rules and regulations for its government which
were then in force or which might thereafter be adopted by
the proper authorities. "6

Returning his attention to Moore and the particular
problem with which he confronted the court, the judge wrote:

The regulation was reasonably applied in this case.
The constitutional boundary line between the right
of the school authorities to search and the right of
a dormitory student to privacy must be based on a
reasonable belief on the part of the college authorities that a student is using a dormitory room for
a purpose which is illegal or which would otherwise
seriously interfere with campus discipline. Upon
this submission, it is clear that such a belief
existed in this case. 7

Judge Johnson then turned to the Fifth Circuit's opinion in Dixon to provide the rationale to sustain his opinion
that dormitory residents are entitled to only qualified protection by the fourth amendment:

This standard of 'reasonable cause to believe' to
justify a search by college administrators--even
where the sole purpose is to seek evidence of suspected violations of law--is lower than the constitutionally protected criminal law standard of 'probable cause. ' This is true because of the special
necessities of the student-college relationship and

because college disciplinary proceedings are not
criminal proceedings in the constitutional sense.
It is clearly settled that due process in college
disciplinary proceedings does not require full-
blown adversary hearings subject to the rules of
evidence and all constitutional criminal guarantees.
'Such a hearing, with the attending publicity and
disturbance of college activities, might be detrimental to the college's educational atmosphere and
impractical to carry out." Dixon v. Alabama
State Board of Education, supra. [8]

Judge Johnson then seemingly undertook to distinguish
this case in the following language:

Assuming that the Fourth Amendment applied to
college discipline proceedings, the search in this
case would not be in violation of it.   It is settled
law that the Fourth Amendment does not prohibit
reasonable searches when the search is conducted
by a superior charged with a responsibility of
maintaining discipline and order or of maintaining
security.   A student who lives in a dormitory on
campus which he 'rents' from the school waives
objection to any reasonable searches conducted pursuant to reasonable and necessary regulations such
as this one. [9]

Moore's action was, of course, dismissed.   The sta-
bility of this case as a lasting legal precedent was opened
to doubt, however, by a subsequent New York action which
reached the United States Supreme Court in the case of
Overton v. New York.

The Overton Case: A Tightening of Criteria

In the Overton case, detectives had obtained search
warrants directing search of two high school students and
their lockers at the Mount Vernon, New York, high school.
They presented the warrant to the vice-principal, who summoned the two students to his office.   The detectives searched
the boys and found nothing of pertinence to their investigation.
One of the boys, asked if he had marijuana in his locker,
responded, "I guess so," or, "Maybe."

A detective, the vice-principal and a school custodian
then accompanied the boy to his locker with a master key

and the detective found marijuana cigarettes in the boy's jacket. It subsequently developed that the search warrant was ineffective insofar as the boy's locker was concerned. The boy's counsel then proceeded to attempt to suppress the evidence at the ensuing youthful-offender proceeding. The trial judge denied the motion, holding that the board of education and the school administration "retained dominion over the use of the lockers and the court finds that the search was legal.."[10], The court of appeals upheld the trial judge and ruled the evidence admissible.[11] The United States Supreme Court, in a two paragraph per curiam opinion, vacated the decision and remanded the case, with Justice Black entering a lone dissent.[12] The conviction was then reaffirmed, however, by the New York courts, and was to "be before the Supreme Court again next term [1969-70]."[13] In its per curiam, the Supreme Court remanded "for further consideration in the light of Bumper v. State of North Carolina, " an opinion issued by the high court in April, 1968.[14] In Bumper, the supreme court stated that "When a law enforcement authority claims authority to search a home under a warrant, he announces that the occupant has no right to resist the search."[15]

The supreme court's reference to Bumper in its Overton per curiam would thus indicate that it considers a valid warrant prerequisite to the search of a high school student's locker. The inevitable legal analogy to be argued is that since a high school administrator cannot authorize search of a student's locker merely because it is school property, then a college administration cannot authorize an official search of a student's dormitory room. The argument that the high school principal occupies the in loco parentis role, whereas the college official does not may lend strength to this argument to bring the college dormitory occupant fully under the protection of the fourth amendment.

People v. Cohen: Warrantless Evidence Excluded

Lippe cites the case of People v. Cohen[16] as more pertinent to the fourth amendment rights of college dormitory residents. In this case, a criminal proceeding, the court ruled inadmissible evidence obtained by a warrantless search of a student's dormitory room at a private college. Here the police had been accompanied by school officials who were concerned about drug use and had requested a police survey. In excluding evidence seized without a warrant, Judge Burstein declared:

> It has been argued that a student impliedly consents to entry into his room by University officials at any time.... Even if the doctrine of implied consent were imported in this case, the consent is given, not to police officials, but to the University and the latter cannot fragmentize, share or delegate it....

> Unitersity students are adults. The dorm is a home and it must be inviolate against unlawful search and seizure. To suggest that a student who lives off campus in a boarding house is protected but that one who occupies a dormitory room waives his constitutional liberties is at war with reason, logic and law. [17]

Lippe reads into the two cases of Moore and Cohen the suggestion, "that college officials may conduct reasonable searches of dormitory rooms without obtaining a search warrant as part of their disciplinary authority but that such power may not be delegated to police officers whose activities are governed by the strict standards of the fourth amendment...."[18]

Legal Commentary

Lippe's personal belief is "that university regulation of personal conduct in nonacademic areas is so peripherally related to the academic interests of the university that any substantial encroachment on the personal freedom of the student may be held unconstitutional as the law of student legal rights evolves."[19]

More particularly, on the subject of privacy in quarters, he has written his opinion that:

> Officials of schools deemed to be 'public' should be bound by fourth amendment standards and required to obtain a search warrant prior to searching a dormitory room. From the student's point of view it makes little difference if his privacy is invaded by a police officer or a college official. Furthermore, it can hardly be argued that college discipline should take priority over effective law enforcement. [20]

Van Alstyne stated in a 1963 article that "It is foreseeable that random and unannounced searching of student rooms may be forbidden. "[21] Five years later, in another law journal article, he observed that:

> Unlike the situation respecting the private landlord who may contractually reserve the right to enter and inspect the premises at any time for reasons satisfactory only to himself, ... it is exceedingly likely that the fourth amendment's interdiction of 'unreasonable searches and seizures' restricts colleges receiving substantial public support from imposing such sweeping conditions upon a student's privacy as those which may be reserved by contract to a private landlord. | Random fishing expeditions without warrant and without excusable emergency, resulting in the seizure of things \subsequently introduced in a disciplinary hearing to provide a basis for expelling a student, are probably forbidden. [22]

While generally preoccupied with the general legal relationship between students and colleges, Goldman has nonetheless observed that "when a university provides dormitory facilities, the contracts it has with its students with respect to the use of such facilities should be judged under the law of landlord and tenant. "[23] Again, he observes, "there is no reason why the university should be permitted to utilize its fiduciary role as an educator in order to give itself greater control over its tenants than a landlord would normally possess. [24]

Monypenny has written that "The role of the university in the direct control of the non-classroom life of the student should be as restricted as possible; in particular he should have rights of privacy and self-regulation of his own leisure time. "[25]

Edward C. Kalaidjian, a New York attorney with an interest in student rights, has written that "the student has the right to be free of unreasonable search and seizure. A tax-supported public college may not compel a waiver of that right as a condition of admission. "[26] Expanding on this, he has further observed:

> The rule seems to be that a university authority requires less information to render a search reasonable than would be required to get a warrant.

> As a practical matter, however, the business of
> search has to be done most judiciously. I don't
> believe university people ought to be popping in and
> out of rooms indiscriminately. They must have
> some very substantial grounds for believing that
> something very serious is going on in the room to
> justify it as a matter of policy and law. [27]

Van Alstyne concurred in this opinion and added a
word about the direction in which the law is moving:

> This development of the law is less than a year
> old. Until a year ago, comfortable counsel might
> have said, 'Why, it's outrageous! There is no
> such thing as a student right to privacy; we have
> this form that every student signs, consenting to
> search of his apartment.' I assure you that such
> consent is absolutely worthless in this area. [28]

Paul D. Carrington, Professor of Law at the University of Michigan, proposed in 1969 that "This is a time for
reappraisal and perhaps a time for shedding burdensome
tasks and functions with which the educational process has
been freighted by an unthinking public." In particular, he
says, "One function that I would expect most institutions to
deem dispensable is the function of the moral disciplinarian." [29]
Pragmatically, he adds, "Educational institutions are sometimes called to exercise greater power over individuals than
they are equipped to exercise." [30]

As early as 1964, Michael T. Johnson, who was later
to join the University of Oklahoma law faculty, was able to
observe that "The cases in this area indicate that for a university to search a student's room without his permission
and seize evidence to be used against him would be illegal." [31]
Johnson was careful to distinguish between criminal due process and disciplinary proceedings, which are civil actions,
and concludes that "It is probable that the student has a
right... to the privilege against unreasonable search and
seizure and its corollary, the exclusionary rule...." [32]
"There is nothing in the language of the fourth amendment,"
he adds, "which would limit its application to instances
wherein the evidence illegally obtained is to be used in
criminal proceedings." [33]

Beaney expressed an attitude which would seem to be
commonly held by many college educators when he wrote that

"While residing in university dormitory facilities, a student
may be required to submit to periodic fire and health inspec-
tions of his quarters, and to have them entered to prevent
harm to persons or property, or when necessary to maintain
order, but students should be able to enjoy security from
casual and prying entries."34   C. Peter Magrath, Dean of
the College of Arts and Sciences and Professor of Political
Science at the University of Nebraska, in 1968 declared that
"colleges and universities which respect the privacy and individual dignity of their students will find it easier to demand the same for their administrators and professors."35

AAUP and ACLU Statements

Both the AAUP and the ACLU have adopted statements
relating to fourth amendment rights of campus dormitory
residents. The Joint Statement, discussed in Chapter V,
contains the following provisions:

>   B.   Investigation of Student Conduct
>
>   1.   Except under extreme emergency circumstances,
>   premises occupied by a student and the personal pos-
>   sessions of students should not be searched unless
>   appropriate authorization has been obtained. For
>   premises such as residence halls controlled by the
>   institution, an appropriate and responsible authority
>   should be designated to whom application should be
>   made before a search is conducted. The applica-
>   tion should specify the reasons for the search and
>   the objects or information sought. The student
>   should be present, if possible, during the search.
>   For premises not controlled by the institution, the
>   ordinary requirements for lawful search should be
>   followed. 36

The ACLU would prefer that the student have the same
privacy in his dormitory room as he would have in off-campus facilities, as reflected by the following 1969 statement:

>   1.   Student Residences.
>
>   a) Although on-campus living is often regarded
>   as an important part of the total educational ex-
>   perience, it should not be compulsory.

b) Dormitory rules with respect to visiting hours, curfew and the use of liquor may be adopted by resident students in their common interest. Any such rules should be drafted so as to leave the maximum freedom of choice to each individual student.

. . . .

4.   Search and Seizure

A student's locker should not be opened, nor his room searched, without his consent except in conformity with the spirit of the Fourth Amendment which requires that a warrant first be obtained on a showing of probable cause, supported by oath or affirmation, and particularly describing the things to be seized.   An exception may be made in cases involving a grave danger to health or safety. [37]

Summary

Probably the case most often cited in support of the opinions and attitudes presented here is the United States Supreme Court's decision in the 1967 case of Camara v. Municipal Court, [38] in which the court struck down the legitimacy of a provision for warrantless administrative searches in public housing units.

The rationale behind requiring a search warrant for the entry of students' dormitory rooms might appear too obvious for mention.   Nonetheless, the following succinct statement by Lippe is perhaps worth consideration:

> The warrant requirement is designed to insure that an independent judicial officer not involved in the situation will make the determination as to whether there is probable cause to infringe on an individual's privacy.   A college official desiring to conduct an administrative search of a student's dormitory room is likely to be just as 'involved' as a police officer and, therefore, should be subject to the warrant requirement. [39]

As to the application of the Camara rule to college dormitories, Lippe has observed that "its rationale in these cases certainly extends to a public college's search of dormi-

tory rooms. The different needs of college authorities and
the police can certainly be reflected in the standards evolved
to govern the issuance of such warrants."[40]

In sum, it would seem safe to conclude that in this
unsettled area of law involving the tax-supported college campus: (1) the student's waiver of the right to privacy in his
dormitory room is unenforceable and will fade into disuse;
(2) existing case law does not support a student claim to the
same privacy in his dormitory room as he enjoys in a private residence, but the law in recent years has moved
steadily in that direction and will no doubt continue to accord the student greater protection; and (3) since the fourth
and fourteenth amendments restrain official actions only,
evolving case law applicable to dormitory-room privacy has
thus far been applied only to dormitories operated by tax-
supported colleges.

Self-Incrimination

In a disciplinary proceeding at the administrative level,
does the college student stand under the aegis of the fifth
amendment's provision against compulsory self-incrimination?
Fewer judicial precedents and less commentary have been
directed to this matter than to the subject of the student's
right to privacy in his dormitory room. Nonetheless, this
issue would seem to rise on the periphery of the evolving
law pertaining to college students.

This question was not overlooked by the Joint Statement, for it includes the proposal that "No form of harrassment should be used by institutional representatives to coerce
admissions of guilt or information about conduct of other suspected persons."[41] The "other persons" provision here
would seem to cloak the student in a very adequate armor of
protection, indeed. But the Joint Statement is a recommendation, rather than a judicial caveat.

Similarly, the ACLU has made a broad policy statement on the subject, observing that "The student should be
advised of his privilege to remain silent and should not be
penalized for exercising this privilege."[42] One may note in
passing that the ACLU refers to silence of an accused student as a privilege, rather than a right.

Van Alstyne stated in 1969 that, "Thus far no university proceeding has been regarded as sufficiently criminal in character that a student could justly claim the privilege against self-incrimination. "43   In amplification, he added that:

> There is, however, the cross-over problem--...the
> very practical problem of the student who is in-
> volved or alleged to be involved in a demonstration
> and also arrested on a downtown charge. I quite
> agree that the university need not suspend its pro-
> ceeding on the basis that the information thus re-
> quired of the student might be used to his incon-
> venience in the downtown prosecution. I agree also
> that if it is a state university putting the student on
> trial, and he is obliged to discuss the transaction
> or risk losing the case on campus, nothing he dis-
> closes may be admitted in evidence downtown or
> even used to furnish a further lead for investigation
> of that charge. 44

On the same point, John P. Holloway, resident legal counsel for the University of Colorado, has stated:

> Where students have sought an injunction postpon-
> ing expulsion hearings until after criminal trials
> are had, it is clear that the courts do not consider
> such hearings a threat to the fifth amendment right
> against self-incrimination, since the fifth amend-
> ment might be invoked in the later criminal ac-
> tions. 45

On the general right of students to fifth amendment protection, Lippe has written:

> Although not entirely clear, it is my understanding
> that a student at a public college may be disci-
> plined or expelled for refusing to testify at a dis-
> ciplinary hearing. This is consistent with a num-
> ber of cases which hold that a public school pupil
> employed may be dismissed for refusing to answer
> questions relating to the conduct of his job. 46

Lippe acknowledges, however, that some uncertainty has been created by the Supreme Court's decision in the case of Spevack v. Klein. 47 Here it was held that a lawyer may not be disbarred for refusing to provide information concerning his professional behavior.

In <u>Furutani v. Ewigleben,</u> [48] a federal district court
in California denied students' application to enjoin a college's
disciplinary proceeding, pointing out that if the students were
obliged to testify in the college proceeding to avoid expulsion,
their testimony could be excluded in the subsequent criminal
trial. This posture was based on the decision of the United
States Supreme Court in <u>Garrity v. New Jersey.</u> [49] The Garrity case involved several New Jersey police officers who
testified in an investigation of irregularities to which no im-
munity statute was applicable.   Under a New Jersey statute,
the officers would have been subject to a removal from office if they had invoked the fifth amendment when questioned
in the investigation.   The police officers involved were subsequently tried for conspiracy to obstruct the administration
of the traffic laws.   At their trial, the testimony which they
had given in the attorney general's investigation was used in
evidence against them and they were convicted.   The United
States Supreme Court reversed on the grounds that the officers' testimony in the attorney general's investigation was
inadmissible in the criminal proceedings. [50]

The court described the predicament of the officers
as placing them "between the rock and the whirlpool," and
concluded:

> We now hold the protection of the individual under
> the Fourteenth Amendment against coerced state-
> ments prohibits use in subsequent criminal pro-
> ceedings of statements obtained under threat of re-
> moval from office, and that it extends to all,
> whether they are policemen or other members of
> our body politic. [51]

Judicial Precedents

Most of the case law dealing with student exemption
from self-incrimination must be accepted as law drawn from
analogy.   This study has led to the discovery of only two
cases in which the court addressed itself directly to the
question.

In the 1942 case of <u>Sherman v. Hyman,</u> [52] the Supreme Court of Tennessee stated that, "Students should not
be compelled to give evidence against themselves or which
may be regarded as detrimental to the best interests of the
school."   While saying this, the court nonetheless ruled

that the accused students had no right to cross-examine witnesses against them. Judge Johnson of the federal district court in Alabama, however, decided in 1968 that a student accused of having marijuana in his room was "denied his right to procedural due process of law" and was entitled to a new hearing, since he had been denied the right to confront and cross-examine witnesses and because of the presumption of guilt which was raised by his refusal to testify on grounds of self-incrimination.[53]

Summary

Grave doubt must surround any assertion of fifth amendment protection against self-incrimination by an accused student in a college disciplinary proceeding. The fifth amendment injunction, "nor shall [any person] be compelled in any criminal case to be a witness against himself," provides a shield only for witnesses in criminal cases. College disciplinary proceedings, although quasi-criminal in nature, are still considered, as Professor Johnson and others have pointed out, to be civil actions. Van Alstyne suggests, however, as indicated above, that it is not beyond the realm of imagination that a college disciplinary proceeding may yet be considered grave enough in its proposed sanction that the accused student will be declared entitled to protection under the fifth amendment. One may imagine, for example, that such a situation might involve a senior medical student denied his degree at the normal time for graduation because of some rule infraction.

Apparently, the law is settled on the issue that statements made in a college disciplinary action cannot be used in a subsequent criminal proceeding to incriminate the student accused in the earlier action.

Additionally, the ACLU quotes the following dicta from Re Gault as being laden with promise of future decisions favorable to college students seeking protection from forcible self-incrimination:

> The privilege can be claimed in any proceeding, be it criminal or civil, administrative or judicial, investigatory or adjudicatory...it protects any disclosure which the witness may reasonably apprehend could be used in a criminal prosecution or which could lead to other evidence that might be

used.   [Emphasis is the Court's.][54]

Notes

1. Richard A. Lippe, "The Student in Court" (Ch. 4) Student Protest and the Law (Ann Arbor, Michigan: The Institute of Continuing Legal Education, 1969), pp. 116-17.

2. 284 F. Supp. 725, 728 (M. D. Ala. 1968), quoting the 1967-68 college bulletin.

3. 284 F. Supp. 725 (M. D. Ala. 1968).

4. Ibid., at 728.

5. Ibid., at 729.

6. Ibid., at 730, quoting Englehart v. Serena, 318 Mo. 263, 300 S. W. 268, 271 (1927).

7. Ibid., at 730.

8. Ibid.

9. Ibid., at 730-31.

10. 20 N. Y. 2d 360.

11. 283 N. Y. S. 2d 22 (1967).

12. 393 U. S. 85 (1968).

13. "End of an Era: The Last Warren Court Term," Civil Liberties, August, 1969, p. 3.

14. 391 U. S. 543 (1968).

15. Ibid., at 550.

16. 52 Misc. 2d 366, 292 N. Y. S. 2d 706 (1st Dist. Ct. Nassau Cty., 1968).

17. 292 N. Y. S. 2d 706, 713 (1968).

18. "The Student in Court," op. cit., p. 119.

19. Ibid., p. 118.

20. Ibid., p. 119.

21. "The Judicial Trend Toward Student Academic Freedom,"
     20 Florida Law Review 290, 297 (1963).

22. "The Student as University Resident," 45 Denver Law
     Journal 582, 588 (Summer, 1968).

23. "The University and the Liberty of Its Students--A Fi-
     duciary Theory," 54 Kentucky Law Journal 643, 681
     (1966).

24. Ibid.

25. "University Purpose, Discipline and Due Process,"
     1967 North Dakota Law Review 739, 750 (1967).

26. "Problems of Dual Jurisdiction of Campus and Commu-
     nity," Student Protest and the Law, op. cit., p. 143.

27. "Panel Discussion--II," Ibid., p. 204.

28. Ibid., p. 205.

29. "The Lawyer's Role in the Design of a University,"
     Ibid., p. 13.

30. Ibid., p. 15.

31. "The Constitutional Rights of College Students," 42
     Texas Law Review 344 (1964), reprinted in Student
     Rights and Responsibilities, op. cit., p. 207 at 215.

32. Ibid., p. 223.

33. Ibid., p. 217.

34. "Students, Higher Education, and the Law," 45 Denver
     Law Journal 511, 522 (1968).

35. "Comment," 45 Denver Law Journal 614, 615 (Summer,
     1968).

36. Joint Statement of Rights and Freedoms of Students, op.
     cit., p. 368.

37.   Academic Freedom and Civil Liberties of Students in
      Colleges and Universities, op. cit., pp. 8-9.

38.   387 U.S. 523 (1967). Pertinent cases also cited by
      Lippe include United States v. Donato, 269 F. Supp.
      921 (E.D. Pa. 1967), aff'd, 379 F. 2d 288 (3d Cir.
      1967) U.S. officials have right to search employee's
      locker in U.S. Mint; and U.S. v. Grisby, 335 F. 2d
      652 (4th Cir. 1964) military authorities may search
      living quarters of marine; Overton v. New York, 20
      N.Y. 2d 360, 283 N.Y.S. 2d 22 (1967) judgment va-
      cated and remanded, 393 U.S. 85 (1968) reargument
      scheduled, 23 N.Y. 2d 869.

39.   "The Student in Court," op. cit., pp. 119-120.

40.   Ibid.

41.   Joint Statement, op. cit., p. 368.

42.   Academic Freedom and Civil Liberties of Students in
      Colleges and Universities, op. cit., p. 10.

43.   "The Constitutional Protection of Protest on Campus,"
      Student Protest and the Law, op. cit., p. 196.

44.   Ibid.

45.   "The School in Court," Ibid., pp. 93-94.

46.   "The Student in Court," Ibid., p. 126.

47.   385 U.S. 511 (1967).

48.   297 F. Supp. 1163 (N.D. Cal. 1969).

49.   385 U.S. 493 (1967).

50.   Edward C. Kalaidjian, "Problems of Dual Jurisdiction
      of Campus and Community," op. cit., p. 138.

51.   Ibid., p. 138.

52.   171 S.W. 2d 822, 826 (1942).

53.   Moore v. Student Affairs Committee of Troy State Uni-
      versity, 284 F. Supp. 725 (1968). See also, Aca-

demic Freedom and Civil Liberties of Students in Colleges and Universities, op. cit., Appendix A, p. 2.

54.   387 U.S. 1 (1967), at 47.

Chapter VII

THE FIRST AMENDMENT
AND EXPANDING SUBSTANTIVE RIGHTS

The legal death of the in loco parentis doctrine vis-a-vis college students has ushered in an almost unbelievable termination of the once stifling administrative paternalism regarding campus matters of first amendment consideration. In a rapid succession of judicial decisions, the federal courts have been especially active in the curtailment of administrative surveillance over campus speech, press, and political activity. This expansion of student rights has also embraced the public-school campus, in spite of the continuing acceptance there of the in loco parentis rationale, [1] extending, at least in some respects, "from kindergarten through high school"--as Justice Black complained in dissent. [2]

"It is in the area of student expression and association that the university's disciplinary power poses its greatest potential threat to society, to the university itself, and possibly to the individual student." So wrote Professor Goldman in his 1968 article published in the Kentucky Law Journal. [3]

In general agreement with this sentiment expressed by Goldman that American universities may pose a threat, rather than a culture medium, to the twentieth century democratic zeitgeist, the Yale Law Journal preceded him by five years in declaring that:

> In some cases, the court ought properly to grant review because of the characteristics of the effect on the student, regardless of the alleged educational characteristics of the university's act. Such need for judicial inquiry is established when it is claimed that the school has infringed such basic interests as freedom of speech--both to speak and to hear--freedom of the press, freedom of assem-

bly, right to political activity, freedom of religion,
or the right of privacy. Our society depends on
its courts to make the ultimate decision as to the
propriety of such infringements--a responsibility
which is not to be delegated to university officials,
even where they claim superiority founded upon educational expertise. [4]

And, in the case of the university, the author could
add:

...society's interest in free and open debate, including the rights of assembly, association and
publication and the right of all to hear and speak
even unpopular ideas is particularly strong. The
university is needed as a source of new ideas
which a democracy constantly requires. Thus relevant legal doctrines, such as the doctrine of university 'reasonable rules,' should be construed as
to further society's interest in freedom of expression, by preventing university incursions upon student freedoms. [5]

The preceding statements were published in 1963. By
the latter part of 1968, the ACLU was to observe that:

Like the right to due process in discipline, the
right of freedom of expression has been expounded
by the courts in cases involving public colleges.
Recent decisions have provided judicial support for
a free student press, students' rights to engage in
lawful demonstrations, and their right to hear outside speakers of their choosing. [6]

The first amendment guarantees of freedom of religion,
speech, press, and assembly and the prohibition against an
establishment of religion have assumed much greater significance in most areas of American existence in the past four
decades. When the United States Supreme Court in 1937
abandoned its role as a censor of social and economic legis-
lation it assumed a new and often-neglected function of protecting dissenting individuals and minority groups in their
espousal of unpopular causes, shielding them against repres-
sive official action from any quarter. With a good deal of
consistency, the federal courts ever since have served this
function, reaching the zenith in this new role during the
Warren years. [7] Many of the more important causes coming

under the federal courts' aegis in recent years have involved
demonstrations of various forms and other types of social
protest aimed incidentally at expanding first-amendment freedoms of the American people.

Actions by both the state and national governments are
limited by first amendment guarantees. However, the courts
have stated on many occasions that first-amendment rights
are not unlimited. Government officials may set reasonable
conditions for the time, place, and manner of exercising
these rights. A college or university is similarly justified
in setting reasonable regulations to protect its educational objectives and to maintain order on campus. Much litigation
has arisen from differences in interpreting the concept of
reasonable to make it apply to difficult situations.

Respective first amendment rights, although distinc-
tively identified in the United States Constitution, are commonly blended together in legal literature and in court opin-
ions--often under the general category of "free expression."
The arbitrary decision was made, for the treatment which
follows, to divide and limit the subject to what would seem
to be the most litigious areas, insofar as the college campus is concerned: freedom of speech, freedom to hear, and
freedom of the press.

The AAUP and ACLU Positions as Criteria

Since the AAUP and ACLU are probably the two most
prominent national organizations consistently expressing an
interest in the rights of college students, it would seem appropriate to advance the stated policy positions of these two
groups on the first amendment rights of college students.
Therefore, in the discussion which follows, AAUP and ACLU
positions have been advanced as criteria against which legal
opinions and judicial decisions may be judged.

Freedom of Speech

Since students, at least in theory, enjoy all the constitutional rights accorded other citizens, some legal writers
today find it difficult to understand how a college can con-
scionably undertake to restrict on-campus and off-campus
student activities involving the lawful exercise of what would
appear to be first amendment rights. Professor Beaney has

noted that "The unpopularity or irrationality of student expression provides no justification for suppression or penalty."[8]
He adds:

> It would be extremely unfortunate if institutions of
> higher learning, having successfully fought so many
> battles with legislatures and trustees in the name
> of academic freedom for the faculty, should fail to
> recognize that freedom for students to express
> ideas without fear of penalty is also essential to a
> free academic community. Obviously, students
> may not always exhibit a full sense of responsibili-
> ty in their zeal to express ideas, but that is hard-
> ly a sufficient reason to stifle their expression. [9]

In 1968 Beaney was looking to the future when he declared that:

> The expansion of first amendment rights by the
> courts in the past 30 years, and the attention
> which the courts are willing to give to claims of
> minorities and dissident individuals, should warn
> colleges and universities to avoid policies and
> practices that overtly or indirectly curtail students'
> exercise of first amendment rights of free speech,
> press, and assembly. [10]

The AAUP and ACLU Positions

On the subject of free expression, the Joint Statement
contains the expected declarations on freedom of inquiry and
discussion in the classroom. Of greater interest to this
study, however, is the subject of out-of-class expression,
since this is the primary arena of free-speech litigation involving college students. On this subject, the statement declares that students should be free to examine and discuss
all questions of interest to them, and to express opinions
publicly and privately. "They should always be free to support causes which do not disrupt the regular and essential
operation of the institution." However, it should be made
clear that they speak only for themselves. [11]

In a section headed, "Off-Campus Freedom of Students," the Joint Statement acknowledges that college students are both citizens and members of the academic community. "As citizens, students should enjoy the same freedom
of speech, peaceful assembly, and right of petition that other

citizens enjoy." As members of the academic community,
they are subject to the obligations growing out of that membership. [12]

The ACLU Statement

The ACLU central statement on freedom of speech is
perhaps broader than that of the Joint Statement--or possibly
one should say it is more militant. Under the heading,
"Students' Personal Freedom Off-Campus," it observes that,
"American college students possess the same right to freedom of speech, assembly, and association as do other residents of the United States. They are also, of course, subject to the same obligations and responsibilities as persons
who are not members of the academic communities."

Student participation in such off-campus activities as
peace marches, civil rights demonstrations, draft protests,
picketing, boycotting, political rallies, non-campus publications, and acts of civil disobedience are not the legitimate
concern of the college. However, students do have a moral
obligation not to misrepresent the views of others in their
academic community. [13]

Legal Commentary

Lawyers and political scientists writing on the subject
of first amendment freedoms for college students are inclined to stand agape at the fact that an institution of higher
learning would even consider infringement on such a basic
right, guaranteed to all by the first and fourteenth amendments. [14] But all are aware of the complexity of the situation today, when no universally accepted definition of speech
is available. It is, after all, quite likely that many university officials are currently engaged in deep soul-searching in
quest of an answer to the question, "Just what are the proper limits on constitutionally protected speech."

Judge Frank M. Johnson of the United States District
Court, Middle District, Northern Division, Alabama, addressed himself briefly to the subject in the 1969 case of
Scott v. Alabama State Board of Education. [15] There he
said, "There seems to be a tendency in this country--and it
is especially prevalent among students--toward the view that
if one only believes strongly enough that his cause is right,
then one may use in advancing that cause any means that
seem effective at the moment, whether they are lawful or

unlawful. ... " Judge Johnson pointed out that those who assume this position must not expect protection from the law,
but must expect to be punished when they violate laws and
college regulations which are part of a system designed to
protect the rights and interests of all.[16]

The United States Supreme Court assumed a similar
position in 1968, when it expressed the view that, "We cannot accept the view that an apparently limitless variety of
conduct can be labeled 'speech' whenever the person engaged
in the conduct intends to express an idea."[17]

As judges are said to do, Bakken selected a precedent to serve his purpose when he concluded that, "The
boards or their delegated representatives are justified in
making rules that will keep the school functioning properly
and the right of free speech cannot be used as a justification for violating the rules."[18] He observes that the courts
have set limits to the enforcement of such rules--the clear
and present danger doctrine. Under this doctrine, he says,
"there must be some reasonable probability that the presence
of unauthorized persons on school grounds would reasonably
lead to ascertainable interference with normal conduct of the
school before the restriction will be sustained in court.

In the mid-1960's the so-called "free-speech" movement at the University of California raised the question of
the legality of common obscenities used in a public place.
At a law conference, Professor Van Alstyne was confronted
with the question, "... to what extent is demonstration which
employs obscene language, amplified by bullhorn, constitutionally protected?"

Van Alstyne's answer was that "Very little" constitutional protection would be enjoyed under the circumstance.
He felt that the United States Supreme court had properly
scaled down the offense of obscenity by applying considerations of time, place and manner. However, "The deliberate
use, before a captive audience, of obscene language that of-
fends their sensibilities may appropriately be made the subject of discipline without violating first amendment standards."

Van Alstyne emphasized the time-and-place aspects of
the question. In the first place, he said, he saw nothing
constitutionally objectionable if a university should ordain
that "there must be no picketing of any kind within 100 yards
of the administration building." But, he added:

The justification must be that under the particular
circumstances the style of communication rises
above the level of mere inconvenience or petty an-
noyance, and is at least in substantial conflict with
the accomplishment of other legitimate uses to be
made of the property. Thus, clearly congestive
picketing, clearly disruptive or raucous demonstrations, clamorously interfering with classes, block-
ing access, are clearly subject to prohibition by a
university as they are by responsible state law. [19]

On another occasion, Van Alstyne spelled out a similar viewpoint. He said, "Second only to their concern with
procedural due process, an increasing number of courts have
moved to circumscribe college power over political freedoms
that are constitutionally reserved to all persons including
students." He identified two areas of student activity to
which the foregoing comment is especially applicable: "(1)
rules that regulate forms of expression or political activity
by the students themselves, on campus; (2) rules that regulate students in terms of whom they may invite to hear on
campus." First amendment protection, he wrote, extends
to those who are otherwise properly on a college campus
which is sufficiently "public" to be subject to the first or
fourteenth amendment. First amendment protection applies,
he said, to protect students in their expression of grievances
which originate in the college community itself, or which are
not especially related to the college. Rules which would undertake to restrain students in this area of liberty, he adds,
must generally satisfy two standards: (1) they must be clear
and specific so as not to chill the exercise of orderly political expression; and (2) they must go no farther than forbidding conduct that is manifestly unreasonable in terms of
time, place, or manner, or forbidding incitements under
such circumstances as to create a clear and present danger
of precipitating a serious violation of the law. [20]

Thus, says Van Alstyne, "a rule that broadly forbids
'any student... [to engage on campus] in any public demonstrations without prior approval of the administration,' is void
on its face. It is a prior restraint devoid of proper standards...." He indicates that the burden of proof would be
on the school to prove that banned demonstrations would disrupt the normal functions of the school. [21]

Lucas points out a serious inconsistency between the
theory of student rights of free speech and campus applica-

tion of those rights. He observed that the overriding first
amendment value of open discussion of public issues probably
provides the same protection for a student criticizing a college official as it does for a non-student. He suggests that
the student may be in a better position than other citizens to
expose academic inadequacies. Nonetheless, he points out,
the few existing decisions concerning student criticism of
college officials "have accorded the student an incredibly narrow range within which he can criticize." He cites Steier v.
New York Education Commissioner, which upheld a student's
expulsion for writing caustic, critical letters to the college
president. Similarly, he cites Jones v. Board of Education,
in which the District Court upheld the expulsion of a student
whose chief error was to call the college president "Super
Tom" and other college officials "Uncle Toms." Finally, he
points out, one of the students readmitted in De Veaux v.
Tuskegee Institute[22] was later expelled because he called one
of the board of trustees a "honkie." "The student," he observes, "would certainly have no remedy at the present stage
of Alabama justice, if the trustee had called him 'nigger.'
It is fair to conclude from these decisions that expansion of
the student's right to criticize and petition his administration must await further clarification in the courts."[23]

     Lucas adds that, "There can be no question that a
university campus is an appropriate setting for student expression in the form of peaceful picketing," but he acknowledges that the development of the law regarding student
picketing has hardly begun. "Narrowly drawn restrictions
are valid," he suggests, "providing they protect legitimate
and substantial state interests."[24]

Cases on Free Speech

     The leading precedent in support of free speech on the
campus is actually an opinion by the United States Supreme
Court in 1969 protecting symbolic speech in the elementary
and secondary schools, Tinker v. Des Moines Independent
Community School District.[25] Briefly, the facts of the case
are as follows. When principals of several Des Moines public schools became aware of a plan by several students to
wear black armbands to publicize their objections to the hos-
tilities in Vietnam and their support for a truce, they adopted
a policy that any student wearing an armband to school would
be asked to remove it, and if he refused to remove it he
would be suspended until he returned without the armband.
Parents of the children sought an injunction restraining en-

forcement of the new policy. After an evidential hearing,
the District Court dismissed the complaint, upholding the
constitutionality of the school authorities' action on the
ground that it was reasonable in order to prevent disturbance of school discipline. 26 The court referred to but declined to follow the Fifth Circuit's ruling in Burnside v.
Byars, 27 infra, where it was held that the wearing of sym-
bols like the armbands cannot be prohibited unless it "ma-
terially and substantially" interferes with the appropriate
discipline in the school.

On appeal, the Eighth Circuit, en banc, was evenly
divided, thus upholding the District Court. The Supreme
Court granted certiorari. Justice Fortas, for the Court,
declared that "the wearing of armbands in the circumstances
of this case was entirely divorced from actually or potentially disruptive conduct by those participating in it. It was
closely akin to 'pure speech.' "28

Although Tinker, as was noted, dealt with public
school pupils below the college level, the Court cited with
apparent approval a number of college cases which have expanded campus liberties, including Dixon, Knight, and Dickey
v. Alabama State Board of Education, 29 which will be discussed later in this chapter.

Remindful of the language of Dixon, Justice Fortas
observed for the majority, "It can hardly be argued that
either students or teachers shed their constitutional rights
to freedom of speech or expression at the schoolhouse
gate. "30 The majority opinion reminded educators: "That
they are educating the young for citizenship is reason for
scrupulous protection of Constitutional freedoms of the individual, if we are not to strangle the free mind at its source
and teach youth to discount important principles of our government as mere platitudes. "31 Also, ". . . undifferentiated
fear or apprehension of disturbance is not enough to overcome the right to freedom of expression. "32 And, in what
might be interpreted as a slap at the philosophy of education
embraced by the Des Moines school officials, Justice Fortas
wrote, "In our system, state-operated schools may not be
enclaves of totalitarianism. "33

"School discipline aside, " the Court said, "the First
Amendment rights of children are co-extensive with those of
adults. "34

Reversing the trial court, the majority thus reinforced the authority of Burnside v. Byars from the Fifth Circuit and apparently excluded first amendment considerations from the prospect of in loco parentis curtailment in the public schools and colleges.

Justice White concurred, and Justices Black and Harlan wrote separate dissenting opinions. Black's dissent was lengthy and heated. He accused the majority of resurrecting the ghost of substantive due process and applying the criterion of "reasonableness."

Other Speech Cases

The Steier case was discussed at some length in Chapter V, with emphasis there placed on procedural aspects. Substantively, the case was exactly what Lucas presented it to be in the preceding quotation. In brief, the Second Circuit let stand the disciplinary expulsion of Arthur Steier from Brooklyn College, his expulsion being based primarily on the fact that he had written letters to the college president in which he was sharply critical of another college official and subsequently wrote a disquieting letter which was published in the student newspaper.

The majority in Steier based the court's decision on an argument couched almost entirely in procedural considerations. However, Judge Clark's dissent was expressed both in procedural considerations and the facts of the case. Without mentioning the first amendment directly, he wrote:

> Steier's several letters, on which the college's action is purportedly based, show perhaps an obstinate and overstated sense of indignation against student discrimination, but nothing indecent, delinquent, or criminal and nothing (I submit) calling for discipline and expulsion, rather than patient response. [35]

In Goldberg v. Regents of University of California, [36] which one writer describes as "of equal importance with the Dixon case," [37] an appellate court in California ruled that students do not have an unlimited right to demonstrate on university property. This was the case which climaxed the "free speech movement" on the Berkeley campus. Goldberg found the California courts yielding to the expertise of the

educator in these terms: "...in an academic community,
greater freedoms and greater restrictions may prevail than
in society at large, and the subtle fixing of these limits
should, in a large measure, be left to the educational institution itself."[38]

However, absolute bans on demonstrations without
prior approval are not constitutionally permissible, except
possibly in the presence of a clear and present danger.   In
Hammond v. South Carolina State College, [39] three students
had been suspended under an administrative regulation requiring prior approval of all campus demonstrations.   The
federal district court found this regulation void on its face
and constituting "prior restraint on the right to freedom of
speech and the right to assemble."   The right of students to
demonstrate for redress of grievances was equated with the
right of citizens to demonstrate at the site of their government.

The apparent conflict between the Goldberg and Hammond cases can probably be explained in terms of the respective regulations of conduct.   In Hammond, the conduct
was more purely protected speech and the rule was broadly
prohibitory.   In Goldberg, the conduct was highly offensive
to many, and the regulation was seemingly reasonable.

A rash of free-speech cases in the federal and state
courts in the late 1960's underscored the fact that the
"speech" provision of the first amendment embraces more
forms of expression than mere oral communication.   For
example, the right of students to wear long hair was firmly
declared for the first time on December 3, 1969, and the
ACLU conjectured that "the case may produce the first Supreme Court ruling on the issue."[40]

The Wisconsin Superintendent of Public Instruction
asked the state attorney general to appeal the decision of the
Seventh Circuit that "the right to wear one's hair at any
length or in any desired manner is an ingredient of personal
freedom protected by the United States Constitution."

The Seventh Circuit cited the "penumbra" of the first
amendment's free-speech guarantee and the ninth amendment's
guarantee of unenumerated personal freedoms as the bases
for its decision.   The opinion held that the Williams Bay,
Wisconsin, school board did not prove a valid interest in
insisting on short hair.   It did not undertake to prove that

long-haired students created disturbances. "To uphold arbitrary school rules...for the sake of some nebulous concept
of school discipline is contrary to the principle that we are
a government of laws which are passed pursuant to the
United States Constitution," the court said. It added that
high school students, like adults, are protected by the Constitution from "arbitrary and unjustified government rules."

The high school advanced its claim to an in loco parentis relationship with students, but the court ruled it inapplicable because it is impossible to comply with a hair-
length regulation during school hours only. The Seventh
Circuit observed that, "Although schools need to stand in
the place of a parent in regard to certain matters during
the school hours, the power must be shared with the parents, especially over intimately personal matters such as
dress and grooming.... In the absence of any showing of
disruption, the doctrine of in loco parentis has no applicability."41

While the Seventh circuit was protecting hirsute high
school students, the United States Supreme Court was erect-
ing a wall of protection against efforts by Iowa school officials to ban the non-disruptive wearing of protest armbands
on campus and in classrooms as a form of expression protected by the first amendment. 42   Other noteworthy free-
speech precedents of the late 1960's included these: Burnside v. Byars, 43 declaring that non-disruptive wearing of
protest buttons on campus and in classrooms is protected by
the first amendment; Power v. Miles, 44 upholding university
demonstration guidelines and ruling that a private university
does not perform such a public function as to render its
regulation of student demonstrations subject to the fourteenth
amendment; State v. Zwicker, 45 in which the supreme court
of Wisconsin upheld disorderly conduct convictions of students for their activities during a demonstration, thus rejecting students' contention that the statute was overly broad;
Schuyler v. University of New York at Albany, 46 in which a
New York appellate court held that university officials have
an inherent right to discipline students who took part in a
boisterous demonstration to harrass a chemical company employment interviewer when the demonstrations had violated
university regulations and interfered with classes; Barker v.
Hardway, 47 in which a federal district court upheld suspension of students for abrasive demonstration at a football
game, although the college president had suspended them
without a hearing, reserving for them the right of appeal to

the faculty committee on student affairs; Evers v. Birdsong,[48] in which a federal district court permanently enjoined a group of non-student demonstration leaders, following a series of disruptive and destructive demonstrations on campus; Jones v. Board of Education, supra., [49] in which a federal district court upheld an expulsion for calling school officials "Uncle Toms" and passing out SNCC literature; and Zanders v. Louisiana State Board of Education, [50] in which a federal district court upheld the expulsion of eighteen students who blockaded a campus building for forty-eight hours.

The Right to Hear

"It is highly doubtful," notes the ACLU, "whether any flat ban against outside speakers or any category of outside speakers, or any particular speaker, will survive a series of recent court rulings."[51]

The problems associated with college speaker bans and various degrees of prior restraint on speakers are as apparent as they are numerous. A visiting speaker can express himself with greater candor without concern about community reprisal than can a permanent member of the college community. The speaker need remain in the environs of his delivery only so long as it takes a limousine to drive him to the airport. But the member of the academic community who drives him to the airport must return to the scene of delivery and be confronted with any hostile reaction which the speech may have engendered in the larger community or on the campus itself. Thus the visiting speaker often leaves in his wake what the college administrator might reasonably consider to be a public relations shambles. One might logically assume that this would present the greatest problem to a community with a long history of value in-breeding. Accordingly, Lucas has observed that, "...it is in the South and Midwest where speaker bans are most likely to flourish."[52]

AAUP and ACLU Positions

The Joint Statement addresses itself to campus speakers in this language:

> Students should be allowed to invite and to hear
> any person of their own choosing. Those routine
> procedures required by an institution before a
> guest speaker is invited to appear on campus

should be designed only to insure that there is an
orderly scheduling of facilities and adequate preparation for the event, and that the occasion is conducted in a manner appropriate to an academic
community. The institutional control of campus
facilities should not be used as a device of censorship. It should be made clear to the academic
and larger community that sponsorship of guest
speakers does not necessarily imply approval or
endorsement of the view expressed, either by the
sponsoring group or the institution. [53]

The ACLU shows a similar awareness of the pressures of public opinion in the larger community in its statement on "Student Sponsored Forums," which declares:

Students should have the right to assemble, to select speakers and guests, and to discuss issues of
their choice. It should be made clear to the public that an invitation to a speaker does not necessarily imply approval of his views by either the
student group or the college administration. Students should enjoy the same right as other citizens
to hear different points of view and draw their own
conclusions.

When a student group wishes to hear a controversial or socially unpopular speaker, the college may
not require that a spokesman for the opposing viewpoint be scheduled either simultaneously or on a
subsequent occasion. [54]

Justification for the practice of inviting guest speakers
to the campus would seem to lie in the fact that individuals
with expertise in a multitude of national issues cannot be
kept in ready supply on each college campus. Lucas has
noted that, "In the spring of 1968, there were no substitutes
for William Sloan Coffin, Dr. Benjamin Spock and Dick
Gregory as social critics, and these men spoke on hundreds
of campuses, although they were excluded from several."

Commentary

Legal commentary on students' right to hear, as
might be expected, remains less plentiful than commentary
on the more celebrated first amendment freedoms. Nonetheless, enough commentary by qualified writers has appeared

to indicate that a weighty preponderance of the legal publi-
cists are convinced that the right of students to hear speakers
of their choice on campus without official interference is well
established. It would perhaps not be too much to say that a
genuine feeling of satisfaction over this development in the
law runs through their writings.

Van Alstyne has given considerable attention to the
subject. In a 1968 article, he wrote: "The courts have
come to recognize that an individual cannot be made to re-
linquish those rights which he holds as a citizen (including
the right to hear) as a condition of attending a college." He
points out that the college may regulate the appearance of invited guest speakers only as much as the government may
regulate public facilities which are otherwise suitable as
meeting places. It may establish neutral priorities. "But
it may neither proceed by rules that are vague or reserve
unchecked discretion to censor, nor may it screen speakers
according to their political affiliation, their subject matter,
or their point of view."[55]

In another article in 1968, Van Alstyne took a closer
view of some of the implications of such a policy when he
wrote that campus speaker bans have been enjoined where
they were so vague as to reserve complete censorship to
the administration[56] and where the university weighed the
political views of a speaker to determine his acceptability,[57]
where the university classified speakers as acceptable or
unacceptable on the basis of their unrelated conduct before
congressional committees, [58] or their having been subjected
to an unadjudicated criminal charge--even one of murder or
homosexual soliciting. [59] He summarized his concept of the
judicial acceptability of speaker regulation in these words:

> Where no physical disorder is imminent, where
> there is no substantial basis for supposing that the
> speaker will himself violate the law or incite
> others to a violation in the course of his remarks,
> where the facilities are otherwise available and
> other guest speakers are generally allowed on cam-
> pus, the student residents interested in hearing a
> given speaker on campus may not be denied. [60]

Other protected forms of expression, Van Alstyne
noted, include peaceful political expression, orderly and non-
disruptive assemblies on campus by students meeting to express a grievance against the college, and critical comment

on the college in the campus newspaper. In its efforts to
affect such forms of expression, he adds, university government is subject to a substantial degree of constraint similar
to that which limits the civil government from which the university derives its powers. As a campus constituent of that
government, the student cannot be made to forfeit his freedom of speech and cannot be made to barter it away as a
condition of being admitted or of remaining. [61]

As early as 1963, the Yale Law Journal expressed an
interest in the subject of the student's right to hear. Five
years before Van Alstyne made the observations cited above,
the Journal observed, drawing on the experience it has
gained in protecting free expresssion, a court might strike
down as unreasonable any regulation which has the effect of
depriving some or all of that freedom. Regulations which
prohibit all campus meetings on political subjects or ban
speakers of an unpopular viewpoint would be unreasonable,
the Journal said. [62]

Commenting on student political organizations in 1968,
Lucas proposed that the college views the active student
group as posing a threat to its unquestioned campus authority and infallibility. [63]

The preceding comments and the following cases would
seem to substantiate the assertion that students have a first
amendment right to hear speakers of their choice--a right
which grows out of the first amendment's free-speech guarantee, and that no administration of any tax-supported college
may legally infringe this right.

Freedom-to-Hear Cases

Recent case illustrations of the viewpoints expressed
above are at hand. A 1965 North Carolina statute requiring
the trustees of the consolidated state university system to
adopt special rules governing the appearance of "known members of the Communist Party" was declared void because of
vagueness by a federal district court in 1968. [64] Similarly,
a rule permitting use of a college auditorium by outside organizations, "insofar as these aims are determined to be
compatible with the aims of Hunter College as a public institution of higher learning," was ruled void for vagueness. [65]

The Human Rights Forum, a student organization at
Auburn University, was granted a charter by the student gov-

ernment on the condition that it not invite outside speakers.
At both Auburn University and the University of Alabama,
the student government determines which student organizations will receive charters.   Approval is not a matter of
course, but may be delayed or denied when unpopular student
groups seek recognition.   Lucas describes these practices
as "patently invalid under prior restraint decisions."[66]

Speaker bans at both the University of Alabama and
Auburn University were sturck down by federal courts in
1969.   In Brooks v. Auburn University,[67] the Fifth Circuit
held that the university president's refusal to allow a speaker invited by a student organization under normal procedures
constituted a restraint in violation of the first amendment.
The speaker, the Reverend William Sloan Coffin, had been
scheduled at an agreed honorarium and travel expenses.   The
court observed that, "Attributing the highest good faith to
[the president] in his action, it is nevertheless clear... that
the right of the faculty and students to hear a speaker, selected as was the speaker here, cannot be left to the discretion of the university president on a pick and choose basis
.... "   This decision upheld the ruling of the United States
District Court, Middle District of Alabama, Eastern Division,
which cited both the first and fourteenth amendments in its
opinion.

The opinion of the district court noted that "The Supreme Court has recognized that hearers and readers have
rights under the first amendment."   The court went on to
say that "There can no longer be much doubt that constitutional freedoms must be respected in the relationships between students and faculty and their university."   Auburn
University may provide disinterested scheduling of campus
speakers, but "the regulations may not be used to deny
either the speakers or the listeners equal protection of the
laws by discriminating among speakers according to the
orthodoxy or popularity of their political or social views."
The court expressed interest in the meaning of the word,
"convicted," in the Auburn speaker regulation and concluded
that, "That part of the regulation which would bar speakers
whose views Auburn could not sanction also sweeps over-
broadly, although it is difficult for this court to see why a
university administration should be thought to have the authority to approve the ideas of a campus speaker as a condition for the speaker's appearance at the invitation of the
students and faculty.[68]

> ...The vice of these regulations, however, is
> really far more basic than their just being vague
> and overbroad. These regulations of Dr. Philpott
> are not regulations of conduct at all.... The
> State of Alabama cannot, through its President of
> Auburn University, regulate the content of the
> ideas students may hear...such action...is uncon-
> stitutional censorship.... While it can be said
> that President Philpott has the ultimate power to
> determine whether a speaker is invited to the cam-
> pus, the First Amendment right to hear of the
> students and faculty of Auburn University means that
> this determination may not be made for the wrong
> reasons or for no reason at all. ...The evidence
> in this case does not reflect any reason for the
> disruption of the academic functions and mission of
> Auburn University by reason of the appearance and
> lecture.... [69]

Just as vagueness and overbreadth were instrumental
in voiding the speaker regulation at Auburn University, the
same criteria were noted by the United States District Court,
Eastern District of Tennessee, Northern Division, in yet
another 1969 decision overruling a campus speaker ban. In
Smith v. University of Tennessee, [70] action was brought by
students and faculty to enjoin the University of Tennessee
from enforcing rules prohibiting students from inviting as
speakers for university-sponsored programs persons who do
not meet established standards. The standards required that
the speaker be competent and that his topic be relevant to
the approved constitutional purpose of the inviting organization; that there be no reason to believe that the speaker
would speak in a libelous, scurrilous, or defamatory manner or in violation of laws which prohibit incitement to riot
and conspiracy to overthrow the government by force, and
that the invitation and timing be in the best interests of the
university.

In finding for plaintiffs in the action, the court ruled
that, "...The First Amendment protection of free speech extends to listeners." It declared further:

> It has long been recognized that in carrying out
> their primary mission of education, state owned
> and operated schools may not disregard the con-
> stitutional rights of students. ...authorities es-
> tablish that the defendant's regulations on student-

invited speakers may not constitutionally be vague
or broad beyond certain limits.

"When a statute or regulation, " the court continued,
"either forbids or requires the doing of an act in terms so
vague that men of common intelligence must necessarily
guess at its meaning and differ as to its application, it violates the due process clause of the Fourteenth Amendment
because of vagueness. "71

Freedom of the Press

Twenty years ago, few student editors, in all probability, gave much thought to the exalted free-press provision
in the first amendment of the United States Constitution.
Student publications constitute a special kind of press.   The
college administrator could convincingly advance the claim
that, since the college assumed financial and domiciliary
responsibility for student publications, this was not the kind
of publishing venture embraced by first amendment considerations.   One may only speculate as to how much the college administrator's viewpoint has changed in two decades.
Certainly there is at least some evidence that the actual
status of college newspapers has changed very little, vis-a-
vis first amendment considerations.

But the law has changed.   Free-press considerations
are inextricably intertwined with the preceding paragraphs
dealing with freedom of expression and the right to hear.
But some distinctive commentary and some distinctive cases
have been addressed to campus press rights as distinguished
from other civil liberties.

The Joint Statement

The section on student publications occupies a prominent place in the Joint Statement, commanding at least three
times as much space as the section on student participation
in institutional government and more than twice as much
space as is devoted to the section on freedom of inquiry and
expression.   The following is an abridgment of the student
publications section:

> Student publications and the student press are a
> valuable aid in establishing and maintaining an at-
> mosphere of free and responsible discussion and of

intellectual exploration on campus. They are a means of bringing student concerns to the attention of the faculty....

Whenever possible the student newspaper should be an independent corporation financially and legally separate from the university.

Institutional authorities, in consultation with students and faculty, have a responsibility to provide written clarification of the role of the student publications, ...

The preceding paragraphs deal generally with the role of the student press. The next three paragraphs become more specific.

1.   The student press should be free of censorship and advance approval of copy, and its editors and managers should be free to develop their own editorial policies and news coverage.

2.   Editors and managers of student publications should be protected from arbitrary suspension and removal because of student, faculty, administrative, or public disapproval of editorial policy or content. Only for proper and stated causes should editors and managers be subject to removal and then by orderly and prescribed procedures. The agency responsible for the appointment of editors and managers should be the agency responsible for their removal.

3.   All university published and financed student publications should explicitly state on the editorial page that the opinions there expressed are not necessarily those of the college, university, or student body. [72]

The ACLU Position

While the ACLU statement on student publications overlaps the position reflected by the Joint Statement, it is nonetheless significantly different in that it might seem to place greater emphasis on student autonomy in press management:

E. Communications Media

All student publications--college newspapers,
literary and humor magazines, academic periodicals and yearbooks--should enjoy freedom of the
press, and not be restricted by either the administration or the student government. This should
be the practice, even though most college publications, except for the relatively few university
dailies which are autonomous financially, are dependent on the administration's favor for the use
of campus facilities, and are subsidized either directly or indirectly by a tax on student funds.

1. College Newspapers

Campus papers subsidized by student fees
should impartially cover news of special student
interest, be free to express their own editorial
opinion, and should serve as a forum for opposing
views on controversial issues as do public newspapers. They may also be expected to deal in
news columns and editorials with the political and
social issues that are relevant to the concerns of
the students as citizens of the larger community.
Neither the faculty, administration, boards of trustees nor legislatures should be immune from criticism.

In no case should the independent decision of the
editors be overruled by pressures from alumni,
boards of trustees, state legislatures, the college
administration, or the student government.

Student initiation of competing publications should
be encouraged.   [Emphasis added]

Wherever possible the student newspaper should be
financially and physically separate from the college,
existing as a legally independent corporation. The
college would then be absolved from legal liability
for the publication and bear no direct responsibility to the community for the views expressed. In
those cases where college papers do not enjoy financial independence, neither the faculty adviser
nor the publications board if the paper has either
or both, nor any representative of the college

should exercise veto power, in the absence of a
specific finding of potential libel as determined by
an impartial legal authority.

Where there is a college publications board, it
should be composed of at least a majority of students selected by the student government or council, or by some other democratic method. Should
the board, or in the case the paper has no board,
an ad hoc committee selected by the faculty and
student government, decide that the editor has
been guilty of deliberate malice or deliberate distortion in one or a number of instances, the validity of this charge must be determined through due
process. [73]

It is interesting to note that the ACLU recommends
the encouragement of competing publications, especially since
such "unofficial" publications today pose a sore bone of contention between sensitive administrators of colleges and public schools on one hand and students backed by parental support on the other.

Commentary on a Free Student Press

Bakken, who views the universe from the narrow window of a student personnel administrator's office, as late as
1968 remained apparently unaware of the student-rights revolution being introduced to the American campus by the federal courts. For, in that year, he could note with equanim-
ity that "There is very little law regarding student publications. [A] California law... provides for such activity. The
operation of student publications is basically dependent upon
the governing boards and exists at their will. "[74]

While Bakken, like many student personnal administrators, apparently viewed student publications as a jewel to
be added to the student dean's crown, he nonetheless apparently viewed them primarily as threats to academic and
civic tranquillity. For he was able to make this sweeping
statement: "Student publications come under the same general authority as do other personnel services listed in this
chapter. There is little to add to this statement. Those
who are guiding the publications should prevent, if possible,
anything that injures a person or a business and may be
classed as slander or libel. "[75] One familiar with the campus scene might feel justified in observing that this state-

ment typifies the empire-building ambitions which occasionally seize some members of the campus bureaucracy. Bakken's casual classification of campus publications as "personnel services" may have roused the ire of a few student editors, but probably caused the collapse of few schools and departments of journalism, which were primarily at least the nominal overseers of publications on the majority of campuses.

In commenting on the Joint Statement before a national conference on law and student protest at Ann Arbor in 1969, Van Alstyne stated that, "The sections of the Statement congruent with recent federal decisions include the statement of policy with regard to the prerogative of the students to support political causes on campus by an orderly means; their prerogative to be critical through the student press, albeit a university-financed press."[76] At the same conference, Tom J. Farar of the Columbia University School of Law suggested limitations on the student press in these words, "The notion of fair allocation of time to present opposing views on important controversial issues should be imposed on college newspapers and perhaps ought to be contemplated more broadly, although it does raise serious constitutional questions."[77]

Van Alstyne expressed the viewpoint that relative freedom of the student newspaper is conditioned by circumstances of ownership and organization, as he explained in this language:

> If the newspaper is wholly financed by the university and is part of its journalistic laboratory, this would seem to give it a greater proprietary control. The school is not attempting merely to use a so-called claim of governmental force to regulate the press, but it is deciding rather, how it elects to spend its money in developing this auxiliary enterprise as part of its program in journalism. It is a very different situation if the student newspaper is an independent corporation which supports itself by advertising, even though much of the advertising comes from the university under a contract reserving them the right to use certain space every day to publish notices of general interest to the campus. The degree of possible control by the university scales way down in that circumstance, especially if other kinds of magazines

and newspapers are also permitted on campus,
which I suspect might be constitutionally compelled. [78]

Lucas has said that when a student editor violates a
college censorship rule which constitutes prior restraint, as
in Dickey, infra., "expulsion is unquestionably beyond the
college's power; and... the college cannot remove the student
as editor under these circumstances." [79]

Referring to an incident in which two high school
students were expelled for publishing remarks critical of
their teachers, Charles Alan Wright declared:

> It seems to me that speech cannot be punishable
> on campus simply because it is vigorous and un-
> complimentary. I fully share the view... that the
> life of a university depends on 'the pursuit of truth
> and knowledge through reason and civility,' and
> that lack of civility leads only to a harmful polari-
> zation of opinion, but it is perfectly clear that the
> first amendment did not enact Mrs. Emily Post's
> book of etiquette. [80]

Aside from the student newspaper, free-press considerations raise the question of handbills on campus. Handbills have frequently constituted a phase of student demonstrations on campus. Lucas is willing to accord handbills
first amendment protection. In 1968 he wrote:

> Student distribution of handbills on campus fre-
> quently accompanies demonstrations. The Supreme
> Court has consistently held that a city cannot ban
> distribution of noncommercial handbills on public
> streets. ...A college campus is arguably even
> more appropriate for picketing and distribution of
> handbills than a busy public street, since the in-
> stitution is supposedly dedicated to the concept of
> free inquiry. Accordingly cases such as Talley v.
> California [362 U.S. 60, (1960).] will probably ap-
> ply with even greater force to protect a student
> leafleteer corps from charges of littering or an-
> noying. [81]

Cases on Campus Press Freedom

As was related in Chapter V, Arthur Steier was dis-

missed from Brooklyn College after he wrote a letter critical of college policies and caused the letter to be published
in the student newspaper.   But it must be remembered that
Steier was decided by the Second Circuit before Dixon had
been decided by the Fifth Circuit.   Or, in the words of
Charles Alan Wright, "In retrospect, the surprising thing is
not that Steier lost his case, but that he lost it to a divided
court. "82

Actually, so few court decisions have dealt with the
tenuous question of freedom of the student newspaper or
freedom of the press on campus that it would be presump-
tuous to say that either a trend or a firm precedent has
been established.   But an examination of the few decisions
in the area will at least demonstrate that the Second Circuit's decision in Steier has fallen in disrepute.

One Supreme Court decision has touched on the subject.   This is Pickering v. Board of Education, 83 which reversed the Illinois Supreme Court by overturning the action
of an Illinois school board in dismissing a teacher for writing and causing to be published a letter criticizing actions of
the school board.

In Pickering, Justice Marshall, speaking for the
Court, declared, "It cannot be gainsaid that the State has
interests as an employer in regulating the speech of its em-
ployees that differ significantly with those it possesses in
connection with the regulation of the speech of the citizenry
in general. "84   The analogy between the position of the
teacher and that of the student, as embraced by these words,
is apparent.   The same might be said for his observation
elsewhere that "Teachers are, as a class, the members of
a community most likely to have informed and definite opinions as to how funds allotted to the operation of the schools
should be spent.   Accordingly, it is essential that they be
able to speak out freely on such questions without fear of
retaliatory dismissal. "85   In Pickering, the Supreme Court
re-examined the evidence on which the Illinois school board
had based its decision to dismiss the teacher.   On re-exam-
ination, the Court concluded that the board had made erroneous findings.

Although Pickering is tangentially a press-freedom
case and presents analogies with the campus situation, it
does not deal with publication on the campus.   For such a
case, one must step down from the Supreme Court to the

United States District Court for the Middle District of Alabama.   Gary Clinton Dickey was editorial page editor for the
student newspaper at Troy State University in Alabama.   In
that role, he was subject to a rule that no editorials be
printed which were critical of the governor or the state legislature.   The rule did not prohibit editorials or articles of
a laudatory nature.

In the spring of 1967, Dickey prepared an editorial
praising the president of the University of Alabama for taking
a public stand in defense of academic freedom for university
professors in the face of criticism of this stand by some
members of the state legislature.   First the faculty advisor
to the student newspaper and then the university president
refused to permit publication of the editorial because it violated the president's rule against criticizing the lawmakers.
The faculty adviser directed that the proposed editorial be
replaced with some material on "Raising Dogs in North
Carolina."   Dickey, instead, left the column blank, except
for the word, "Censored," printed diagonally across the
column.   For this "insubordination," he was suspended for
one year.   The federal court, in a strong opinion by Judge
Johnson, ordered his reinstatement.   The action was later
dismissed as moot when Dickey transferred to Auburn University while the appeal was pending.   The Fifth Circuit,
ordering the dismissal, declared that this took away from
the decision below "any precedential effect."   Nonetheless,
Judge Johnson's opinion in the Dickey case is twice cited
in the Tinker case, supra. [86]   In Dickey, Judge Johnson declared:

> A state cannot force a college student to forfeit
> his constitutionally protected right of freedom of
> expression as a condition to his attending a state-
> supported institution.   State school officials cannot
> infringe on their students' right of free and un-
> restricted expression... where the exercise of such
> right does not 'materially and substantially inter-
> fere with requirements of appropriate discipline in
> the operation of the school.'   The defendants in
> this case cannot punish Gary Clinton Dickey for
> his exercise of this constitutionally guaranteed
> right by cloaking his expulsion in the robe of "in-
> subordination.' [87]

In sum, the district court held Dickey's suspension
invalid because it was made pursuant to an unreasonable

rule which bore no relation to maintaining order and discipline on campus. The court held that the college could not establish a student newspaper and then subject it to arbitrary censorship, although Judge Johnson did suggest that Dickey could have been removed as editor.

Of Judge Johnson's decision in Dickey, Lucas has written this estimate:

It is apparent from Dickey that the challenged regulation inhibited free inquiry in discussion of governmental activities, that it constituted an officially imposed form of orthodoxy by limiting inquiry to praise, and that there was no evidence that censorship of this character was required to maintain law and order on the campus. These observations, however, provide only a partial answer, for Dickey could have distributed leaflets, made speeches, written letters to the editor, demonstrated, and engaged in unlimited forms of expression. The college only asked that his editorial privileges be limited to the broad sphere beyond criticism of the state governor or legislature. Yet this request carves the heart out of the first amendment and severly limits defense of academic freedom. As Justice Jackson so eloquently stated in Barnette: 'Freedom to differ is not limited to things that do not matter much. That would be a mere shadow of freedom. The test of its substance is to differ as to things that touch the heart of the existing order.'[88]

Three recent high school press-freedom cases are worthy of mention. These would seem to be addressed squarely to the subject of freedom of the press on campus. They are Sullivan v. Houston Independent School District,[89] Vought v. Van Buren Public Schools,[90] and Baughman v. Freienmuth.[91] In Sullivan, a federal district court ruled that two students engaged in first-amendment activity in its purest form and that they had been expelled by school officials for exercise of their rights because the authorities disliked the contents of the paper they published and distributed off school premises. The court found regulation of that conduct a questionable proposition and ruled that, at any rate, the school may not exercise more control of off-campus conduct than it may exercise over on-campus conduct. It held that discipline must be based on a standard of substantial

interference with normal operations of the school.[92] In
Vought, a federal district court in Michigan ruled that an
expelled student's first amendment rights had been violated
and he had been denied due process when dismissed for
possessing a copy of an "obscene" tabloid newspaper; the
court ruled the school's position "preposterous on its face."[93]
In Baughman, the parents of five students seek to enjoin enforcement of a school regulation which requires that all literature distributed on school grounds have prior approval of
the school's principal.[94]

Notes

1. On December 3, 1969, the Seventh Circuit ruled that,
   "Although schools need to stand in place of a parent
   in regard to certain matters during the school hours,
   the power must be shared with the parents, especially over intimately personal matters such as dress
   and grooming...." [Breen v. Kahl, 419 F. 2d 1034,
   1037 (1969)].

2. Tinker v. Des Moines Independent Community School
   District, 89 S. Ct. 733, 741 (1969).

3. "The University and the Liberty of Its Students--A Fiduciary Theory," op. cit., p. 643.

4. "Private Government on Campus--Judicial Review of
   University Expulsions," op. cit., p. 1395.

5. Ibid., pp. 1397-98.

6. Academic Freedom and Civil Liberties of Students in
   Colleges and Universities, op. cit., Appendix B, p. 5.

7. See H. Abraham, Freedom and the Court (1967), for a
   survey of post-1937 leading decisions by the United
   States Supreme Court.

8. William N. Beaney, "Students, Higher Education, and
   the Law," op. cit., p. 523.

9. Ibid.

10. Ibid., p. 524.

11. Joint Statement, as reprinted in Student Protest and the
     Law, op. cit., p. 218.

12. Ibid., p. 220.

13. Academic Freedom and Civil Liberties of Students in
     Colleges and Universities, op. cit., p. 8.

14. See comment by Beaney, supra.

15. Civil Action No. 2865-N, as reprinted in Student Pro-
     test and the Law, op. cit., p. 315.

16. Ibid., at 322.

17. United States v. O'Brien, 391 U.S. 367, 376 (1968).

18. Clarence J. Bakken, The Legal Basis for College Stu-
     dent Personnel Work (Washington, D.C.: The Ameri-
     can College Personnel Association, 2d ed., 1968), p.
     39.   In effect, Bakken's description of the judicial
     rationale issuing from the courts today is correct.
     However, it is especially noticeable in the leading
     school free-speech decision, Tinker v. Des Moines
     Independent Community School District (80 S. Ct. 733),
     the Court achieves the effect of the "clear and pre-
     sent danger" doctrine, but attaches the label of "rea-
     sonableness" to its rationale, which inspired a heated
     dissent from Justice Black.

19. This dialogue is taken from "Panel Discussion--II,"
     Student Protest and the Law, op. cit., pp. 202-203.

20. "The Judicial Trend Toward Student Academic Free-
     dom," op. cit., pp. 298-299.

21. Ibid., p. 299, quoting Hammond v. South Carolina
     State College, 272 F. Supp. 947 (D.S.C. 1967).

22. Civil No. 758-E (M.D. Ala. 1968).

23. Roy Lucas, "Comment," op. cit., pp. 627-628.

24. Ibid., pp. 628-629.

25.   89 S. Ct. 733 (1969).

26.   258 F. Supp. 971 (1966).

27.   363 F. 2d 744, 749 (1966).

28.   89 S. Ct. 733, 736 (1969).

29.   273 F. Supp. 613 (D. C. M. D. Ala. 1967).

30.   89 S. Ct. 733, 736.

31.   Ibid., at 737.

32.   Ibid.

33.   Ibid., at 739.

34.   Ibid., at 741.

35.   271 F. 2d 13, 22 (1959).

36.   57 Cal. Rptr. 463 (Ct. App. 1967).

37.   John P. Holloway, "The School in Court, " Student Pro-
      test and the Law. op. cit., p. 83, 91.

38.   57 Cal. Rptr. 463 (Ct. App. 1967) at 472.

39.   Breen v. Kahl; 272 F. Supp. 947 (D. S. C. 1967).

40.   "Circuit Affirms Long Hair Win, " Civil Liberties,
      February, 1970, p. 1.

41.   419 F. 2d 1034, 1038 (7th Cir. 1969).

42.   Tinker v. Des Moines Ind. Comm. Sch. Dist., 393 U.
      S. 503 (1969), supra.

43.   363 F. 2d 744 (5th Cir. 1966).

44.   407 F. 2d 73 (2d Cir. 1968).

45.   164 N. W. 2d 512 (Wisc. 1969).

46.   297 N. Y. S. 368 (App. Div. 1969).

47.   283 F. Supp. 228 (S. D. W. Va. 1968).

48.   287 F. Supp. 900 (S. D. Miss. 1968).

49.   279 F. Supp. 190 (M. D. Tenn. 1968).

50.   281 F. Supp. 747 (W. D. La. 1968).

51.   Academic Freedom and Civil Liberties of Students in
Colleges and Universities, op. cit., Appendix A, p. 4.

52.   Roy Lucas, "Comment," 45 Denver Law Journal 622,
638.

53.   "Joint Statement on Rights and Freedoms of Students,"
taken here from reprint of statement in Student Protest and the Law, op. cit., p. 218.

54.   Academic Freedom and Civil Liberties of Students in
Colleges and Universities, op. cit., pp. 5-6.

55.   "Judicial Trends Toward Student Academic Freedom,"
op. cit., at 301 (1968).

56.   Dickson v. Sitterson, 280 F. Supp. 486 (M. D. N. C.
1968).

57.   Danskin v. San Diego Unified School District, 28 Cal. 2d
536, 171 P. 2d 885 (1946). Buckley v. Meng, 35
Misc. 2d 467, 230 N. Y. S. 2d 924 (Sup. Ct. 1962).

58.   Dickson v. Sitterson, supra, n2.

59.   Student Liberal Federation v. Louisiana State University, Civil No. 68-300 (E. D. La. 1968); Stacy v. Williams, 306 F. Supp. 963 (N. D. Miss. 1969).

60.   "The Student as University Resident," 45 Denver Law
Journal 582, 587 (Summer, 1968).

61.   "Judicial Trends Toward Academic Freedom," op. cit.,
at 301.

62.   "Private Government on Campus--Judicial Review of
University Expulsions," 72 Yale Law Journal 1362,
1366 (1963).

63. Roy Lucas, "Comment," op. cit., p. 632.

64. Dickson v. Sitterson, 280 F. Supp. 486 (M. D. N. C. 1968).

65. Buckley v. Meng, 30 Misc. 2d 476, 230 N. Y. S. 2d 924 (Sup. Ct. 1962).

66. 412 F. 2d 1171 (5th Cir. 1969).

67. 296 F. Supp. 188 (M. D. Ala. 1969).

68. Ibid.

69. 296 F. Supp. 188, 195-196 (M. D. Ala. 1969), as reported in The Education Court Digest, June, 1969, p. 5.

70. 300 F. Supp. 777 (E. D. Tenn. 1969).

71. Ibid., at 781.

72. Joint Statement, op. cit., p. 219.

73. Academic Freedom and Civil Liberties of Students in Colleges and Universities, op. cit., pp. 6-7.

74. Bakken, Student Personnel Work, op. cit., p. 49.

75. Ibid.

76. "The Constitutional Protection of Protest on Campus," Student Protest and the Law, op. cit., p. 183.

77. "Panel Discussion--I," Student Protest and the Law, op. cit., p. 160.

78. Ibid., p. 161.

79. Lucas, op. cit., p. 637.

80. "The Constitution on the Campus," 22 Vanderbilt LR 1027, 1055 (October, 1969).

81. Lucas, op. cit., p. 630.

82. "The Constitution on the Campus," op. cit., at 1030.

83. 88 S. Ct. 1731 (1968).

84. Ibid., at 1734.

85. Ibid., at 1736.

86. 393 U. S. 503, 514n2. (1969).

87. 273 F. Supp. 613, 618 (M. D. Ala. 1967).

88. Lucas, op. cit., p. 636.

89. 307 F. Supp. 1328.

90. 306 F. Supp. 1388 (E. D. Mich. 1969).

91. Civil Action 21484 (D. Md. 1969).

92. 307 F. Supp. 1328 (S. D. Texas, Houston Div. 1969).

93. 306 F. Supp. 1388 (E. D. Mich. 1969).

94. College Law Bulletin, January, 1970, p. 37.

Chapter VIII

CONCLUSIONS

The Fifth Circuit's broad mandate for constitutional protection, expressed in Dixon, opened a Pandora's Box of procedural and substantive rights for college students. After eleven years in the judicial market-place Dixon has proved that it was more than a decision bearing the label, "good for this case only." The Fifth Circuit's caveat of campus rights has been accepted as authoritative precedent by United States District Courts, Circuit Courts, and state courts. It has received acquiescence from the United States Supreme Court.

The several decades of sporadic state-court litigation in the student-rights area have been characterized by some legal writers as a nadir of legal logic and justice vis-a-vis student-college relationships. Legal scholarship is not required to enable one to see the transparent weaknesses of the contract and in loco parentis theories of student-college relations which for many years enabled American college campuses to deny students reasonable procedural protections. To the civil libertarian, the fact that state courts went along with this scheme of arbitrary social control places in question the entire system of popular selection of state judges and degrades the state judicial systems to a level of arbitrary social control. Beyond doubt, the college student has been arbitrarily discriminated against in the matter of individual liberties.

The history of college administration in the United States is marked with frequent examples, well documented in court records, of arbitrary treatment of college students so flagrant as to be correctly identified as intolerance. It is probably less than satisfactory to dismiss the record by drawing the too-obvious conclusion that intolerance is an occupational hazard faced by the college administrator. For the college administrator must exist in a milieu of state legislatures, boards of control, alumni, taxpayers and parents, as well as students. One might well ask, too, if the student culture is affected by a unique dynamics which has justified, fully or partially, the tight rein held on college students by campus administrators. Empirical evidence to support such a hypothesis is either lacking, or else has not received wide publicity.

Presumably, a primary theoretical function of the board of control for a tax-supported college is to serve as a "buffer" between the college and the general public, to absorb and deflect public pressures by exponents of conformity. Detailed study of the effectiveness of college boards in this role would seem to be warranted by the facts reported in this study. Study, too, of the ideal interest representation on a college board of control would seem to be indicated. A strong argument can be advanced for providing board representation for students and faculty, two clientele groups commonly unrepresented on college boards.

Veblen, a caustic critic of American higher education, pointed out that university boards are made up largely of businessmen, men of wealth and clergymen, and that their primary function is the control of expenditure budgets. He observed that "their pecuniary surveillance comes in the main to an interference with the academic work, the merits of which these men of affairs on the governing board are in no special degree qualified to judge."[1] He declares further that "their sole effectual function [is] to interfere with the academic management in matters that are not of the nature of business and that lie outside their competence."[2]

Arthur Schlesinger, Jr., has written the following insightful evaluation of the role of the board of trustees of Columbia University:

> At Columbia, the all-powerful board of trustees, composed of men from banks, corporations and government, act as representatives of [the] ruling class. To be sure, certain reforms are possible within the university, but these are mostly either to give the illusion of democracy, as in student and faculty senates and judicial boards, or to grant more privileges to students, such as longer dormitory visiting hours or later curfew. University administrators can well afford to make such concessions, because of their lack of social significance.[3]

The Conveyance Theme

One of the more pertinent conclusions to be drawn
from this study surrounds the fact that Dixon was born in a
Negro-rights context, but served as the vehicle to convey a
broad spectrum of individual rights not merely to Negroes,
but to all college students. It has been pointed out that the
facts indicate that Dixon was suspended from Alabama State
College because he was a Negro out of place, not because
he was a student out of place. But the caveat of individual
rights issued by the Fifth Circuit through Judge Rives was
addressed to students rather than to Negroes or Negro students.

It has been pointed out that Dixon v. Alabama State
College marked a 180-degree about-face in the law embracing a significant American minority group. But, although
the case was pressed by the N. A. A. C. P., it turned out that
the beneficiary minority group was not the American Negro,
but the American college student.

In a sense, prior to 1961 and the Fifth Circuit's decision in this case, college matriculation amounted to an extreme form of expatriation in an area of the student's life.
That is to say, when one assumed the role of student at a
tax-supported institution of higher learning, he surrendered
some of his rights of citizenship and many of his rights as
a person, in the language of the fourteenth amendment. Of
course the sanctions to which he exposed himself did not
include imprisonment. But after matriculation he nonetheless stood exposed to the application of such sanctions as
are available to college authorities. The point to be made
is that the college-bound high school graduate was expected
to surrender rights in this area of his life without parallel
in the experience of his vocation-bound high school classmate. In a day when little material significance was attached to the attainment of higher learning, slight significance was accorded by the courts to the matter of whether
one was a student in good standing or a former student expelled by arbitrary action of the college administrator. Expulsion was almost assumed to be in the best interest of the
college and the general student body.

Dixon climaxed an attempted use of the college discipline power for imposing politically inspired punishment--
punishment of a group of Negro students who had "stepped
out of place." Dixon, then, poses an example of a federal

court using the judicial power for the protection of a minor-
ity--Negroes who were students. And yet, because of the
circumstances of the case, the Fifth Circuit was compelled
to address itself, not to the rights of Negroes, but to the
rights of students. It had no option in that matter. Thus
the clamor for the rights of one group--the Negroes--led to
the conveyance of broad and sweeping rights to another
group--college students--and within a decade has contributed
to the expansion of individual liberties of students at all
levels of the public-school system. It is highly unlikely that
any other court decision has ever been accompanied by so
apparent a transfer or conveyance of civil liberties from one
group to another.

By 1969 apparently more student-college cases lean-
ing on the authority of Dixon had been brought to protect the
rights of white students than to protect Negroes. One of the
more important of these actions[4] was brought in the name of
a student of Latin-American extraction. But this case, like
many another, was free of racial implications. Indeed, by
1969 the emphasis of student-college court actions had shifted
from procedural questions like that which had provided the
grist for Dixon. Substantive rights had become the new is-
sue--freedom of the campus press, freedom of assembly,
freedom to speak and to hear. These are individual rights
less susceptible to racially discriminatory restrictions than
was evident in such cases as Dixon, where procedural overtones were paramount.

While Dixon gave birth to a student-rights revolution
in the setting of the college campus, by 1969 many of the
challenges to public-school authority were springing from the
high schools, rather than the colleges. The in loco parentis
doctrine, invalidated in its applicability to college students
at tax-supported institutions, has retained much of its validity as applied to public-school pupils. But even so, the doctrine has been closely circumscribed, until today public-
school pupils cannot be denied essential first amendment
rights either on-campus or off-campus in the absence of a
showing by school authorities that such restriction is necessary in pursuit of the educational aims of the public schools.
Thus public-school pupils from kindergarten through high
school have apparently won freedom from official regulation
of what they say--either literally or symbolically--, what
they read or publish, and how they dress and groom themselves. Thus the federal courts have largely ruled out the
official peevishness and prudery which has long served to

stereotype public-school teachers and administrators in the
United States. Although Dixon has served as a guiding light
to the courts in this liberalization movement, court cases
conveying these new freedoms for pupils have been generally
free of racial characteristics.

The Authority of Dixon

Since 1961 Dixon has stood as an unchallenged authority in its area of public policy. Shepardizing Dixon in
March, 1970, one could find neither a state case nor a federal case which had sought to rebuff the Fifth Circuit in this
important decision or to impeach its revolutionary doctrine.
On the other hand, several cases had tended to expand the
procedural rights enunciated by Judge Rives, and Dixon had
served to support a remarkable succession of substantive
rights for college students and public-school pupils. No
doubt inspired by the Fifth Circuit's findings in Dixon, the
courts have displayed challenging creativity while moving in
several directions to curb arbitrary administrative actions
in tax-supported schools.

Not to be overlooked as an important factor in future
litigation is the fact that on October 24, 1969, the Seventh
Circuit demolished an important underpinning of college and
public-school disciplinary codes when it subjected such standards to the test of vagueness and overbreadth. [5] Since
some college personnel authorities have defended vagueness
as essential in campus codes, and since vagueness is a common characteristic of such ordinances, one might assume
that college administrators of disciplinary codes are required
to seek an entirely new philosophy of discipline.

The Dixon rationale suffers the defect of never having
been considered on all four points by the United States Supreme Court. This is not to say, however, that the court
has had no opportunity to reverse the Fifth Circuit. In
three respects, the Court might be said to have acquiesced
to the rationale conveyed in Dixon: (1) It denied certiorari
to the state of Alabama when its granting would have placed
the issue directly before the Court for review; (2) The Supreme Court did not use the convenient forum of its Tinker
opinion in 1969 to undercut the rationale of Dixon; (3) The
Court did use Tinker to extend a compatible rationale downward into the elementary and secondary schools.

Of course, the fact that Dixon has not been directly challenged by any court does not mean that it has been followed without exception. It was demonstrated in Chapter V that Judge Carswell, President Nixon's ill-fated second appointee to the Fortas seat on the Court, distinguished the facts in Due v. Florida A and M University so as to sidestep the Fifth Circuit while paying "lip service" to Dixon. One can only guess at the importance of this action in political struggle which ended in Carswell's being barred from a seat on the Supreme Court.

Voluntary Compliance With Dixon

What is the record of voluntary compliance with the Dixon rationale by college authorities? Unfortunately, little empirical evidence is available to reflect on this important question. It is certainly an area which warrants further study. The literature indicates that many of the larger universities are complying. A survey of the most recent student-rights cases, however, suggests that a large number of smaller colleges have not been touched by the new doctrine. The one publicized study has indicated that compliance is minimal. A related study of the attitude of college board members indicates that a significant number of these officials hold personal values which are antipathetic to the principles announced in Dixon.

On the other hand, the Joint Statement, which has been discussed in the foregoing pages, seems to hold the greatest promise as an extra-legal description of the constitutional rights of college students. No evidence is available to indicate how many colleges have altered their student codes in response to the Joint Statement.

In response to the new legal alignment, as well as to campus disorders which have sometimes involved violence, some colleges and universities have promulgated new codes embracing behavior in the academic community. 6

In all probability, the greatest effect of the judicial decrees of the constitutional rights of college students has been one which defies measurement to any degree--the administrator's fear of being sued and the out-of-court responsiveness by college administrators to student-retained counsel. The martinet college administrator who once answered only to his controlling board is becoming increasingly aware

that he may now be required to answer to a disinterested
federal judge as well.

The New Status of In Loco Parentis

In consequence of Dixon and subsequent student-rights
cases, it is reasonable to draw three conclusions concerning
the new status of the in loco parentis doctrine: (1) Many
college administrators still consider it the governing rule regarding student-college relationships. This is reflected as
a consistent theme running through legal literature on the
subject and is confirmed by the increasing frequency with
which student-rights cases are being reported by the federal
courts; (2) The legal legitimacy of the doctrine is dead, at
least insofar as tax-supported colleges are concerned. The
in loco parentis doctrine has been superseded by the new
constitutional rights doctrine at least insofar as student discipline is concerned; (3) Although the in loco parentis rationale survives as a viable description of the relationship
between educators and pupils in elementary and secondary
schools, it was demonstrated in this study that first amendment cases, especially in the areas of symbolic speech,
press, and grooming have significantly undermined its legitimacy here.

Student Rights and Juvenile Rights

One must be careful not to confuse the rapid growth
in procedural rights for juveniles with the expanding right of
college students. Gault and other recent decisions expanding
juvenile procedural rights addressed themselves to criminal
proceedings. College discipline cases, even in their most
severe form, remain in the realm of civil law, despite the
fact that Van Alstyne, as was shown, believes students should
be entitled to the full protections afforded criminal-charge
defendants.

The Law Versus Public Opinion

Evidences of a broad-based public opinion in support
of the Dixon rationale are conspicuously lacking. No legislative action embracing the public-policy direction of Dixon
had been learned of at the time of this writing. Some insight into public attitudes on the subject may be gained from

the experience of United States District Judge James E.
Doyle of Wisconsin's Western District. After delivering a
number of student-rights decisions in harmony with the Dixon precedent, and after being sustained in two important decisions within a period of three months, Judge Doyle might
well have expected public plaudits. What he received, however, was quite different. Disturbed by Judge Doyle's rulings, the lower house of the Wisconsin legislature passed a
resolution calling for a constitutional amendment to make
federal judgeships elective, rather than appointive. Assembly Speaker Harold Froehlich, in arguing for the measure,
may have expressed the feelings of millions of his fellow
citizens when he declaimed, "Judge Doyle is using the United
States Constitution to protect people who are trying to tear
down our society."[7] This statement probably reflects a
characteristic of middle-class conservatism much more
broadly held than civil libertarians would like to admit.

Student Rights and the Private College

        Since the injunction of the fourteenth amendment ad-
dresses itself to state governments, and thus inhibits only
state and local governments and their agencies, the rationale
of Dixon and related cases applies only to tax-supported colleges and schools. The courts have been careful to spell
out this distinction. Therefore, colleges which operate without the support of public funds remain immune to the constitutional-rights doctrine.

        However, "private" colleges, including those related
to churches and other non-public institutions, commonly
operate under a charter issued by the state. They certainly serve a public function--education. Increasingly, they
are being funded by tax moneys. Consequently, the commonest opinion expressed by legal writers dealing with the
subject is that developing case law will move inevitably to
bring the so-called "private" colleges and universities within the purview of the fourteenth amendment and the rationale
of Dixon and other constitutional-rights cases. At the time
of this writing, no breach has been noted on this front.

        Of course, several arguments might be advanced to
establish the view that it is relatively unimportant that non-
public colleges be included in this new doctrine. It has been
pointed out that private colleges have shown less of a trend
toward authoritarianism than tax-supported colleges have.

colleges are moti-
economic and geo-
end public colleges,
highly competitive
s.

rights movement--
tial gains may be ex-
ed to fourth and fifth

ng are protected
students living in
share in this protec-
vs.

nsion of student rights
inst self-incrimination.
o the college campus,
a matter of right

amine the pivotal court
ents in relation to tax-
supported colleges, to describe the 180-degree turn in the
law concerning procedural rights for college students and to
sketch the course of subsequent case law in that same general area. It has perhaps left untouched more questions than
it has undertaken to examine. The general area of student-
college relationships is one pregnant with research possibilities in many disciplines. In the areas of law and political
science, a few of these research possibilities perhaps de-
serve to be mentioned:

(1) A continuing study of voluntary compliance with
the new direction of the law by college administrations which
have not been sued would seem to be warranted. Simple
surveys such as that by Van Alstyne, cited in this study,
would seem to offer great possibilities in measuring the extent of voluntary compliance;

(2) A challenging area of research would involve the degree of awareness and acceptance of the Joint Statement by faculties and administrations. The relationship between acceptance of the principles of the Joint Statement and frequency of litigation at respective institutions might well be worth noting;

(3) The adoption of the procedure of ombudsmanship for student representation to college faculties and administration and the effectiveness of this practice would appear to offer fruitful research possibilities. Case studies in this area might be especially valuable to beleaguered college administrations;

(4) A comprehensive treatment of the subject of college and university constitutions and handbooks insofar as they deal with student rights should prove rewarding. It would be of much interest and potential practical value for administrators to know precisely how other institutions define and promulgate codes of student rights;

(5) Study would seem warranted into the subject of the means being utilized to finance expensive litigation against colleges and universities failing to comply with the new judicial rationale of student rights. One might perceive the germs of student unions in cooperation efforts to bring recalcitrant administrators into court.

Notes

1. The Higher Learning in America, op. cit., p. 47.

2. Ibid., p. 48.

3. "Joe College Is Dean," Saturday Evening Post, September 21, 1968, p. 72.

4. Esteban v. Central Missouri State College, 272 F. Supp. 649 (W. D. Mo. 1967).

5. Soglin v. Kauffman, 418 F. 2d 163 (7th Cir. 1969).

6. See, e.g., the 1969 "Rules of the Board of Higher Education of the City of New York," and "Columbia University Interim Rules Relating to Rallies, Picketing and Other Mass Demonstrations," appendixes C and

D, Student Protest and the Law, op. cit.

7. "The Law," Time Magazine, March 23, 1970, p. 64.

BIBLIOGRAPHY

Cases

Anthony v. Syracuse University, 224 App. Div. 487, 130 Misc. 249, reversed, 231 N. Y. Supp. 435 (1928).

Bluett v. Board of Trustees, 10 Ill. App. 2d 207, 134 N. E. 2d 634 (1956).

Breen v. Kahl, 196 F. Supp. 702 (W. D. Wisc.) sustained, 419 F. 2d 1034 (7th Cir. 1969).

Brooks v. Auburn University, 296 F. Supp. 188 (M. D. Ala. 1969).

Brown v. Board of Education, 347 U. S. 483, 74 S. Ct. 686, 98 L. Ed. 873 (1954).

Bumper v. State of North Carolina 391 U. S. 543 (1968).

Burnside v. Byars, 363 F. 2d 744 (5th Cir. 1966).

Cecil v. Bellevue Hospital Medical College, 60 Hun 107, 14 N. Y. Supp. 490 (1891).

Cohen, People v., 52 Misc. 2d 366, 292 N. Y. S. 2d 706 (1st Dist. Ct. Nassau Cty. 1968).

Dickey v. Alabama State Board of Education, 273 F. Supp. 613 (M. D. Ala. 1967).

Dixon v. Alabama State Board of Education, 186 F. Supp. 945, reversed 294 F. 2d 150 (5th Cir.) cert. denied, 368 U. S. 930 (1961).

Due v. Florida A and M University, 233 F. Supp. 196 (D. C. Fla. 1963).

Esteban v. Central Missouri State College, 277 F. Supp. 649 (W. D. Mo. 1967).

Esteban v. Central Missouri State College, 290 F. Supp. 622 (W. D. Mo. 1968).

Furutani v. Ewigleben, 297 F. Supp. 1163 (N. D. Cal. 1969).

Garrity v. New Jersey, 385 U. S. 493 (1967).

Gault, In re, 387 U. S. 1 (1967).

Goldberg v. Regents of University of California, 57 Cal. Rptr. 463 (Ct. App. 1967).

Goldenkoff v. Alabany Law School, 198 A. D. 460, 191 N. Y. S. 549 (New York 1921).

Goldstein v. New York University, 38 Misc. 93 (1902).

Gott v. Berea College, 156 Ky. 376, 161 S. W. 204 (1913).

Hammond v. South Carolina State College, 272 F. Supp. 947 (D. S. C. 1967).

Hill v. McCauley, 3 Pa. C. C. Rep. 77 (C. P. Cumberland Cy. 1887).

Jones v. State Board of Education of Tennessee, 277 F. Supp. 190, 407 F. 2d 834, 90 S. Ct., 779 (1970).

The King v. Chancellor of the University of Cambridge, 6 T. R. 89, 10 Eng. Rep. 451 (K. B. 1732).

Knight v. State Board of Education, 200 F. Supp. 174 (M. D. Tenn. 1961).

Koblitz v. Western Reserve University, 21 Ohio C. C. R. 144, 11 Ohio C. C. Dec. 515 (1901).

Miranda v. Arizona, 384 U. S. 436 (1966).

Monroe v. Pape, 365 U. S. 167 (1961).

Moore v. Student Affairs Committee of Troy State University, 284 F. Supp. 725 (M. D. Ala. 1968).

United States v. O'Brien, 391 U. S. 367 (1968).

Overton v. New York, 20 N. Y. 2d 360, aff'd, 283 N. Y. S. 2d 22 (1967), vacated and remanded, 393 U. S. 85 (1968), reargument scheduled, 23 N. Y. 2d 869 (1969).

Powe v. Miles, 407 F. 2d 73 (2d Cir. 1968).

Sherman v. Hyman, 180 Tenn. 99, 171 S. W. 2d 822 (Tennessee 1942), cert. denied, 319 U. S. 748 (1943).

Soglin v. Kauffman, 295 F. Supp. 978, sustained, 418 F. 2d 163 (7th Cir. 1969).

Spevack v. Klein, 385 U. S. 511 (1967).

Steier v. New York Education Commissioner, 271 F. 2d (2d Cir. 1959), cert denied, 381 U. S. 966 (1960).

Sullivan v. Houston Independent School District, 307 F. Supp. (S. D. Texas, Houston Div. 1969).

Swanson v. McGuire, 188 F. Supp. 112 (N. D. Ill. 1960).

Tanton v. McKenney, 226 Mich. 245, 197 N. W. 510 (Michigan 1924).

Tinker v. Des Moines Independent Community School District, 258 F. Supp. 971 (S. D. Iowa), 383 F. 2d 988 (8th Cir.), 393 U. S. 503 (1969).

Truitt v. Illinois, 278 F. 2d 819 (7th Cir. 1960).

Vought v. Van Buren Public Schools, 306 F. Supp. 1388 (E. D. Mich. 1969).

Articles from Journals and Collections

Beaney, William M. "Students, Higher Education, and the Law." 45 Denver Law Journal 511 (1968).

Buess, Thomas E. "A Step Toward Guaranteed Student Rights--The University as Agency." Student Lawyer Journal. (May, 1968), p. 7.

Byse, Clark. "Procedure in Student Dismissal Proceedings: Law and Policy." Journal of College Student Personnel. (March, 1963), 134.

Carrington, Paul D. "The Lawyer's Role in the Design of a University." Student Protest and the Law. Edited by Grace W. Holmes. Ann Arbor, Michigan: The Institute of Continuing Legal Education (1969).

Cohen, Stanley S. "Constitutional Law--Due Process--Expulsion of Students at Tax-Supported Schools Without a Hearing." 35 Temple Law Quarterly 437. (Summer, 1962).

"Developments in the Law--Academic Freedom." 81 Harvard Law Review 1134 (1968).

Erdreich, Ben Leader. "Case Notes." 14 Alabama Law Review 126 (1962).

Farar, Tom J., et al. "Panel Discussion--I." in Student Protest and the Law, supra. 149.

Goldman, Alvin A. "The University and the Liberty of Its Students--A Fiduciary Theory." 54 Kentucky Law Journal 643 (1966).

Heyman, Ira Michael. "Some Thoughts on University Disciplinary Proceedings." 54 California Law Review 73 (1966).

Holloway, John P. "The School in Court." in Student Protest and the Law, supra. 83.

Johnson, Michael T. "The Constitutional Rights of College Students." 42 Texas Law Review 344 (1964).

Kalaidjian, Edward C. "Problems of Dual Jurisdiction of Campus and Community." in Student Protest and the Law, supra (1969).

Katz, Joseph, and Sanford, Nevitt. "The New Student Power and Needed Educational Reforms." Phi Delta Kappan. (April, 1966), 397.

Kauffman, Joseph F. "The New Climate of Student Freedom and Rights." Educational Record. (Fall, 1964), 360.

Keniston, Kenneth. "The Sources of Student Dissent." in The Age of Protest. Edited by Walt Anderson. Pacific Palisades, Calif.: Goodyear Publishing Co. (1969), 227.

Knapp, Stephen R. "The Nature of 'Procedural Due Process' as Between the University and the Student." III The College Counsel 25 (No. 1. 1968).

Ladd, Edward T. "Civil Liberties: Yet Another Piece of Baggage for Teacher Education?" Journal of Teacher Education. XX (Summer, 1969), 139.

Lippe, Richard A. "The Student in Court." in Student Protest and the Law, supra. 105.

Lucas, Roy. "Comment" (William W. Van Alstyne, "The Student as University Resident"). 45 Denver Law Journal 582 (Summer, 1968).

McGrath, C. Peter. "Comment" (William W. Van Alstyne, "The Student as University Resident") supra. 614.

McKay, Robert B. "The Student as Private Citizen." 45 Denver Law Journal 558 (1968).

Monypenny, Phillip. "University Purpose, Discipline and Due Process." 43 South Dakota Law Review 739 (1967).

Myerson, Martin. "The Ethos of the American College Student: Beyond the Protests." in Higher Education and Modern Democracy. Edited by Robert A. Goldwin. Chicago: Rand-McNally & Company. (1965).

O'Leary, Richard E. "The College Student and Due Process in Disciplinary Proceedings." 1962 University of Illinois Law Forum 438 (1962).

Powell, Robert S., Jr. "Comment" (Phillip Monypenny, "The Student as Student"). 45 Denver Law Journal 669 (Summer, 1968).

"Private Government on Campus--Judicial Review of University Expulsions." 72 Yale Law Journal 1362 (1963).

"Readmission of Students Rejecting the Draft." School and Society. (October 12, 1968).

"Recent Cases." 75 Harvard Law Review 1429 (1962).

"Recent Cases." 58 North Dakota Law Review 348 (April, 1962).

Riesman, David, and Jencks, Christopher. "The Viability of the American College." in The American College. Edited by Nevitt Sanford. New York: John Wiley & Sons, Inc. (1962).

Seavey, Warren A. "Dismissal of Students: 'Due Process.' " 90 Harvard Law Review 1406 (1957).

"Soaring College Enrolments: A Critical Problem for the States," State Government. (October, 1954). 201.

Stamp, Neal R. "Comment" (Monypenny, supra). 45 Denver Law Journal 663 (Summer, 1968).

Strahan, Richard D. "School Board Authority and Behavioral Codes for Students." Texas School Board Journal. (March, 1970). 9.

Thompson, Ralph, and Kelly, Samuel P. "In Loco Parentis and the Academic Enclave." Educational Record. (Fall, 1969). 449.

Van Alstyne, William W. "The Constitutional Protection of Student Protest on Campus." in Student Protest and the Law, supra. 181.

_____. "The Demise of the Right-Privilege Distinction in Constitutional Law." 81 Harvard Law Review 1439 (1968).

_____. "The Judicial Trend Toward Academic Freedom." 20 Florida Law Review 290 (1963).

_____. et al. "Panel Discussion--II." in Student Protest and the Law, supra. 201.

_____. "Procedural Due Process and State University Students." 10 UCLA Law Review 368 (1963).

_____. "The Student as University Resident." 45 Denver Law Journal 582 (Summer, 1968).

"What the Courts Are Saying About Student Rights." NEA Research Bulletin, (October, 1969). 86.

Wright, Charles Alan. "The Constitution on the Campus." 22 Vanderbilt Law Review 1027. (October, 1969).

Books

Abraham, Henry J. Freedom and the Court. New York:
Oxford University Press. 1967.

_____. The Judiciary. Boston: Allyn and Bacon. 1969.

Academic Freedom and Civil Liberties of Students in Colleges and Universities. New York: American Civil
Liberties Union (Working paper, June, 1969).

Anderson, Walt, ed. The Age of Protest. Pacific Palisades, Calif.: Goodyear Publishing Co. 1969.

Bakken, Clarence J. The Legal Basis of College Student
Personnel Work. 2d ed. Washington, D. C.: American College Personnel Association. 1968.

Blair, J. W., Jr., ed. Student Rights & Responsibilities.
Cincinnati, Ohio: Associated Student Government.
1968.

Brady, Thomas F., and Snoxell, Laverne F. Student Discipline in Higher Education. Washington, D. C.:
American College Personnel Association. 1965.

Cohen, Morris, and Cohen, Felix S. Readings in Jurisprudence and Legal Philosophy. New York: Prentice-
Hall, Inc. 1951.

Goldwin, Robert A., ed. Higher Education and Modern
Democracy. Chicago: Rand-McNally & Company.
1965.

Hofstadter, Richard, and Hardy, C. DeWitt. The Development and Scope of Higher Education in the United
States. New York: Columbia University Press.
1952.

Holmes, Grace W., ed. Student Protest and the Law. Ann
Arbor, Michigan: The Institute of Continuing Legal
Education. 1969.

Jencks, Christopher, and Riesman, David. The Academic
Revolution. Garden City, New York: Doubleday &
Co. 1968.

212

Konvitz, Milton R. Expanding Liberties. New York: The
    Viking Press. 1966.

Sanford, Nevitt, ed. The American College. New York:
    John Wiley & Sons, Inc. 1962.

Veblen, Thorstein. The Higher Learning in America. New
    York: Sagamore Press, Inc. 1957.

Magazines and Newspapers

Commager, Henry Steele. "The Nature of Academic Free-
    dom, " Saturday Review. August 27, 1966. 14.

"Circuit Affirms Long Hair Win." Civil Liberties. Febru-
    ary, 1970.

"End of an Era. The Last Warren Court Term." Civil
    Liberties. August, 1969. 3.

"Interpreter in the Front Line." Time. May 12, 1967. 72.

"The Jinxed Seat: Who's Next?" Newsweek. December 1,
    1969. 24.

"The Law." Time. March 23, 1970. 64-66.

Levitas, Michael. "2-S--Too Smart to Fight?" The New
    York Times Magazine. April 24, 1966. 27.

"Life and Death Grades." Time. March 25, 1966. 70.

"News and Views." Commonweal. January 31, 1969. 544.

News Report. The New York Times. April 14, 1964. 27.

News Report (Judge Wisdom's appointment). The New York
    Times. March 15, 1957. 15:1.

Obituary (Judge Ben F. Cameron). The New York Times.
    April 14, 1964. 27.

"Trail Blazers on the Bench." Time. December 5, 1960.
    14.

Documents

General Order on Judicial Standards of Procedure and Substance in Review of Student Discipline in Tax-Supported Institutions of Higher Education. 45 F. R. D.
133. United States District Court for the Western
District of Missouri (en banc). (1968).

Higher Education for American Democracy. Vol. I, Report
of the President's Commission on Higher Education.
Washington, D. C.: U. S. Government Printing Office.
1947.

Joint Statement of Rights and Freedoms of Students. 53 A.
A. U. P. Bulletin 365. 1967. Reprinted in several
sources.

Interview

The writer is indebted to Irving Achtenberg, Kansas
City counsel for the ACLU for an extensive interview in his
office in the Spring of 1967 and a telephone interview on
February 22, 1970. Since Achtenberg was ACLU counsel in
the two Esteban cases, while the writer was teaching on the
faculty at the defendant Central Missouri State College, these
interviews were very helpful in inspiring and carrying forth
this study.

Correspondence

Gray, Fred D. Montgomery, attorney, who initiated the action in Dixon. Letter dated May 20, 1969.

Monroe, W. J., First Assistant Attorney General for Oklahoma. Letter dated February 24, 1970.

Van Alstyne, William W., Letter dated February 27, 1969.

Van Waes, Robert, Associate Secretary, A. A. U. P. Letter
dated May 20, 1970.

Selected List of References Not Cited

Cases

Baltimore University v. Colton, 98 Md. 623, 57 Atl. 14 (1940).

Baker v. Bryn Mawr College Trustees, 1 Pa. D & C 383 (Dist. Ct. 1922), aff'd. per curium, 278 Pa. 121, 122 Atl. 220 (1923).

Barker v. Hardway, 283 F. Supp. 228 (S. D. W. V. 1968).

Buckley v. Meng, 230 N. Y. S. 2d 924 (Sup. Ct. 1962).

Buttny v. Smiley, 281 F. Supp. 280 (D. Colo. 1968).

Carr v. St. John's University, 17 A. D. 2d 632, 231 N. Y. S. 2d 410 (Sup. Ct. App. Div. 2d Dept. 1962).

Connelly v. University of Vermont, 244 F. Supp. 156 (D. Vt. 1956).

Danskin v. San Diego Unified School District, 28 Cal. 2d 885 (1946).

Dehaan v. Brandeis University, 150 F. Supp. 626 (D. Mass. 1957).

Dickson v. Sitterson, 280 F. Supp. 486 (M. D. N. C. 1968).

Edde v. Columbia University, 8 Misc. 2d 795, 168 N. Y. S. 2d 558, cert. denied, 359 U. S. 956 (1959).

Egan v. Moore, 245 N. Y. S. 2d 622 (App. Div. 1963), aff'd., 14 N. Y. 2d 775 (1964).

Englehart v. Serena, 300 S. W. 268 (Sup. Ct. Mo. 1927).

Ferrell v. Dallas Independent School District, 261 F. Supp. 545 (N. D. Texas 1966), 392 F. 2d 697 (5th Cir. 1968), cert. denied, 89 S. Ct. 98 (1968).

Finot v. Pasadena City Board of Education, 58 Cal Rptr 520 (1967).

Frank v. Marquette University, 209 Wisc. 372, 245 N. W. 125 (1932).

Gannon v. Georgetown College, 28 App. D. C. 87 (1906).

Gleason v. University of Minnesota, 104 Minn. 359 116 N. W. 650 (1908).

Green v. Howard University, 203 F. Supp. 609 (D. D. C. 1967).

Griffin v. County School Board, 377 U. W. 218 (1964).

Guillory v. Tulane University, 203 F. Supp. 855 (1962), reversed on rehearing, 212 F. Supp. 674 (E. D. La. 1962).

Hannah v. Larche, 363 U. S. 420 (1960).

Ingersoll v. Clapp, 81 Mont. 220, 263 Pac. 439 (1928).

Kerr v. Enoch Pratt Free Library of Baltimore, 149 F. 2d 212 (4th Cir. 1945).

Keyishian v. Board of Regents, 385 U. S. 589 (1967).

Madera v. Board of Education, 276 F. Supp. 356, reversed, 386 F. 2d 778 (2nd Cir. 1967).

Matter of Lesser v. Board of Education, 18 A. D. 2d 388 (1963).

Niedermeyer v. Curators of State University, 61 Mo. App. 654 (Kan. Cy. Ct. App. 1895).

Pass v. Pass, (Miss.) 118 So. 2d 769 (C. A. 5th 1961).

Robinson v. University of Miami, 100 So. 2d 442 (Fla. 1958).

Sigma Chi Fraternity v. Regents of University of Colorado, 258 F. Supp. 515 (D. Colo. 1966).

Snyder v. Board of Trustees, 288 F. Supp. 927 (N. D. Ill. 1968).

Stacy v. Williams, 306 F. Supp. 963 (N. D. Miss. 1969).

Stetson University v. Hunt, 88 Fla. 510, 102 So. 637 (1924).

Timkoff v. Northwestern University, 33 Ill. App. 224, 77 N. E. 2d 345 (1945).

University of Miami v. Militania, 184 So. 2d 701 (Fla. 1966).

University of Notre Dame du Lac v. Twentieth Century-Fox Film Corp., 256 N. Y. S. 2d 301 (1964).

Wasson v. Trowbridge, 382 F. 2d 807 (2nd Cir. 1967).

Webb v. State University of New York, 125 F. Supp. 910 (N. D. N. Y. 1954).

West v. Board of Trustees of Miami University, 181 N. E. 144, (Ohio Ct. App. 1931).

White v. Portia Law School, 174 N. E. 187 (Mass. S. J. D. 1931).

Woods v. Simpson, 146 Md. 547, 126 A. 882 (1924).

Woody v. Burns, 188 So. 2d 56 (Fla. 1966).

Wright v. Texas Southern University, 277 F. Supp. 110 (S. D. Texas 1967).

Zanders v. Louisiana State Board of Education, 281 F. Supp. 747 (W. D. La. 1968).

Articles from Journals and Collections

"Academic Freedom--Its Constitutional Context." 40 University of Colorado Law Review 600. (Summer, 1968).

"Academic Freedom: A Symposium." 28 Law and Contemporary Problems 439. (Summer, 1963).

"Are Rights of Students Expanding?" 38 Oklahoma Bar Association Journal 1585. (1967).

Blackburn, M. "Some Thoughts on the Administrative Process as a Means of Revoking the Public Education Benefit." 47 Nebraska Law Review 528. (May, 1968).

Brennan, W. J., Jr. "A Judge Looks at Student Dissent." 19 Harvard Law School Bulletin 9. (June, 1968).

"Campus Censorship." 42 North Carolina Law Review 179 (1963).

217

"Campus Law." 54 California Law Review 40 (1966).

Chambers, M. M. "The Legal Right of a Student to a Diploma or a Degree." Educational Law and Administration. January, 1936. 7.

"College Disciplinary Proceedings." 18 Vanderbilt Law Review 819. (March, 1965).

"The College Student and Due Process in Disciplinary Proceedings," 13 South Dakota Law Review 87. (Winter, 1968).

Costanzo, J. F. "Wholesome Neutrality: Law and Education." 43 North Dakota Law Review 605. (Summer, 1967).

"Degree of Discretionary Authority Possessed by University Officials in Disciplinary Matters--the Availability of Mandamus." 21 Southwest Law Journal 664. (Fall, 1967).

"Due Process and the Dismissal of Students at State-Supported Colleges and Universities." 3 Georgia State Bar Journal 101. (August, 1966).

"Due Process in Public Colleges and Universities--Need for Trial-Type Hearings." 13 Howard Law Journal 414. (Spring, 1967).

"Educational Aspects of In Loco Parentis." 8 Journal of College Student Personnel 231 (July, 1964).

"Expulsion of College and Professional Students--Rights and Remedies." 38 Notre Dame Law 174. (March, 1963).

"Expulsion of Students from Private Educational Institutions." 35 Columbia Law Review 898 (1935).

Fish, Donald W. "College Disciplinary Proceedings." 18 Vanderbilt Law Review 819. (March, 1965).

Kurland, F. B. "The Revolting Student." 16 University of Chicago Law School Record 10. (Spring, 1968).

_____. "The University of the Future." 14 University of Chicago Law School Record 1. (Winter, 1966).

Landford, Terry F. "Who Are Members of the University Community?" 45 Denver Law Journal 545. (Summer, 1968).

Levi, E. H. "The Critical Spirit." 14 University of Chicago Law School Record 1. (Winter, 1966).

Monypenny, Phillip. "The Student as a Student." 45 Denver Law Journal 649. (Summer, 1968).

_____. "Toward a Standard for Student Academic Freedom." 28 Law and Contemporary Problems 625 (1963).

"North Carolina Speaker Bias Law: A Study in Context." 55 Kentucky Law Journal 225. (Winter, 1966).

"Procedural Limitations on the Expulsion of College and University Students." 10 St. Louis University Law Journal 542. (Summer, 1966).

Reichstein, K. J. "Appeals Day: A Study of Academic Justice." 2 Law and Society Review 259. (February, 1968).

"Student Rights and Campus Rules." 54 California Law Review 1. (March, 1966).

Van Alstyne, William W. "Political Speakers at State Universities--Some Constitutional Considerations." 111 University of Pennsylvania Law Review 328. (January, 1963).

_____. "Student Academic Freedom and the Rule-Making Powers of Public Universities: Some Constitutional Considerations." 2 Law in Transition 1. (Winter, 1965).

Wilson, Logan. "Campus Freedom and Order." 45 Denver Law Journal 502. (Summer, 1968).

APPENDICES

Appendix A

Joint Statement
on Rights and Freedoms
of Students

In June, 1967, a joint committee, comprised of representatives from the American Association of University Professors, U. S. National Student Association, Association of American Colleges, National Association of Student Personnel Administrators, and National Association of Women Deans and Counselors, met in Washington, D. C., and drafted the Joint Statement on Rights and Freedoms of Students published below.

The multilateral approach which produced this document was also applied to the complicated matter of interpretation, implementation, and enforcement, with the drafting committee recommending (a) joint efforts to promote acceptance of the new standards on the institutional level, (b) the establishment of machinery to facilitate continuing joint interpretation, (c) joint consultation before setting up any machinery for mediating disputes or investigating complaints, and (d) joint approaches to regional accrediting agencies to seek embodiment of the new principles in standards for accreditation.

Since its formulation, the Joint Statement has been endorsed by each of its five national sponsors, as well as by a number of other professional bodies. The endorsers are listed below (sponsors are indicated by an asterisk):
* *U. S. National Student Association
* *Association of American Colleges
* *American Association of University Professors
* *National Association of Student Personnel Administrators
* *National Association of Women Deans and Counselors

American Association for Higher Education
Jesuit Education Association
American College Personnel Association
Executive Committee, College and University Department, National Catholic Education Association
Commission on Student Personnel, American Association of Junior Colleges

Preamble

Academic institutions exist for the transmission of knowledge, the pursuit of truth, the development of students, and the general well-being of society. Free inquiry and free expression are indispensable to the attainment of these goals. As members of the academic community, students should be encouraged to develop the capacity for critical judgment and to engage in a sustained and independent search for truth. Institutional procedures for achieving these purposes may vary from campus to campus, but the minimal standards of academic freedom of students outlined below are essential to any community of scholars.

Freedom to teach and freedom to learn are inseparable facets of academic freedom. The freedom to learn depends upon appropriate opportunities and conditions in the classroom, on the campus, and in the larger community. Students should exercise their freedom with responsibility.

The responsibility to secure and to respect general conditions conducive to the freedom to learn is shared by all members of the academic community. Each college and university has a duty to develop policies and procedures which provide and safeguard this freedom. Such policies and procedures should be developed at each institution within the framework of general standards and with the broadest possible participation of the members of the academic community. The purpose of this statement is to enumerate the essential provisions for student freedom to learn.

I.   Freedom of Access to Higher Education

The admissions policies of each college and university are a matter of institutional choice provided that each college and university makes clear the characteristics and ex-

pectations of students which it considers relevant to success
in the institution's program.   While church-related institutions
may give admission preference to students of their own per-
suasion, such a preference should be clearly and publicly
stated.   Under no circumstances should a student be barred
from admission to a particular institution on the basis of
race.   Thus, within the limits of its facilities, each college
and university should be open to all students who are qualified according to its admission standards.   The facilities and
services of a college should be open to all of its enrolled
students, and institutions should use their influence to secure
equal access for all students to public facilities in the local
community.

II.   In the Classroom

The professor in the classroom and in conference
should encourage free discussion, inquiry, and expression.
Student performance should be evaluated solely on an academic basis, not on opinions or conduct in matters unrelated
to academic standards.

A.   Protection of Freedom of Expression.   Students
should be free to take reasoned exception to the data or
views offered in any course of study and to reserve judgment
about matters of opinion, but they are responsible for learning the content of any course of study for which they are enrolled.

B.   Protection Against Improper Academic Evaluation.
Students should have protection through orderly procedures
against prejudiced or capricious academic evaluation.   At the
same time, they are responsible for maintaining standards of
academic performance established for each course in which
they are enrolled.

C.   Protection Against Improper Disclosure.   Information about student views, beliefs, and political associations which professors acquire in the course of their work as
instructors, advisers, and counselors should be considered
confidential.   Protection against improper disclosure is a
serious professional obligation.   Judgments of ability and
character may be provided under appropriate circumstances,
normally with the knowledge or consent of the student.

III. Student Records

Institutions should have a carefully considered policy as to the information which should be part of a student's permanent educational record and as to the conditions of its disclosure. To minimize the risk of improper disclosure, academic and disciplinary records should be separate, and the conditions of access to each should be set forth in an explicit policy statement. Transcripts of academic records should contain only information about academic status. Information from disciplinary or counseling files should not be available to unauthorized persons on campus, or to any person off campus without the express consent of the student involved except under legal compulsion or in cases where the safety of persons or property is involved. No records should be kept which reflect the political activities or beliefs of students. Provision should also be made for periodic routine destruction of noncurrent disciplinary records. Administrative staff and faculty members should respect confidential information about students which they acquire in the course of their work.

IV. Student Affairs

In student affairs, certain standards must be maintained if the freedom of students is to be preserved.

A. Freedom of Association. Students bring to the campus a variety of interests previously acquired and develop many new interests as members of the academic community. They should be free to organize and join associations to promote their common interests.

1. The membership, policies, and actions of a student organization usually will be determined by vote of only those persons who hold bona fide membership in the college or university community.

2. Affiliation with an extramural organization should not of itself disqualify a student organization from institutional recognition.

3. If campus advisers are required each organization should be free to choose its own adviser, and institutional recognition should not be withheld or withdrawn solely because of the inability of a student organization to secure

an adviser. Campus advisers may advise organizations in the exercise of responsibility, but they should not have the authority to control the policy of such organizations.

4. Student organizations may be required to submit a statement of purpose, criteria for membership, rules of procedures, and a current list of officers. They should not be required to submit a membership list as a condition of institutional recognition.

5. Campus organizations, including those affiliated with an extramural organization, should be open to all students without respect to race, creed, or national origin, except for religious qualifications which may be required by organizations whose aims are primarily sectarian.

B. Freedom of Inquiry and Expression.

1. Students and student organizations should be free to examine and to discuss all questions of interest to them, and to express opinions publicly and privately. They should always be free to support causes by orderly means which do not disrupt the regular and essential operation of the institution. At the same time, it should be made clear to the academic and the larger community that in their public expressions or demonstrations students or student organizations speak only for themselves.

2. Students should be allowed to invite and to hear any person of their own choosing. Those routine procedures required by an institution before a guest speaker is invited to appear on campus should be designed only to insure that there is orderly scheduling of facilities and adequate preparation for the event, and that the occasion is conducted in a manner appropriate to an academic community. The institutional control of campus facilities should not be used as a device of censorship. It should be made clear to the academic and larger community that sponsorship of guest speakers does not necessarily imply approval or endorsement of the views expressed, either by the sponsoring group or the institution.

C. Student Participation in Institutional Government. As constituents of the academic community, students should be free, individually and collectively, to express their views on issues of institutional policy and on matters of general interest to the student body. The student body should have clearly defined means to participate in the formulation and application of institutional policy affecting academic and student affairs. The role of the student government and both its general and specific responsibilities should be made explicit, and the actions of the student government within the areas of its jurisdiction should be reviewed only through orderly and prescribed procedures.

D. Student Publications. Student publications and the student press are a valuable aid in establishing and maintaining an atmosphere of free and responsible discussion and of intellectual exploration on the campus. They are a means of bringing student concerns to the attention of the faculty and the institutional authorities and of formulating student opinion on various issues on the campus and in the world at large.

Whenever possible the student newspaper should be an independent corporation financially and legally separate from the university. Where financial and legal autonomy is not possible the institution, as the publisher of student publications, may have to bear the legal responsibility for the contents of the publications. In the delegation of editorial responsibility to students the institution must provide sufficient editorial freedom and financial autonomy for the student publications to maintain their integrity of purpose as vehicles for free inquiry and free expression in an academic community.

Institutional authorities, in consultation with students and faculty, have a responsibility to provide written clarification of the role of the student publications; the standards to be used in their evaluation, and the limitations on external control of their operation. At the same time, the editorial freedom of student editors and managers entails corollary responsibilities to be governed by the canons of responsible journalism, such as the avoidance of libel, indecency, undocumented allegations, attacks on personal integrity, and the techniques of harassment and innuendo. As safeguards for the editorial freedom of student publications the following provisions are necessary:

1. The student press should be free of censorship and advance approval of copy, and its editors and managers should be free to develop their own editorial policies and news coverage.

2. Editors and managers of student publications should be protected from arbitrary suspension and removal because of student, faculty, administrative, or public disapproval of editorial policy or content. Only for proper and stated causes should editors and managers be subject to removal and then by orderly and prescribed procedures. The agency responsible for the appointment of editors and managers should be the agency responsible for their removal.

3. All university published and financed student publications should explicitly state on the editorial page that the opinions there expressed are not necessarily those of the college, university or student body.

V.   Off-Campus Freedom of Students

A. Exercise of Rights of Citizenship. College and university students are both citizens and members of the academic community. As citizens, students should enjoy the same freedom of speech, peaceful assembly, and right of petition that other citizens enjoy and, as members of the academic community, they are subject to the obligations which accrue to them by virtue of this membership. Faculty members and administrative officials should insure that institutional powers are not employed to inhibit such intellectual and personal development of students as is often promoted by their exercise of the rights of citizenship both on and off campus.

B. Institutional Authority and Civil Penalties. Activities of students may upon occasion result in violation of law. In such cases, institutional officials should be prepared to apprise students of sources of legal counsel and may offer other assistance. Students who violate the law may incur penalties prescribed by civil authorities, but institutional authority should never be used merely to duplicate the function of general laws. Only where the institution's interests as an academic community are distinct and clearly involved should the special authority of the institution be asserted. The student who incidentally violates institutional regulations in the course of his off-campus activity, such as those relating to class attendance, should be subject to no greater penalty than would normally be imposed. Institutional action should be independent of community pressure.

VI. Procedural Standards in Disciplinary Proceedings

In developing responsible student conduct, disciplinary proceedings play a role substantially secondary to example, counseling, guidance, and admonition. At the same time, educational institutions have a duty and the corollary disciplinary powers to protect their educational purpose through the setting of standards of scholarship and conduct for the students who attend them and through the regulation of the use of institutional facilities. In the exceptional circumstances when the preferred means fail to resolve problems of student conduct, proper procedural safeguards should be observed to protect the student from the unfair imposition of serious penalties.

The administration of discipline should guarantee procedural fairness to an accused student. Practices in disciplinary cases may vary in formality with the gravity of the offense and the sanctions which may be applied. They should also take into account the presence or absence of an Honor Code, and the degree to which the institutional officials have direct acquaintance with student life, in general, and with the involved student and the circumstances of the case in particular. The jurisdictions of faculty or student judicial bodies, the disciplinary responsibilities of institutional officials and the regular disciplinary procedures, including the student's right to appeal a decision, should be clearly formulated and communicated in advance. Minor penalties may be assessed informally under prescribed procedures.

In all situations, procedural fair play requires that the student be informed of the nature of the charges against him, that he be given a fair opportunity to refute them, that the institution not be arbitrary in its actions, and that there be provision for appeal of a decision. The following are recommended as proper safeguards in such proceedings when there are no Honor Codes offering comparable guarantees.

A. Standards of Conduct Expected of Students. The institution has an obligation to clarify those standards of behavior which it considers essential to its educational mission and its community life. These general behavioral expectations and the resultant specific regulations should represent a reasonable regulation of student conduct but the student should be as free as possible from imposed limitations that have no direct relevance to his education. Offenses should be as clearly defined as possible and interpreted in a manner consistent with the aforementioned principles of relevancy and reasonableness. Disciplinary proceedings should be instituted only for violations of standards of conduct formulated with significant student participation and published in advance through such means as a student handbook or a generally available body of institutional regulations.

B.   Investigation of Student Conduct.

1.   Except under extreme emergency circumstances, premises occupied by students and the personal possessions of students should not be searched unless appropriate authorization has been obtained. For premises such as residence halls controlled by the institution, an appropriate and responsible authority should be designated to whom application should be made before a search is conducted. The application should specify the reasons for the search and the objects or information sought. The student should be present, if possible, during the search. For premises not controlled by the institution, the ordinary requirements for lawful search should be followed.

2.   Students detected or arrested in the course of serious violations of institutional regulations, or infractions of ordinary law, should be informed of their rights. No form of harassment should be used by institutional representatives to coerce admissions of guilt or information about conduct of other suspected persons.

C.   Status of Student Pending Final Action. Pending action on the charges, the status of a student should not be altered, or his right to be present on the campus and to attend classes suspended, except for reasons relating to his physical or emotional safety and well-being, or for reasons relating to the safety and well-being of students, faculty, or university property.

D.   Hearing Committee Procedures. When the misconduct may result in serious penalties and if the student questions the fairness of disciplinary action taken against him, he should be granted, on request, the privilege of a hearing before a regularly constituted hearing committee. The following suggested hearing committee procedures satisfy the requirements of "procedural due process" in situations requiring a high degree of formality:

1.   The hearing committee should include faculty members or students, or, if regularly included or requested

by the accused, both faculty and student members. No member of the hearing committee who is otherwise interested in the particular case should sit in judgment during the proceeding.

2. The student should be informed, in writing, of the reasons for the proposed disciplinary action with sufficient particularity, and in sufficient time, to insure opportunity to prepare for the hearing.

3. The student appearing before the hearing committee should have the right to be assisted in his defense by an adviser of his choice.

4. The burden of proof should rest upon the officials bringing the charge.

5. The student should be given an opportunity to testify and to present evidence and witnesses. He should have an opportunity to hear and question adverse witnesses. In no case should the committee consider statements against him unless he has been advised of their content and of the names of those who made them, and unless he has been given an opportunity to rebut unfavorable inferences which might otherwise be drawn.

6. All matters upon which the decision may be based must be introduced into evidence at the proceeding before the Hearing Committee. The decision should be based solely upon such matter. Improperly acquired evidence should not be admitted.

7. In the absence of a transcript, there should be both a digest and a verbatim record, such as a tape recording, of the hearing.

8. The decision of the Hearing Committee should be final, subject only to the student's right of appeal to the President or ultimately to the governing board of the institution.

Appendix B

Academic Freedom and Civil Liberties
of Students
in Colleges and Universities

American Civil Liberties Union

Preface

This pamphlet is the fifth publication concerned with
academic freedom for students in institutions of higher learning prepared by the Academic Freedom Committee of the
American Civil Liberties Union.

The Union has long sought to gain for students a recognition of rights that, until recently, were held to apply to
teachers only. Traditionally, academic freedom for students
is the right to study the evidence supporting or critical of
accepted beliefs, to discuss and question this evidence, to
hear speakers of all points of view, to express opinions
through all media without censorship, and to organize to
exercise these rights. In its broadened sense, academic
freedom is analogous to civil liberties in the community at
large, encompassing not only the right to free inquiry, expression, and dissent, but the right to due process and equal
treatment. Academic freedom, in other words, assures for
teachers and students the full enjoyment of their constitutional liberties.

In 1941, the ACLU published a survey entitled, "What
Freedom for American Students?," describing the restraints
on students' activities and freedom of expression imposed on
the nation's campuses. In a subsequent statement, "Civil
Liberties of Teachers and Students--Academic Freedom"
(1949), it equated students' rights with faculty rights, em-
phasizing that the freedom to learn is as vital to the educational process as the freedom to teach.

232

The present pamphlet was first published in 1956.
Concerned with the protection of academic freedom for college and university students at all levels, it is addressed also to administrators and faculty, who play a vital role in
the maintenance of academic freedom on the campus.

As long-time guardian of civil liberties, the ACLU
uses its resources--those of the national office and of its
many affiliates and chapters throughout the country--to offer
advice and assistance when, in its judgment, academic freedom has been infringed upon or denied to one or more students. The Union does not work exclusively through the
courts. In cases involving academic freedom, the ACLU
prefers direct negotiation, supplemented when needed, by
publicity and the influence of other interested organizations.

Other current ACLU publications prepared by the Academic Freedom Committee are: "Academic Freedom, Academic Responsibility, Academic Due Process in Institutions
of Higher Learning: A Statement of Principles Concerning
the Civil Liberties and Obligations of Teachers and Desirable Procedures Involving Academic Freedom in Public and
Private Colleges and Universities" (1966); and the recently
released "Academic Freedom in the Secondary Schools" (1968).

Introduction[1]

In this period of great tension, unrest among college
students involving confrontations and bordering in some cases
on rebellion has swept from one American campus to another.
Students have been asserting the right to participate in deci-
sion-making in matters relating to student life and discipline,
to the formulation of academic policies, and the governance
of their institutions. Many students strongly oppose what
they consider the distortion or perversion of the university's
proper purposes in serving ends established by agencies
other than the academic community. They have condemned,
inter alia, the university's ties to military agencies, secret
research, the status on campus of Reserve Officers Training
Corps, recruitment for the military or defense industries
and the failure adequately to educate black and other disadvantaged Americans.

The American Civil Liberties Union and its Academic
Freedom Committee recognize that many of the protesters,
who include not only undergraduate and graduate students but

some (particularly younger) faculty members, are moved by deep conviction and urgent concern in the attempt to correct what they deem educational inequities and, beyond that, to eliminate or limit the social, economic and political injustices of our society. Whatever differences of opinion exist with respect to and on how best to serve these causes, the ACLU is convinced that methods of protest which violate and subvert the basic principles of freedom of expression and academic freedom are abhorrent and must be condemned.

We believe in the right, and are committed to the protection of, all peaceful forms of protest, including mass demonstrations, picketing, rallies and other dramatic forms. But actions which deprive others of the opportunity to speak or be heard, involve take-overs of buildings that disrupt the educational process, incarceration of or assaults on persons, destruction of property and rifling of files are anti-civil-libertarian and incompatible with the nature and functions of educational institutions.

Fundamental to the very nature of a free society is the conviction expressed by Mr. Justice Holmes that "the best truth is the power of the thought to get itself accepted in the competition of the market." When men govern themselves they have a right to decide for themselves which views and proposals are sound and which unsound. This means that all points of view are entitled to be expressed and heard. This is particularly true in universities which render great services to society when they function as centers of free, uncoerced, independent and creative thought and experience. Universities have existed and can exist without bricks and mortar but they cannot function without freedom of inquiry and expression.

For these reasons, the American Civil Liberties Union has from its very inception defended free expression for all groups and all points of view, including the most radical and the most unpopular within the society and the university. To abandon the democratic process in the interests of "good" causes, without a willingness to pay the penalty for civil disobedience, is to risk the destruction of freedom not just for the present but for the future, not just for our social order but for any future social order as well. Freedom, the world has learned to its sorrow, is a fragile plant that must be protected and cultivated.

It should be axiomatic that if the college or univer-

sity[2] is to survive as a free institution without recourse to
the law-enforcement authorities, without interposition by the
courts or interference from legislators, it must strive to
create its own workable, forward-looking, self-governing society. That there should be a purposeful movement in this
direction was underscored in the letter addressed to President Nixon, on May 2, 1969, by the faculty, students and
administrative staff of Amherst College, following "an extraordinary two days of debate, discussion, and meditation."
In this letter, which was signed by President Calvin H.
Plimpton, the Amherst college community declared:

> It is clear that we have much to do to set our own
> house in order. We are convinced, and have shown
> during these days, that changes, even fundamental
> ones, can take place without physical duress. It
> will require all our care and energy... to combine
> change with continuity, to provide students with a
> real and regular role in influencing their education
> and the college's government, and to honor both in-
> tellectual discipline and creativity...

In its letter to President Nixon, the Amherst College
community stressed its belief that "part of this turmoil in
universities derives from the distance separating the American dream from the American reality."

It is obvious that our universities and colleges do not have
the power or means to redress the ills of our society. But the
more forward-looking are re-examining their structure and policies to preserve and extend the freedom and autonomy of the university community. In this connection, the ACLU has already
endorsed measures which would enhance the role of faculty and
students in the governing of academic institutions, which would
deprive ROTC of academic standing, and which call for continuing scrutiny of curricula and extra-curricula programs. (The
ACLU has also condemned the draft as a form of involuntary ser-
vitude not justified by "overriding need of national security.")

In this time of challenge and change, the Academic
Freedom Committee trusts that its completely revised pamphlet on Academic Freedom and Civil Liberties of Students in
Colleges and Universities will be of service to faculty, administrators and students alike. Given the diversity of institutions of higher education--public and private, secular
and religious, their differing traditions, size and aims--we
realize that no set of formulas or prescriptions will fit all

situations. But we believe that there are certain fundamental
principles applicable to the rights, freedoms and responsibilities of students in institutions of higher education. These
we have attempted to set forth in a series of guide-lines as
a basis for discussion and decision in all academic communities, private as well as public.

I. The Student as a Member
of the Community of Scholars

The student's freedom to learn is a counterpart of the
faculty member's freedom to teach. An academic community
dedicated to its ideals will safeguard the one as vigorously
as it does the other. [3]

A. Admission Policies

Admission policies should be clearly defined, publicly
stated, and uniformly administered to assure proper consideration for all applicants. Admission to either publicly or
privately operated colleges or universities should not be denied on the basis of ethnic origin, race, religion or political
belief or affiliation. In screening for admission individuals
who are members of disadvantaged minority groups, colleges
may properly apply methods for judging their academic potential different from the usual methods employed for appraising
applicants who have had the ordinary educational advantages.
The ultimate criterion for the admission of students in general should be their capacity to benefit from the educational
experience.

B. Freedom in the Classroom

Free and open discussion, speculation, and investigation are basic to academic freedom. Students as well as
teachers should be free to present their own opinions and
findings, and teachers should evaluate student performance
with scrupulous adherence to professional standards.

C. Safeguarding the Privileged Student-Teacher Relationship

The essential safeguard of academic freedom is mu-
tual trust and the realization by both student and teacher that
their freedom is reciprocal. Any abrogation of or restriction on the academic freedom of the one will, inevitably, ad-
versely affect the other.

1. Inquiries by Outside Agencies.

Because the student-teacher relationship is a privileged one, the student does not expect that the views he expresses, either orally or in writing, and either in or outside the classroom, will be reported by his professors beyond the walls of the college community. If he anticipated that anything he said or wrote might be disclosed, he might not feel free to express his thoughts and ideas.

The following standards are recommended as general guidelines: when questioned directly by representatives of government agencies or by prospective employers of any kind, public or private, or by investigative agencies or other persons, or indirectly by the institution's administrative officers in behalf of such agencies, a teacher may safely answer questions which he finds clearly concerned with the student's competence and fitness for the job. There is always the chance, however, that even questions of this kind will inadvertently cause the teacher to violate academic privacy. Questions and answers in written form make it easier to avoid pitfalls, but the teacher's alertness is always essential. Ordinarily, questions relating to the student's academic performance as, for example, the ability to write clearly, to solve problems, to reason well, to direct projects--pose no threat to educational privacy. But questions relating to the student's loyalty and patriotism, his political or religious or moral or social beliefs and attitudes, his general outlook, his private life, may if answered, violate the student's academic freedom and jeopardize the student-teacher relationship.

As a safeguard against the danger of placing the student in an unfavorable light with government agencies or employers of any category, teachers may preface each questionnaire with a brief pro forma statement that the academic policy to which they subscribe makes it inadvisable to answer certain types of questions about any or all students. Once this academic policy becomes widespread, presumptive inferences about individual students will no longer be made by employers.

Even when the student requests his teacher to disclose information in addition to his academic performance because he thinks it would be to his advantage, such disclosure should not be made, since that student may be persuaded by an outside agency to request disclosure on this assumption when, in fact, such disclosure would not be to

his benefit; disclosure in individual cases would raise doubts
about students who had made no such request. A satisfactory
principle, therefore, would foreclose disclosures in all cases.

Faculty senates or other representative faculty bodies,
it is hoped, will take cognizance of the teacher disclosure
problem, recommend action which will leave inviolate the
teacher-student relationship and protect the privacy of the
student.

2. Use of Electronic Recording Devices.

Television cameras, tape recorders, and similar devices are being used with increasing frequency for educational purposes in colleges and universities. For example, language and speech teachers are making extensive use of
speech recordings to help their students master foreign lan-
guages or recognize personal speech defects. The use of
such equipment, in an ethical manner, for legitimate educational purposes is not to be criticised; but faculty members
and students must exercise caution to prevent the misuse of
sight or sound recordings, as, for example, to discredit a
teacher or a fellow student. Students who wish to use tape
recorders for the purpose of recording class lectures and/or
discussions should do so only with the explicit knowledge and
consent of the teacher and participants, and then only for
that purpose. Faculty and student committees should establish guidelines for the use of electronic recording devices
and for the disposition of records which are made.

D. The Student's Role in the Formulation of Academic Pol-
icy

Colleges and universities should take whatever steps
are necessary to enable student representatives to participate
in an effective capacity with the faculty and administration in
determining at every level, beginning with the departmental,
such basic educational policies as course offerings and curriculum; the manner of grading; class size; standards for
evaluating the performance of faculty members; and the relative allocation of the institution's resources among its various educational programs.

E. The Ethics of Scholarship

So that students may become fully aware of the ethics
of scholarship, the faculty should draw up a clear statement

as to what constitutes plagiarism, setting forth principles the
students will understand and respect, and made readily available to students. Any student charged with such a violation
should be accorded a due process hearing as outlined in
Chapter III.

II. Extracurricular Activities

Students receive their college education not only in
the classroom but also in out-of-class activities which they
themselves organize through their own press and other media
of communications, and their association with fellow students.
It is vital, therefore, that their freedom as campus citizens
be respected and ensured.

A. Student Government

Student government in the past has had as one of its
chief functions the regulation of student-sponsored activities,
organizations, publications, etc. In exercising this function,
no student government should be permitted to allocate resources so as to bar or intimidate any campus organization
or publication. In the exercise of any newly-won authority
to participate in university policy decisions, the student government should represent the will of the majority of students.

1. Election Procedures.

Delegates to the student government should be elected
by the entire student body and should not represent merely
clubs or organizations. Designation of officers, committees,
and boards should be by majority vote, should be non-discriminatory, and should not be subject either to administrative or faculty approval. Any enrolled student, without regard to his scholastic standing, should be eligible for elec-
tion to student office.

In universities, graduate students should be represented in the student government unless they prefer their
own student body.

2. Funding.

Operational funds should be supplied by the students
themselves or the college administration. No student government, nor its national affiliate, should be subsidized by any
governmental agency.

B.   Student Clubs and Societies

    1.   The Right to Organize.

Students should be free, without restraint by either the
college administration or the student government, to organize
and join campus clubs or associations for educational, political, social, religious or cultural purposes. No such organization should discriminate on grounds of race, religion,
color or national origin. The fact of affiliation with any ex-
tra-mural association should not in itself bar a group from
recognition, but disclosure of such fact may be required. If
its funds in whole or in part are derived from such an organization, this information should be made public. The administration should not discriminate against a student because
of membership in any campus organization.

The guidelines in this section should apply to student
organizations that seek official university recognition, sub-
sidy, or free use of university facilities. They do not necessarily apply to off-campus organizations or those which do
not have these privileges. (See Sections III and IV).

    2.   Registration and Disclosure.

A procedure for official recognition and registration
of student organizations should be established by the student
government. The group applying for recognition should be
required only to submit the names of its officers and, if
considered advisable, an affidavit that it is composed of a
minimum number of students. The names of officers should
not be disclosed without the consent of the individuals involved. [4]

    3.   Use of Campus Facilities.

Meeting rooms and other campus facilities should be
made available, so far as their primary use for educational
purposes permits, on a non-discriminatory basis, to regis-
tered student organizations. Bulletin boards should be provided for the use of student organizations; school-wide circu-
lation of all notices and leaflets should be permitted.

    4.   Advisers for Organizations.

No student organization should be required to have a
faculty adviser, but if it wishes one, it should be free to

choose for itself. An adviser should consult with and counsel the organization but should have no authority or responsibility to regulate or control its activities.

C.   Student-Sponsored Forums

Students should have the right to assemble, to select speakers and guests, and to discuss issues of their choice. It should be made clear to the public that an invitation to a speaker does not necessarily imply approval of his views by either the student group or the college administration. Students should enjoy the same right as other citizens to hear different points of view and draw their own conclusions. [5]

When a student group wishes to hear a controversial or socially unpopular speaker, the college may not require that a spokesman for the opposing viewpoint be scheduled either simultaneously or on a subsequent occasion.

D.   Protests and Political Activity

Students should be free through organized action on campus to register their political views or their disapprobation of university policies, but within peaceful limits. The use of force on a college campus--whether by students, the campus police, or outside police called in by the administration--is always to be regretted. Outside police should not be summoned to a campus to deal with internal problems unless all other techniques have clearly failed and then preferably on the basis of rules made in advance with the participation, consultation and concurrence of representatives of students and faculty who have been selected in a truly representative fashion.

Failure of communication among administration, faculty and students has been a recurrent cause of campus crises. Prompt consultation by the administration with faculty and student spokesmen may serve to prevent potentially disastrous confrontations which disrupt the orderly processes of the institution.

1.   Ground Rules.

Picketing, demonstrations, sit-ins, or student strikes, provided they are conducted in an orderly and non-obstructive manner, are a legitimate mode of expression, whether politically motivated or directed against the college administration, and should not be prohibited. Student organizations and individual students should be allowed, and no special permission required, to distribute pamphlets or collect names for petitions concerning either campus or off-campus issues.

Demonstrators, however, have no right to deprive others of the opportunity to speak or be heard; to take hostages; physically obstruct movement of others; or otherwise disrupt the educational or institutional processes in a way that interferes with the freedom of others.

2. Tripartite Regulations.

Regulations governing demonstrations should be made by a committee of administrators, representative faculty, and democratically selected students. The regulations should be so drawn as fully to protect the students' First Amendment rights and at the same time ensure that the academic process not be disrupted.

E. Communications Media

All student publications--college newspapers, literary and humor magazines, academic periodicals and yearbooks-- should enjoy full freedom of the press, and not be restricted by either the administration or the student government. This should be the practice, even though most college publications, except for the relatively few university dailies which are autonomous financially, are dependent on the administration's favor for the use of campus facilities, and are subsidized either directly or indirectly by a tax on student funds.

1. College Newspapers.

Campus papers subsidized by student fees should impartially cover news of special student interest, be free to express their own editorial opinion, and should serve as a forum for opposing views on controversial issues as do public newspapers. They may also be expected to deal in news columns and editorials with the political and social issues that are relevant to the concerns of the students as citizens of the larger community. Neither the faculty, administration, boards of trustees nor legislatures should be immune from criticism. [6]

In no case should the independent decision of the editors be overruled by pressures from alumni, boards of trustees, state legislatures, the college administration, or the student government.

Student initiation of competing publications should be encouraged.

Wherever possible a student newspaper should be financially and physically separate from the college, existing as a legally independent corporation. The college would then be absolved from legal liability for the publication and bear no direct responsibility to the community for the views expressed. In those cases where college papers do not enjoy financial independence, neither the faculty adviser nor the publications board if the paper has either or both, nor any representative of the college should exercise veto power, in the absence of a specific finding of potential libel as determined by an impartial legal authority.

Where there is a college publications board, it should be composed of at least a majority of students selected by the student government or council, or by some other democratic method. Should the board, or in case the paper has no board, an ad hoc committee selected by the faculty and student government, decide that the editor has been guilty of deliberate malice or deliberate distortion in one or a number of instances, the validity of this charge must be determined through due process.

2.   Radio and Television.

Campus radio and television stations should enjoy and exercise the same editorial freedom as the college press. Stations whose signals go beyond the campus operate under a license granted by the Federal Communications Commission and, therefore, must conform to the applicable regulations imposed by the Commission.

F.   Artistic Presentations

The same freedom from censorship enjoyed by the communications media should be extended to on-campus artistic presentations.

III.   Students' Political Freedom Off-Campus

American college students possess the same right to

freedom of speech, assembly, and association as do other
residents of the United States. They are also, of course,
subject to the same obligations and responsibilities as persons who are not members of the academic communities.

A.   The Right of Public Dissent

Student participation in off-campus activities such as
peace marches, civil rights demonstrations, draft protests,
picketing, boycotts, political campaigning, public rallies,
non-campus publications, and acts of civil disobedience are
not the legitimate concern of the college or university. Students, like teachers, have the right to identify themselves
as members of a particular academic community. But they
also have the moral obligation not to misrepresent the views
of others in their academic community.

B.   Arrests and Convictions

Students who are arrested or convicted for off-campus
acts of social or political protest should not be further penalized by their colleges through such disciplinary measures as
suspension or dismissal, withdrawal of scholarships, nota-
tions on their records, or be subjected in any other manner
to additional punishment. (See also V, C.)

When a student has been indicted for an act based on
his conscience-motivated beliefs, the college may provide
him with legal advice if requested. Even though the student
is prepared to accept full responsibility for his personal actions, the college has an interest in seeing that his legal
rights are protected.

IV.   Personal Freedom

College students should be free to organize their
personal lives and determine their private behavior free
from institutional interference. In the past many colleges,
with the approval of parents and the acquiescence of students, have played the role of surrogate parents. But this
function is now being strongly challenged. An increasing
number of institutions today recognize that students, as part
of the maturing process, must be permitted to assume responsibility for their private lives--even if, in some instances, their philosophy or conduct is at variance with traditional standards.

The college community should not regard itself as the arbiter of personal behavior or morals, as long as the conduct does not interfere with the rights of others. Regulation is appropriate only if necessary to protect the health and safety of members of the academic community or the fulfillment of the basic academic process. Any such rules should be adopted by elected representative student committees, or by committees on which these students have a majority voice.

Some Specific Areas of Personal Behavior:

1. Student Residences.

    ✦ a) Although on-campus living is often regarded as an important part of the total educational experience, it should not be compulsory.

        b) Dormitory rules with respect to visiting hours, curfew and the use of liquor may be adopted by resident students in their common interest. Any such rules should be drafted so as to leave the maximum freedom of choice to each individual student.

2. Personal Appearance.

    Dress and grooming are modes of personal expression and taste which should be left to the individual except for such occasions as are designated by the students themselves.

3. Pregnancy.

    If a student is pregnant she should be free to decide in consultation with her own physician or with college health authorities, when to take leave of her studies.

4. Search and Seizure.

    A student's locker should not be opened, nor his room searched, without his consent except in conformity with the spirit of the Fourth Amendment which requires that a warrant first be obtained on a showing of probable cause, supported by oath or affirmation, and particularly describing the things to be seized. An exception may be made in cases involving a grave danger to health or safety.

V.   Regulations and Disciplinary Procedures

Regulations governing student conduct should be in harmony with and essential to the fulfillment of the college's educational objectives. Students should participate fully and effectively in formulating and adjudicating college regulations
governing student conduct. Reasonable procedures should be
established and followed in enforcing discipline.

A.   Enacting and Promulgating Regulations

1.   Regulations should be clear and unambiguous.
Phrases such as "conduct unbecoming a student," or "actions
against the best interests of the college," should be avoided
because they allow too much latitude for interpretation.

2.   The range of penalties for the violation of regulations should be clearly specified.

3.   Regulations should be published and circulated to
the entire academic community.

B.   Academic Due Process

1.   Minor infractions of college regulations, penalized
by small fines, or reprimands which do not become part of
a student's permanent record, may be handled summarily by
the appropriate administrative, faculty, or student officer.
However, the student should have the right to appeal.

2.   In the case of infractions of college regulations
which may lead to more serious penalties, such as suspension, expulsion, or notation on a student's permanent record,
the student is entitled to formal procedures in order to prevent miscarriages of justice.

These procedures should include a formal hearing by
a student-faculty or a student judicial committee. No member of the hearing committee who is involved in the particular case should sit in judgment.

Prior to the hearing the student should be:[7]

a.   Advised in writing of the charges against him,
including a summary of the evidence upon which the charges
are based.

        b. Advised that he is entitled to be represented, and advised at all times during the course of the proceedings by a person of his own choosing.

        c. Advised of the procedures to be followed at the hearing.

        d. Given reasonable time to prepare his defense.

At the hearing, the student (or his representative) and the member of the academic community who had brought charges (or his representative) should have the right to examine and cross-examine witnesses and to present documentary and other evidence in support of their respective contentions. The student should be advised of his privilege to remain silent and should not be penalized for exercising this privilege. The college administration should make available to the student such authority as it may possess to require the presence of witnesses and the production of documents at the hearing. A full record should be taken at the hearing and it should be made available in identical form to the hearing panel, the administration, and the student. After the hearing is closed, the panel should adjudicate the matter before it with reasonable promptness and submit its findings and conclusions in writing. Copies thereof should be made available in identical form and at the same time, to the administration and the student. The cost should be met by the school.

3. Appeals either from summary or formal proceedings may be carried to a designated administrative officer, who may affirm or reverse the committee's decision but not increase the penalty.

C. Avoidance of Double Punishment

A student who is charged with committing a crime on or off-campus should not be subject to sanctions for the same offense by both the courts and the college unless the offense is so serious in nature that such dual action is necessary for the protection of the institution. In this event, disciplinary hearings by the college should be postponed until the termination of criminal proceedings against the student to forestall the possibility that testimony and other evidence at a college hearing would be subject to disclosure by way of subpoena in a subsequent court proceeding.

D. Law Enforcement on the Campus

Although a college cannot be considered sacrosanct
against policemen, and the proper function of law officers
cannot be impeded in crime detection, every effort should be
made to resolve campus disciplinary problems without recourse to outside authority. A Campus Law Enforcement
Committee composed of representatives of the administration,
faculty, and student body should establish guidelines and procedures for summoning off-campus law enforcement authorities. This committee should also determine the duties and
prerogatives of campus police.

Members of the academic community should not function surreptitiously as agents for law enforcement authorities
on campus. Nothing is more detrimental to the climate of
free association essential in a college community.

VI.   Students and the Military

Colleges have an educational function to perform and
should not become an adjunct of the military. Such a development would constitute a threat to their survival as centers
of critical inquiry. At the same time, institutions of higher
learning must recognize the existence of the draft as it applies to students.

A. Extent of Cooperation with the Selective Service System

Information concerning the student's enrollment and
standing should be submitted to Selective Service by the college only at the request of the student. 8

B. Unconstitutional Reclassification

Draft boards should be considered by colleges to have
violated the First Amendment when they cancel the deferment
of students who have participated in anti-war demonstrations.9

C. College Reinstatement of Draft Resisters

Students imprisoned for refusing on grounds of conscience to be drafted to fight in any war, or in a particular
war, or to accept the alternative service provided by law
for conscientious objectors, should be eligible for readmission to their colleges on completion of their sentences, with-

out prejudice to opportunities for financial aid. [10]

D. Recruitment on Campus

Unless a college bars all occupational recruitment of students, the Army, Navy and Air Force should be allowed the same campus facilities as other government agencies and private concerns. [11]

E. ROTC

On campuses where Reserve Officer Training programs exist, student enrollment should be on a voluntary basis. Academic credit should be granted only for those ROTC courses which are acceptable to, and under the academic control of, the regular faculty. ROTC instructors should not hold academic rank unless they are members of an academic department subject to the regular procedure of appointment and removal.

VIII. Confidentiality of Student Records in General

1. No record, including conviction in a court of law, shall be noted[12] unless there is a demonstrable need for it which is reasonably related to the basic purposes and necessities of the university. Relevant records, such as academic, disciplinary, medical, and psychiatric, should be maintained in separate files.

2. No mention should be made in any university record of a student's religious or political beliefs or association.

3. Access to student records should be confined to authorized university personnel who require such access in connection with the performance of their duties. Particular safeguards should be established with respect to medical, (including psychiatric) records. All persons having access to student records should be instructed that the information contained in the records must be kept confidential, and should be required to sign and date their adherence to this procedure.

4. Persons outside the university may not have access to student records without the student's written permission, except in response to a constitutionally valid subpoena. [13]

5. The rules regarding the keeping and release of records should be made known and available to the university community.

Notes

1. Revised Introduction to "Academic Freedom and Civil
   Liberties of Students in Colleges and Universities."

2. As used in this pamphlet, the words "college" and "university" are used interchangeably to refer to all institutions of higher education.

3. "The First Amendment, " Mr. Justice Brennan wrote
   in a 1967 Supreme Court decision "does not tolerate
   laws that cast a pall of orthodoxy over the classroom. " (Keyishian v. The Board of Regents of New
   York, 385 U.S. 598).

4. See footnote 6 for action taken by the ACLU when
   HUAC subpoenaed from the University of Michigan,
   University of California at Berkeley and Stanford University, the names of student members and officers
   of anti-Vietnam war organizations.

5. In overturning a ban against a Communist speaker at
   the University of Buffalo, a New York court held:
   "We believe that the tradition of our great society
   has been to allow our universities in the name of academic freedom to explore and expose their students
   to controversial issues without government interference. " (Egan v. Moore, 235 N.Y.S. 2d. 1962).

6. In a recent case involving the expulsion of a student
   editor, a Federal court said: A state cannot force
   a college student to forfeit his constitutionally protected right of freedom of expression as a condition
   for his attending a state-supported institution. "
   (Dickey v. Alabama State Board of Education, 1967).
        For example, in August, 1966, the U.S. House
   Committee on Un-American Activities subpoenaed
   from the University of Michigan, the University of
   California at Berkeley, and Stanford University,
   copies of certification or statements of membership
   filed with the university by campus political organizations known to be critical of America's involvement
   in the war in Vietnam. The ACLU sent a letter to
   over 1, 000 university and college presidents protesting this action by HUAC as one of the most serious
   breaches of academic freedom in recent decades,
   calling upon institutions to resist, in every possible

legal manner, such subpoenas should this investigation
by HUAC be extended to other universities and colleges. A substantial number of institutions responded
to this letter by affirming their interest in affording
students protection, and indicating that they would
want to resist such subpoenas within all possible legal means. Many cited administration policy on confidentiality of student records, such as not keeping
membership lists of opinion-oriented groups or of any
student groups, and/or not releasing information without prior consent of individuals involved. In some
instances, officers' names are kept for identification
purposes only and some institutions destroy all such
records at the end of each year.

Several organizations also expressed support of the
Union's position. In a statement released July, 1967,
the American Council on Education, referring to the
HUAC subpoenas, said: "It is... in the interests of
the entire academic community to protect vigilantly
its traditions of free debate and investigation by safeguarding students and their records from pressure
that may curtail their liberties.... Colleges and universities should discontinue the maintenance of membership lists of student organizations, especially those
related to matters of political belief or action. If
rosters of this kind do not exist, they cannot be subpoenaed, and the institution is therefore freed of some
major elements of conflict and from the risks of contempt proceedings or a suit."

This issue is of continuing concern in light of the
subpoenas issued in May, 1969, by the Senate Permanent Subcommittee on Investigations to five universities
(Stanford, Harvard, Columbia, Cornell and the University of California at Berkeley) for documentation
on persons and groups allegedly involved in student
disorders.

7.   Pending disposition of the charges a student may be
     suspended only in exceptional circumstances.

8.   In a letter to the Union, dated December 2, 1968, Dep-
     uty Director of Selective Service, Daniel O. Omer,
     stated: "The responsibility for keeping a selective
     service board informed regarding the current student
     status of a registrant is upon the registrant himself
     and not upon the college."

9. On November 28, 1967, the ACLU protested as unconstitutional the recommendation to draft boards from Selective Service Director General Lewis B. Hershey, dated October 26, 1967, that any student adjudged to have interfered "illegally" with draft processes or military recruitment be deprived of his deferment and reclassification on the ground that his action was not "in the national interest." A previous attempt by General Hershey to misuse the draft laws to punish students when protesting U.S. involvement in the Vietnam war was blocked by court order in 1966 when the U.S. Court of Appeals in the Second Circuit ruled that the reclassification of two University of Michigan students who had staged a sit-in at the Ann Arbor draft board was "illegal" and violated the students' right of free speech. The Court also held that "It is not the function of local boards in the Selective Service System to punish registrants by reclassifying them 1-A because they protested as they did over the Government's involvement in Vietnam." In another decision bearing on this issue, the Supreme Court ruled (in December, 1968) that persons qualifying for statutory exemptions can go to court to contest reclassificatory actions of their draft boards. The Court ordered exemption restored to divinity student James J. Oestereich, who had been reclassified 1-A after he had returned his draft card to the Department of Justice during an anti-war protest. The ACLU contended before the Court that punitive use of the Selective Service System is unconstitutional. The decision does not cover non-exempt persons, including students; several such cases are now in the lower courts.

10. In a letter sent to college and university presidents throughout the country on April 21, 1968, the ACLU declared that a student whose convictions against the war in Vietnam are "so deeply rooted" that he chooses prison rather than military duty is entitled to resume his education when free. "To refuse him the opportunity, after he has paid the penalty imposed by society, would be to punish him twice for the same offense," in violation of the spirit of the Fifth Amendment's safeguard against double jeopardy. The Union held that a policy of readmitting students who had violated the draft laws "does not embody political implications or judgments; nor does it encourage violation of the law."

11. The ACLU believes that any decision to exclude some
     recruiters, arising primarily from a political contro-
     versy, poses questions of civil liberties concern.
     Whether based on the imposition of an ideological
     test, concern for the physical safety of students, dis-
     ruption of the orderly processes of the institution, or
     protection of students from threat of reprisal by draft
     reclassification, selective exclusions strike against
     the concept of the open university, are discriminatory
     in their application, and suggest a possible infringe-
     ment of the spirit of the equal protection clause of
     the Constitution.

12. In October, 1966, the United States Civil Service Com-
     mission dropped all inquiries concerning arrests from
     its federal employment application forms, stating that
     such queries "infringed the spirit of due process and
     was particularly hurtful to those citizens who were
     arrested not for committing ordinary crimes, but as
     reprisal for exercising First Amendment rights of
     speech and association in civil rights demonstrations."

13. The term "constitutionally valid subpoena" is used to
     exclude subpoenas based on political investigation or
     other situations which, in the opinion of the Union,
     are unconstitutional. (See footnote 6 for ACLU
     protest against HUAC subpoenas in 1966.)

INDEX

Academic freedom, 10
Achtenberg, Irving, 132, 133; 142 n36
Alabama Law Review, 113
American Association of University Professors, 126, 135-136,
    152, 154, 164, 166, 174
American Civil Liberties Union, 9, 27, 82, 118, 122, 123,
    126, 135, 152, 154, 157, 163, 164, 165, 166, 172,
    174, 181-183
American College, The, 36
Anthony v. Syracuse University, 8, 25, 39, 48, 50, 60, 63-
    70, 72, 102
Assembly, freedom of, 198
Authoritarianism, see Paternalism

Bakken, Clarence J., 167, 183
Barker v. Hardway, 173
Baughman v. Frienmuth, 188, 189
Beaney, William M., 23, 45, 151-52, 164, 165
Bentham, Jeremy, 80
Bentley, Richard, 72
Black, Justice Hugo L., 124, 148, 162, 171
Bluett v. Board of Trustees, 53, 75
Brady, Thomas F., 9, 134; 141 n30
Breen v. Kahl, 189 n1
Brennan, Justice W. L., 124
Brooks v. Auburn University, 178
Brown v. Board of Education, 25, 45, 64, 81, 92, 119
Buess, Thomas E., 18, 56
Bumper v. State of North Carolina, 148
Burnside v. Byars, 170, 171, 173
Burstein, Judge, 148
Byse, Clark, 60, 64, 70

Caldwell, Judge, 73
California Cafeteria and Restaurant Workers Union v. McElroy,
    104
Camara v. Municipal Court, 153
Cameron, Judge Ben F., 104-107, 112, 116n

255

Carrington, Paul D., 151
Carswell, Judge G. Harrold, 122; 140 n11; 200
Clark, Judge, 110, 171
Coffin, William Sloan, 175, 178
Cohen, Felix S., 80
Cohen, Morris R., 80
College Law Bulletin, 7
Columbia Law Review, 8
Commager, Henry Steele, 10, 11
Constitutional theory, 51-52, 54, 200
Contract, 80
Contract theory, 1, 2, 37, 38-40, 44, 47, 48, 51, 53, 56,
    66, 68, 73, 74, 98, 102, 118, 150, 195
Cranney v. Trustees of Boston University, 106

Denver Law Journal, 8, 9, 54
DeVeaux v. Tuskegee Institute, 169
Dickey v. Alabama State Board of Education, 170, 185-188
Dickey, Gary Clinton, 187, 188
Dixon v. Alabama State Board of Education, 1, 2, 3, 5, 6,
    7, 24, 25, 27, 37, 51, 52, 60, 64, 65, 78, 79, 81,
    82, 91, 92, 94, 96, 99, 107, 110, 111, 112, 113,
    114, 116n, 118, 119, 120, 121, 122, 123, 124, 126,
    135, 137, 139; 140 n11; 147, 170, 185, 195, 197, 198,
    199, 200, 201, 202
Dormitory rooms, privacy in, 143-154
Doyle, Judge James E., 202
Due v. Florida A&M University, 122, 139, 200

Educational Law and Administration, 8
Eisenhower, President Dwight David, 112
Embrey, Elroy, 95
Enrolment growth, college, 21, 26
Erdreich, Ben Leader, 113
Evers v. Birdsong, 174

Farar, Tom J., 184
Fiduciary theory, 52-56
Fortas, Justice Abe, 170, 200
Froehlich, Harold, 202
Furutani v. Ewigleben, 156

Gault, In re, 28
Gibson, Judge, 109, 111
Gleason v. University of Minnesota, 102
Goldberg v. Regents of University of California, 171, 172
Goldenkoff v. Albany Law School, 58n
Goldman, Alvin L., 17, 23, 38, 42, 45, 46, 53, 55, 70, 72,

256

150, 162
Goldstein v. New York University, 57n, 65
Gomillion v. Lightfoot, 112
Gott v. Berea College, 45, 73
Gregory, Dick, 175
Grooming regulations, 153-154, 201

Hair, see grooming regulations
Hammond v. South Carolina State College, 171, 172
Harlan, Justice John Marshall, 171
Harvard Law Review, 4, 8, 18, 41, 43, 44, 46, 52, 77,
    113, 138
Hear, right to, 174-180, 198
Heyman, Ira Michael, 47
Higher Education for American Democracy, report, 12
Hill v. McCauley, 60-63, 64, 70, 102
Hofstadter, Richard, 26
Holloway, John P., 81; 140 n14; 155
Human Rights Forum, 177
Hunter, Judge Elmo B., 123, 127, 132, 133, 134

In loco parentis see under loco

Jackson, Justice Robert H., 188
Jefferson, Thomas, 13-15
Jencks, Christopher, 10, 11, 17, 22, 29, 30, 32, 78, 79
Johnson, Judge Frank M., 97, 98, 99, 102, 111, 112, 144,
    146, 157, 166, 167, 187, 188
Johnson, Michael T., 19, 21, 151, 157
Joint Anti-Fascist Refugee Committee v. McGrath, 105
Jones v. State Board of Education of Tennessee, 123, 124,
    126, 169, 174
Juvenile rights, 201

Kalaidjian, Edward C., 150
Katz, Joseph, 30, 83
Kauffman, Joseph F., 30, 83
Kelly, Samuel P., 83
Keniston, Kenneth, 81, 84
Kentucky Law Journal, 17, 162
King's Bench, 72
Knapp, Stephen R., 49, 50
Knight v. State Board of Education, 121, 122, 137, 139, 170
Koblitz v. Western Reserve University, 48, 50, 59n, 73
Konvitz, Milton R., 28, 91

Ladd, Edward T., 82
Lee, Bernard, 95

Property, nature of, 80
Public opinion and student rights cases, 201-202

Reynolds v. Sims, 112
Riesman, David, 10, 11, 17, 22, 26, 29, 31, 32, 78, 79
Right-privilege controversy, 24
Rives, Judge Richard Taylor, 24, 25, 51, 54, 70, 91, 99-
    104, 113, 119-120

Sadler, Judge, 62-63, 70
Sanford, Nevitt, 30, 83
Schlesinger, Arthur, Jr., 196
Schuyler v. University of New York at Albany, 173
Scott v. Alabama State Board of Education, 166
Sears, Justice, 40, 68, 102
Seavey, Warren A., 17-18, 41, 52, 54, 76, 103, 113
Sherman v. Hyman, 156
Smith, Judge, 64
Smith v. University of Tennessee, 179
Snoxell, Laverne F., 9, 134; 141 n30
Soglin v. Kauffman, 124-125; 142 n35
Speech, freedom of, 164-180, 198, 201
Spevack v. Klein, 155
Stamp, Neal R., 22
State v. Zwicker, 173
Status theory, 37, 40, 45, 47-49, 53, 56
Statutory theory, 37, 50, 52
Steier, Arthur, 108-110, 171, 186
Steier v. New York State Education Commission, 106, 107-
    110, 116n, 118, 169, 171, 186
Substantive rights, 19

Talley v. California, 185
Tanton v. McKenney, 58n, 74
Temple Law Quarterly, 114
Tennessee Law Review, 8
Texas Law Journal, 19
Thompson, Ralph, 83
Thomte, Dennis, 114
Tinker v. Des Moines, 9, 59n; 142 n35; 169-170, 187, 199
Trenholm, H. Councill, 94, 95, 96, 100
Truitt, v. Illinois, 94
Truman, Harry S., 112
Trust theory, 37, 50, 52

UCLA Law Review, 8
University of Pennsylvania Law Review, 8
University of Virginia, 13

Van Alstyne, William W., 3, 4, 8, 19, 24, 29, 42, 46, 92, 93, 118, 125, 126, 149, 151, 154-155, 157, 167, 176, 177, 184, 201, 203
Vanderbilt Law Review, 7, 59n
Veblen, Thorstein, 78, 196
Voluntary compliance, 200
Vought v. Van Buren Public Schools, 188, 189

Warren Court, 27
White, Byron, 171
Wildovsky, Aaron, 31
Wisdom, Judge Minor, 112
Wright, Charles Alan, 1, 51, 59n, 185, 186
Wulf, Melvin L., 27
Wyzanski, Judge, 106

Yale Law Journal, 41, 43, 49, 162, 177

Zanders v. Louisiana State Board of Education, 174